Toward a
Future for
Religious
Education

CONTRIBUTORS   *Bernard Cooke*
David Elkind
William B. Friend
Jeffrey Keefe
Christopher Kiesling
James Michael Lee
C. Ellis Nelson
Didier Piveteau
Patrick C. Rooney

Toward a Future for Religious Education

Edited by James Michael Lee and Patrick C. Rooney

1970   PFLAUM PRESS, Dayton, Ohio

Library of Congress Catalog Card Number: 73-93008
Pflaum Press
38 West Fifth Street
Dayton, Ohio   45402
© 1970 by James Michael Lee and Patrick C. Rooney.
Printed in the United States of America

Contents

An Appreciation

The term "communion of saints," though a theological concept, is a particularly appropriate operational description of the myriad conjointed activities involved in editing a book. Cooperation among a host of people at every phase and level forms the "communion" phase of the editorial enterprise. And the devotion, hard work, painstaking critical comments, and hawkeye reading far into the night—these are the stuff of which saints are made. Fortunately for the editors, a wonderful communion of real saints hovered constantly over the work, from tender manuscript to final page proofs, to bring about the freshborn volume. To be sure, if one is not a saint before working on a book, he or she becomes one by the time the book finally comes out.

Many persons combined to bring this little volume into completed form. Neil G. McCluskey, pioneer Dean-Director of the Institute for Studies in Education here at Notre Dame, continually displayed wonderful kindness toward and gentle understanding of the sometimes frayed nerves of his Education Chairman from the moment of the book's inauguration right down to the very last moment. Noreen Dugan and Mary Fallon augmented their sainthood noticeably in their tireless and devoted efforts, particularly during the final stages. Nancy Wesolowski, typist supreme, gained the palm of martyrdom in rendering the all-too-frequent illegible scrawls into type. Kay Coleman increased her patience quotient all during the many months of writing and editorial work. Finally, the faithful old warhorse, Pobdwm, dear paht-nah in so many, many ventures, once again came through magnificently in the editorial and typing clutches. And to the many, many other members of the communion of saints, known and unknown, who helped us through this book, we are deeply grateful.

—James Michael Lee
—Patrick C. Rooney

ACKNOWLEDGMENTS

The editors wish to express their appreciation to the following for permission to reproduce copyrighted materials:

Herder and Herder of New York for excerpts from *Teaching All Nations*, edited by Johannes Hofinger.

Educational Technology Magazine of Englewood Cliffs, New Jersey, for material from "Computer Assisted Instruction" by Gerald T. Gleason in the November, 1967, issue.

The Bishops' Committee on the Liturgy of the National Conference of Catholic Bishops of the United States for material from the article, "The Place of Music in Eucharistic Celebrations."

The United States Catholic Conference for material from the Encyclical Letter of Pius XII, *Mediator Dei*.

Foreword
James Michael Lee

This book represents an approach to catechetics which some of us believe is at once unique and new. The approach I am referring to is the social-science approach to religious instruction. To the best of my knowledge, this approach has not heretofore been expounded—at least as systematically—as in the present volume.

There are many characteristics which constitute the social-science approach to the teaching of religion. These will become evident as the reader progresses through the various chapters of this book. By way of introduction, I would like to touch briefly on three of the more important characteristics. These characteristics will become more evident as the reader works his way through this volume and fleshes out and expands for himself these characteristics into a larger and more embracing set. The purpose of my *Foreword,* then, simply is to prepare the reader, albeit sketchily, for what he will encounter in the nine chapters of this book.

The social-science approach radicates catechetics in the teaching-learning process. By this I mean that the central task of religious instruction becomes the conscious and deliberative facilitation of specified behavioral goals. Accepting the content of theology, whether old or new, the prime function of religious instruction is the study into and the implementation of a planned structuring of the learning situation. Quite obviously, theology plays a vital and indispensable role in this kind of catechetics; however, it is theology which is being inserted into the social-science approach, rather than vice versa, as is typically the case.

Second, the social-science approach views the environment in which the learning of religion takes place as constituting a key factor—and indeed in some ways the controlling force—in the here-and-now learning process, and not merely as a supportive milieu for "getting across" the subject matter of religion. The elements of social time and social space, with all their ramifications, are crucial to the type of teaching-learning which takes place. To be sure, the classroom group is in itself a unique psychosocial system, with its own peculiar psychosocial structure. Again, theology is indispensable here; but the shift in emphasis that I am suggesting is one in which theology is utilized as only one directional force in the classroom group. This, of course, substantially differs from the typical emphasis, in which the classroom milieu is perceived simply as a motivational tool to interest the students in religion, or to "get them going" to carry out the theological themes of the lesson.

Third, the social-science approach views religious instruction as a conscious and deliberative effort by the teacher and by the students to effect selected behavioral modifications in the learners. The classroom becomes the planned milieu for facilitating in the students this change in behavior. Theology remains as a mode of prime importance; however, theology is used as only one of the factors in the social structuring of the learning environment, instead of as the *terminus ad quem* of the classroom activity.

Each of the chapters forms a complementary vector to this social-science thesis, which undergirds the book as a whole. Patrick Rooney's chapter throws into bold relief the influence of the entire Christian school structure in reinforcing, broadening, or extinguishing the behavioral outcomes acquired in the religion class. Jeffrey Keefe analyzes the nature and genesis of attitudes and values, with particular emphasis on the capabilities and directions of the religion class to effect attitude reinforcement or change. My own contribution is to examine the nature of the teaching process in order to shed some light on what the social-science approach means in the concrete circumstances of both the teaching-learning situation in general and the teaching act in particular.

The chapters by Didier Piveteau, Christopher Kiesling, and Bernard Cooke form together a complementary emphasis on the notion that the Bible is the Bible, the liturgy is the liturgy, and the Word is the Word, only to the extent that it is being lived in the personal and social circumstances of students in the here-and-now situation. Ellis Nelson's essay provides a fascinating look into the strategies of Protestant religious instruction and indicates that the non-Roman Christian denominations have utilized for some time certain social-science processes.

William Friend's contribution surveys the range of audio-visual materials, and provides concrete assistance to the religion teacher on the more effective use of these aids in religious instruction. Finally, David Elkind, a Jewish psychologist, sheds light on the effects which a social-science approach has on the basic ways in which research and evaluation of religious instruction is done.

To be perfectly candid, I must admit that the social-science approach which I am advocating has already encountered considerable opposition from the catechetical Establishment in the Roman Catholic sector of religious education. (Perhaps opposition is not the correct word here; a more accurate description, I think, would be that the catechetical Establishment does not seem to grasp the nature and thrust of this approach.) There seem to be two principal groups composing this Establishment, namely the theologians and the old-time pedagogs. The theologians, quite naturally, tend to think in terms of the categories posited by the humanistic disciplines, notably philosophy and theology. The social-science categories, especially those of be-havior modification, environmental structuring, pedagogical process, and operational traits are quite foreign to this mentality. Sometimes the theologians attempt to transpose these and other social-science categories into their own system, with the result that they either garble or miss the mark. The old-time pedagogs, on the other hand, view social science as merely an updated version of the old methods approach in catechetics. These per-sons, often found in the ranks of experienced religion teachers or of housewives and businessmen who have had their fling at CCD teaching, seem to lump all the categories of teaching into bald methodology, making no distinction between teaching methods, teaching strategies, and teaching processes. Some of the more progressive of the old-time pedagogs have done a little —but usually a very little—reading on dynamics of the coun-seling process, and awkwardly attempt to replace therapeutic techniques for teaching strategies and processes.

This volume of essays attempts to elaborate on certain of the key emphases of the social-science approach to education. Some of the chapters deliberately aim at plunging the reader into the social-science mentality. This is not to say, however, that one short book will convert the catechetical Establishment to the social-science approach to teaching religion, or even assist them to gain an adequate understanding of it. Additional study, re-flection, and complementary reading of pertinent educational and other social-science books are, of course, necessary. But it is my own personal belief—one shared by my fellow contributors to this book—that the social-science approach represents the most fruitful direction for the future of religious instruction. Such a redirection from the present thrust of catechetics will engender, of course, considerable controversy and contention. But such is the fate of any new approach, particularly if it tends to be somewhat revolutionary. It is the hope of all of us who contributed to this volume that this work will constitute a beginning, however modest, of the social-science approach to the teaching of religion.

1 Religious Instruction in the Context of Catholic Schooling

Patrick C. Rooney

Introduction

There can be little doubt that the students of the present generation are remarkably different than those in most previous generations. These differences have been detailed over and over again in the popular press and are a cause of great concern among educators, as well as among the adult population in general. It is not uncommon to hear moans, complaints and just plain bewilderment expressed over the life-style, values and the attitudes of our young people, who find closer affinity and empathetic response to Benjamin from *The Graduate* than they do to the more traditional folk heroes of American society. Perhaps more than at any other time in American history, we are faced with a crisis in understanding the youth of our nation. There is a generation gap, which, with each new public demonstration or dramatic confrontation with the "Establishment," seems to grow wider and wider.

Reactions on the part of the adult population to the generation gap and its attendant public disorders have not been entirely favorable. Accusations that the new generation is degenerate, immoral, addicted to the use of strange drugs and free sex, unpatriotic and anarchistic are bantered about as freely as Saturday's football scores. On the other hand, there are at least some adults who see the current life-style of young Americans as challenging, exciting, and potentially the most fruitful change that has ever occurred in American society. Without too much difficulty, therefore, it can be said that the present epoch in the American dream of life, liberty, and the pursuit of happiness is one of discord and discontent. The American people now live in an era of rapid change—and perhaps even revolution —where the basic values, traditions, and structures of established society become the object of radical questioning, as we desperately grope our way toward some semblance of meaningful self-understanding in a technological and urban world.

In this chapter I am going to try to deal with the generation gap specifically as it applies to Christian educators in Catholic schools. I believe that many Christian educators, although imaginatively attempting to make their teaching creative and challenging, simply are prohibited by much of what happens within the normal Catholic school. This is not to say that Catholic schools should be closed. I want to make clear at the very outset that this chapter will not deal with the burning problem of the existence of Catholic schools. Rather, I will be speaking about an entirely different subject: the relationship between a school's religious education program and its normal day-to-day operational atmosphere.

THE CATHOLIC SCHOOL MILIEU

For the past ten years or so, the teaching of religion in the typical Catholic school has undergone a tremendous change. Recently, there has been renewed criticism of some of the newer programs designed for use in the Catholic schools, and much of this criticism has been accurate.[1] The point here, however, is that, with the "new" religion being taught in most schools, there has not been a corresponding look at the typical regime of the Catholic school. By "regime" is meant the rules and regulations which govern the day-to-day operation of a school and the conduct of its students.

---

[1] See especially Gabriel Moran, *Vision and Tactics* (New York: Herder and Herder, 1968).

Roots of the Tension

One of the principal preoccupations of the "new" religion has been a striving to present the authentic gospel of Christ, a gospel which has infinite respect for the value of the person, a gospel which has concern for others as its keynote. Now, of course, most educators would agree that this effort has not succeeded in any exceptional way, but at least there has been some kind of start in the recent past toward a more authentic presentation of Christianity in the Catholic school, even admitting all the shortcomings which are rather clear to everyone.

Many religious educators now feel that a new stage in the catechetical movement is beginning.[2] There is great expectation and hope that this new stage will lead to a sounder religious education than has appeared so far. As advances are made, however, I think it will become increasingly important to take a long, hard look at the ordinary regime of the Catholic school. Does what happens in the course of a normal school day and over the period of the academic year promote or hinder what the religion teachers of this country are trying to accomplish in the classroom? This question is of paramount importance, and I raise it because I believe that many of the frustrations and obstacles of which religion teachers constantly speak can be traced back ultimately to a marked discrepancy between what the teachers are saying concerning the nature of Christianity and what the students actually experience in the Catholic school milieu.

It is somewhat surprising that not too many people speak or write about this problem. My surprise seems justified by the apparently large numbers of religion teachers who privately agree that there is, indeed, a tension between what they are trying to accomplish and the way the Catholic school in general

---

[2]This new stage, it appears, will be very concerned about adult education. The subtitle of the above-cited book by Gabriel Moran is "Toward an Adult Church," and the famous (Dutch) *New Catechism* (New York: Herder and Herder, 1967) is billed as "Catholic Faith for Adults."

operates. Perhaps there is some hesitation on the part of religion teachers to talk about those rules and regulations which may be an obstacle to the success of their teaching because these teachers feel that such a discussion could be construed as a direct and even severe attack upon the policies of school administrators or other authorities responsible for the rules. This supposition, in turn, is based upon the experience that many school administrators are somewhat touchy, if not defensive, when the faculty discusses issues which are the direct responsibility of the administrators. This is not to blame school administrators for being touchy about their administration. They are called upon so often by so many different people to give an account of their policies that after a while even the best administrator will feel that any discussion of his or her policies constitutes some kind of attack. But this uneasiness in the face of open discussion is fundamentally another problem and cannot be dealt with at this moment.

I hope that no one will read into this essay an attack upon school authorities, for this chapter is intended simply to bring out a fundamental Catholic school problem into the public forum. This problem—the dynamic interplay between the religion class and the wider Catholic school milieu—has been raised previously, but somewhat quietly. Interestingly, the problem surfaced through a letter concerning this problem written by an extremely perceptive Catholic high school student to his school newspaper. The fact that all of us had to wait for a student to bring this issue out into the open tells us a great deal about ourselves, as well as a great deal about the generation we are now attempting to educate.

This young man's position is so well expressed that it might be well to quote his short statement in full:

Upon being asked about our school while I was a freshman, I answered, "It's a perfect place." However, during my four years here I have found it, on the contrary, quite imperfect. As shown by many faculty members, it is a place to: "Do what I say, not what I do."

First there is this question about "love." We were told by our religion teacher on Ash Wednesday that the one thing he has never heard about our school is "what Christians they are." Well Father, I think I know why. Here is an example: A student is told to stay after school for talking in study hall. He asks the proctor if it can be put back one day because he has to work that night at the family business so that his father may go to night school. He is given a blunt, "No!"

Another religion teacher tells us about the true Christian man who stops and helps anyone in need rather than being on time for his appointment. Why then, does a member of a car pool who is thirty seconds late for school have to stay after school because the driver of the car decided to wait for one of the members who was late?

I also believe there is a mix-up in our school's scale of values. Why does a person caught cheating just receive a warning "look at your own paper," but a boy with long hair or without cuffs on his pants is sent to the disciplinarian? Am I to leave this school thinking that, according to the rules, the best students are the ones who always look proper and well groomed, even though they act like children? Wouldn't it be better if this school stressed me, the person, rather than me, the well-groomed shell?

Or how about the students who criticized one of the faculty members for having something to say about Vietnam and saying it, but when asked about the new star, Tiny Tim, they replied that what he does is OK because "he's making money"? Well then, is the faculty member wrong because he is not making money? Although I realize that this school is not the cause of this type of thinking, I'm sure that if our school would have taught us the proper way to think, that much of this would have been solved.

Then there are the students, just like the above-mentioned teachers, who also worry too much about their hair and clothes. I think maybe you should have more important things to worry about, such as growing up, becoming mature, or becoming a Christian.

Another paradox of our school is that I know, as sure as I'm writing this, that I will be criticized or that someone will say, "If you don't like it, then get out." However, somehow I feel that instead of telling me to run away from the problem they should teach me to face it.[a]

This is as good a statement of the problem as anyone might make. How long will religion teachers be able to discuss in their religion classes the meaning and value of persons, the idea of love one for another, when this attitude is so easily extinguished by the general Catholic school milieu; how long can they go on proposing that students, for their own happiness, should grow into compassionate and sensitive human persons, all the while knowing that when the students leave a particular classroom and return to the ordinary life of the school they perhaps will be subjected to some of the most trivial, irrational, and unjust actions ever imposed upon man. For example, just what kind of crime is it when a student, on an errand for some teacher, is caught going up the down staircase at a time when all the other students are in class? What kind of compassion, understanding, and love is shown to such a student when for this horrendous crime he is detained for an hour after school? How often in the future will that student offer help to a teacher in need of supplies or some such thing? And what will that student think when he hears from his religion teacher that Christians, and especially Catholics, are characterized by their love and justice toward each other?

There is a serious problem here, and one which I hope is now sufficiently clear so that I may undertake a study of its origins, followed by a look at some of the options which religion teachers have open to them to effectively confront the issue.

---

[a]This is a bona fide example, but I did not feel that identifying either the student or the school would serve any purpose.

FOCAL POINTS OF TENSION

The New Catechetics

The first and most obvious origin for this tension between the religion classroom and the regime of the school is what is happening within the religion classroom itself. Due in large measure to the impact of the catechetical movement, religion teachers are moving closer and closer to presenting the actual ideas and goals developed by Jesus Christ for man to find happiness in this life.

The catechetical movement began in Europe around the start of this century with a concentration upon the methodology involved in the teaching of religion. This concern for methodology developed into what is known as the Munich Method, the basic outline of which has been summarized by Klemens Tilmann:

> "Observation, thought, action" are the three steps . . . indispensable to the acquisition of all true knowledge, and thus to teaching . . . The new method of religious instruction originating in Munich required that each doctrine treated be introduced by a story illustrating the truth in question. Starting with the story, the truth itself is arrived at by a process of thought and explanation. And finally the way from this truth to action must be pointed out. With two steps added to the three major ones, the teaching of any particular doctrine should normally run according to the following psychological scheme.
> INTRODUCTION . . . the purpose is to focus the student's attention on the object of the lesson.
> PRESENTATION of an illustrative story.
> EXPLANATION. The object of the lesson is developed from the story.
> SUMMARY. The truth that has been learnt is stated briefly.
> APPLICATION to life of what has been learned.[4]

---

[4] Klemens Tilmann, "Origin and Development of Modern Catechetical Methods," in Johannes Hofinger, editor, *Teaching All Nations,* translated by Clifford Howell (New York: Herder and Herder, 1961), p. 86.

The concern for a new method in catechetics continued until 1936, when Josef Jungmann published his now famous work, *The Good News and Our Proclamation of the Faith.* This book caused a great deal of controversy, much of it irrelevantly directed against Jungmann's call for an entirely new kind of theology called "kerygmatic theology," as opposed to scientific, scholastic theology. It was unfortunate that the controversy had to revolve around this point, and that Jungmann was attacked for trying to destroy the intrinsic unity of theology as a discipline. This kind of arguing really missed Jungmann's basic thesis. Indeed, Jungmann himself was later to admit that he really was not deeply concerned whether theology is one or many; rather, his fundamental concern revolved around the value of the ideas expressed by theologians. Jungmann's point was that theology, and hence catechetics, should not deal entirely with abstract ideas, but should make every effort to show the implications and meaning of Christian truths for daily life. As Jungmann himself put it:

> It is not enough to show the necessity and reasonableness of the faith, nor enough to expound every point of doctrine and every commandment down to the very last division; but that it is singularly important to achieve first of all *a vital understanding* of the Christian message, bringing together "the many" into a consistent, unified whole, that then *there may be joyous interest and enthusiastic response* in living faith.[5]

Jungmann is concerned, then, to present faith as something living, real, and vital.

Jungmann's point of view eventually won wide acclaim among catechists and Christian educators. After World War II—since 1956 to be exact—the International Center for Studies in Religious Education, "Lumen Vitae," in Brussels has crystal-

---

[5]Josef Jungmann, *The Good News: Yesterday and Today,* translated, abridged and edited by William A. Huesman (New York: Sadlier, 1962), pp. 5-6.

lized the thesis of Jungmann into a training program for religious educators. Further, since World War II there developed that most familiar catechetical idea known as salvation history, proposed through the four great signs of scripture, liturgy, doctrine, and witness. In the United States, these ideas were quickly channeled into textbooks and programs presenting salvation history to the students in Catholic schools. I am not going to attempt a defense of the salvation history approach. In fact, I think it is almost totally indefensible, because it is, after all, simply the substitution of one tightly knit closed system for another closed system. The point I am making, however, is that since religion teachers have been talking about salvation history in Catholic schools for some years now, and although the students are obviously very tired of hearing about it, these teachers ought to reflect seriously upon just what the students have been hearing.

I suppose the "bible" in the salvation history approach is the well-known Eichstätt meeting, whose papers were published in 1961. These papers list the "basic principles" of modern catechetics. A few of the more pertinent ones are these: [1] Catechesis proclaims the merciful love of the Father for us and the Good News of God's Kingdom; [2] Catechesis teaches us to respond to God's call by an inner change of heart manifested in a life of faith and hope and of loving obedience to his commands; [3] Catechesis makes the Christian aware of his responsibility for the world and the betterment of its condition; [4] Catechesis leads the Christian to share the faith with others; [5] Catechesis introduces the catechumen [student] into a living community and helps him to strike root in it.[6]

I would like to contend that contrary to many critics of the salvation history approach, the weakness of these principles of Eichstätt—and indeed of the whole salvation history movement as it has typically appeared in textbooks, and as religion teachers

---

[6]Johannes Hofinger, "Basic Principles of Modern Catechetics," in Hofinger, *Teaching All Nations,* pp. 394-400.

have expounded it in their classrooms—is not that all of this has been totally ineffective, but that, in a certain way, it has been too effective.

I am referring to the fact that many persons engaged in the teaching of religion have gone to great lengths to point out to their students that this salvation history and this message of Christ can and does—or at least should—show up in daily life in any number of ways. Primary among these ways is that Christians are persons who have a tremendous respect for others, a great capacity for compassion and kindness, and a loving regard for everyone with whom they deal. I suspect that there are many students today who would not object to believing this. They would be all in favor of a program that results in genuine kindness one for another. They certainly are not against the dignity of other human persons, and, in fact, they are probably more in favor of it than many previous generations.

Why then, do these students find the religion class, especially the salvation history type religion class, so difficult to endure? Let me say again that they frequently "turn off" the religion teacher because the teaching is inept and dull. The lesson often is irrelevant and sounds like the teacher is trying to sell something. But these are by no means the only reasons why religion teachers are not succeeding.

What I am suggesting is that another and equally important reason for the overall lack of success of the religion class is that the students see and hear their teachers talking a good game, but a game that no one in the rest of the school appears to be playing. They do not *experience* in the rest of their school life the warmth, the compassion, and the dignity of Christianity of which the religion teacher speaks so much. There is a great gap between what the students hear the religion teacher say and the way the student is expected to behave in the school in general. I would suggest that this gap is so great that the only option these boys and girls have is to think that the religion teacher is simply unbelievable.

So, in this sense, the renewal in catechetics, with its concentration on the joyful message of Christ, has been too effective. It has had a high degree of negative effectiveness because
it has shown quite clearly and quite accurately to today's
students just how inconsistent twentieth century Christians can
be. It has proven to them beyond a shadow of a doubt that
Catholic teachers want their students to do what they say and
not what they do. In short, the content of many contemporary
religion courses has evolved into a somewhat deeper understanding of Christianity, with a marked concentration on personalistic values. It is this new kind of religion class which has
caused the students to feel a gap between theory and practice
right in the hallowed halls of Catholic schools.

Secular Education

Another set of causes for the increasingly wide gap between
what Christian educators say and the actual experience of Christianity by today's students revolves around recent developments
in secular education. This set of causes may not be as apparent
as the progress in the teaching of religion, but it is, nonetheless,
a subtle influence upon the state and goals of religious education today. That the influence is only subtle and perhaps indirect
is, of course, unfortunate, because it indicates that Catholic educators, especially in the area of religion teaching, really are not
taking full advantage of the insights and experiences of their
secular colleagues.

One of the great concerns in contemporary secular education
is a probing analysis of the whole teaching-learning process.
With the so-called "knowledge explosion" affecting almost all
academic subjects, secular educationists have come to the gradual realization that teaching and learning cannot be a simple
matter of communicating a certain number of facts or information concerning a particular subject. There are just too many
facts and too much information in all areas of investigation to
allow contemporary teachers the luxury of engaging solely in the
communication of information. Rather, what is called for is the

ability on the part of the teacher to engage students in the process of knowledge, in the life stream of the specified disciplines.

This effort to enter into the process of knowledge has led secular educational theorists to investigate every aspect of the teaching-learning situation. Preliminary results of such investigation have produced a body of literature dealing with the inter-relationships of teacher and student as together they seek the level of personal development required by a technological society. Hence, today there is great interest and enthusiasm for analyzing what exactly happens, verbally and nonverbally, between teacher and student in the typical classroom.[7] Fortunately, the scientific investigation of classroom behavior has gone beyond the realm of simple interest and enthusiasm. As a result increasingly sophisticated instruments of verbal classroom interaction analysis are being developed to pinpoint clearly those activities of the teacher which promote real engagement in a process and those which do not.[8]

Inevitably, the thrust toward a more authentic understanding of the teaching-learning process has generated renewed interest in the goals and purposes of education, and it is in this area that secular educationists today have much to say to religious educators. To be sure, there is a remarkable convergence of aspirations between secular and religious education. For instance, as I pointed out earlier, the religious educator today is concerned with the personal development of his students, with their human growth and their ability to live in a Christian relationship with other persons. It does not take much imagination to perceive that this type of objective is very similar to the purpose of secondary education as outlined by a leading educationist: "to produce a free, reasoning person who can make up his own

---

[7] A good introduction to this field is Edmund J. Amidon and John B. Hough, editors, *Interaction Analysis: Theory, Research and Application* (Reading, Mass.: Addison-Wesley, 1967).

[8] See, for instance, Ned A. Flanders, *Interaction Analysis in the Classroom* (Ann Arbor, Michigan: School of Education, University of Michigan, 1962).

mind, who will understand his cultural tradition, and who can live compassionately with his fellowman. In judging a school, I would want to know first what its graduates care about most."[9] Similarity of concern and interest between secular and religious educators does not stop, however, simply at the level of goals and objectives. It extends even to certain specific questions and problems facing schoolwork today. In particular it has extended itself to the very problem I have been discussing in this chapter:

> The school itself as an institution cannot contradict what it is trying to teach in the classroom. It cannot teach the value of freedom of inquiry and at the same time censor books and ideas. It cannot teach the value of individual dignity and disregard student opinion. It cannot call for responsible behavior without allowing students—and teachers—to have responsibility. It cannot be built around the governmental structure of a boss who dictates school policy and then expect to produce students who really believe in a majority rule, or even that a human being matters.[10]

It is evident, then, both from the standpoint of the "new" religion and from contemporary secular educational theory, that today's students are exposed to attitudes, values, and goals which explicitly deal with human relationships and personal growth. Children and youth are more and more in a process of developmental formation whose specific aim is the creation of competent, compassionate, Christ-like human persons. A certain experiential gap obviously exists between this type of formation and the concrete demands of the school as an institution. Is this gap in itself sufficient to explain the unrest and dissatisfaction students feel when they believe themselves to be the victims of a do-what-I-say-but-not-what-I-do mentality?

Theory-Practice Gap

An honest answer to this question only can be that the theory-

---

[9] Edward J. Gordon, "Conflicting Values in the Secondary School," in Alfred de Grazia and David A. Sohn, editors, *Revolution in Teaching* (New York: Bantam, 1964), p. 51.

[10] *Ibid.*, p. 55.

practice gap, especially in regard to religious education, cannot be the sole explanation for the apparent irrelevancy of the religion teacher today. I say this because it seems to me that there is always at least some discrepancy between what Christianity should be and the way Christians actually are in the concrete, workaday world. The latter never quite live up to the former, and it has been this way ever since Jesus Christ decided to form the nucleus of his church around twelve grubby and somewhat unintelligent Galileans. It was certainly this way in those dim days of yesteryear when the present adult generation was struggling with the mental gymnastics required to memorize question 124 of the *Baltimore Catechism:*

124. What is charity?

Charity is the virtue by which we love God above all things for his own sake, and our neighbor as ourself for the love of God. Charity is divine friendship uniting man to God and man to fellowman in bonds of mutual affection. Our neighbor includes all living human beings, even our enemies, the souls in purgatory, the blessed in heaven and the angels.[11]

Surely, there were at least a few students in that bygone age who realized that the actual practice of the church and of church schools really did not unite man to his fellowman in bonds of mutual affection. Why today can the contemporary generation no longer tolerate such a gap? When the present adult generation was younger they seemed to be able to live with, or at least to ignore, the blatant contradictions which existed between Christian ideals and Christian practice. What is it in the constitution of the "now generation" that makes it virtually impossible for them to adjust or compromise religious theory and religious practice?

American Culture and Society

I believe the main reason why the present generation cannot

[11]Confraternity of Christian Doctrine, *A Catechism of Christian Doctrine* (Paterson, N.J.: St. Anthony Guild Press, 1941), pp. 93-94.

stand a divergence between what they hear, on the one hand, and what they see being done, on the other, is that today's young people appear to be exceptionally mature Americans. This means, first of all, that contrary to all appearances, the youth of today actually have accepted and live according to the cultural heritages and mental attitudes of this country, and they probably do this to an extent which far surpasses any previous generation. Obviously such a contention needs careful explanation, for it seems both grossly inaccurate and highly simplistic. However, I believe that this assertion is in reality extremely complex, and from a metaphysical point of view, it may be seen as perceptively accurate.

To state that the present generation has learned its lesson of Americanization well is to contend that it has a very direct approach to life and life-problems. By "direct" I mean that the present generation takes at face value all of the sensory and reflective impressions of any one given experience. They equate these impressions in that all of them together form one total experience. In other words, the present generation has acquired an outstanding American characteristic: the ability to live each moment or particular experience all at once. In a rough way, this is one of the fundamental theses of Marshall McLuhan in his *Understanding Media.* For the contemporary man, there is and must be a real and obvious convergence between all sensory perceptions in any one experience and the reflective meaning of that experience. Put into its most concrete terms, this indicates that students today cannot tolerate a do-what-I-say-but-not-what-I-do attitude. For them an experience based upon this premise would be a lie, and the modern student would find such an experience utterly incomprehensible.

McLuhan, of course, states that the reason for this kind of total approach to experience resides in the overwhelming presence of modern mass communications, and I would agree definitely with such an evaluation of the situation. But I would like to point out another set of causes or reasons why this approach to life can actually be termed typically American. George Santayana in his *Character and Opinion in the United States* says: "When a way of thinking is deeply rooted in the soil and embodies the instincts or even the characteristic errors of a people, it has a value quite independent of its truth; it constitutes a phase of human life and can powerfully affect the intellectual drama in which it figures."[12] Commenting on these lines, the American Catholic philosopher, John J. McDermott, points out that "in the case of America, to which Santayana's text primarily refers, the stakes are somewhat higher than that of an intellectual drama."[13]

These statements of Santayana and McDermott form a starting point for a short analysis of the American mentality and the American metaphysical attitude, which I now will attempt to make. I want to make clear, first of all, as Santayana indicates, that I will not be concerned with the ultimate truth or value of the American approach. It will be a matter of simply describing what already is. Secondly, along with McDermott, in speaking about the American mentality or the American metaphysical style, I actually am discussing something far more important than an intellectual drama. My analysis here concerns a way of life, a stance in the face of reality, an approach to the existing world which deeply involves every power of the human person.

Perhaps the most obvious characteristic of American young people today, and theoretically of every American citizen, is that they do not conform to the metaphysical style of ancient Greece. They are not, in other words, Aristotelians. This means that Americans in general are not given over to speculating about "being as such," and indeed, this form of speculation does not seem to be of much value to the ordinary American. Reflection of an exceptionally abstract variety on experiences whose connection to real life problems and situations is not

---

[12]Quoted in John J. McDermott, *The American Angle of Vision* (West Nyack, New York: Cross Currents Press, 1965), p. 433.
[13]*Ibid.*

readily perceived is not part of the American life-style.

I am making this point because, although Americans by natural inclination shy away from abstract speculation, they can be trained to accustom themselves to the thought-patterns of ancient Greece. At one time most church functionaries in the Roman Catholic Church were so trained, and this included American Catholic religious educators. American catechists grew up and lived in one kind of culture, but they had to take on the thought forms and mental sets of a completely different culture in order to attain their goal of service to the church.[14] In a real sense, then, Catholic religious educators were culturally deprived. They were deprived of their native, innate culture, at least in regard to their role as Christian teachers, and had to acquire the thought forms, values, and approaches to problem-solving of another society, another way of life.

The cultural deprivation of American Catholic educators led them to teaching concepts such as the hypostatic union, the necessary distinctions for an understanding of predestination, and whether or not God is a substance, an accident, or prime matter itself. When American Catholic students displayed little interest in these matters, they were being more authentically American than their teachers.

I presume that it is safe to say that the era of Catholic teachers being trained in such an out-of-date philosophical framework is over. There should no longer be any concern that American catechists are actually ancient Greeks in disguise. But if the day of this Greek infiltration is over, there still looms the possibility that American catechists have fallen victims to another kind of cultural deprivation.

Earlier in this chapter, I pointed out how the modern cate-chetical movement brought with it from Europe a program of catechesis based upon the idea of salvation history as this is manifested in the four great signs of revelation. This system

---

[14]This idea was first put forward by Leslie Dewart in his *The Future of Belief* (New York: Herder and Herder, 1966), and can be applied to all aspects of Roman Catholic life.

seems to have failed miserably with the students now occupying Catholic schools, and many critics of the approach have claimed that the reason for the failure was that teachers really did not understand salvation history themselves. Whereas this may be one of the factors in the failure of the salvation history system, I do not think it is a sufficient explanation. If a closer scrutiny of salvation history is undertaken, and the question asked what kind of metaphysics or world view does all this presuppose, the answer would have to be that whatever it is, it is not an American approach to the real world.

At its root the salvation history system is based upon a Christian version of philosophical existentialism. This is, of course, a very appealing philosophical framework, and it is especially appealing to anyone who has spent long, tedious, dry hours juggling Greek metaphysical concepts. The existential point of view manifests itself in the salvation history system through the constant repetition of phrases such as "the joyful proclamation of the good news." It appears in religion textbooks by means of prolonged discussions on the paschal mystery, the lordship of Christ, and that early summary of Christian teaching known as the apostolic kerygma. All of these indicate an existentialist framework because they are each attempts to probe and to experience the primitive core of some reality. They are, in other words, the effort to relive or to live-in the being, existence, or whatever it may be called, of some thing. In this case the thing in question is salvation history, the good news or message of Christianity.

Existential philosophy is one great contribution to contemporary thought and life, and I do not want to give the impression of regarding it with something less than esteem. The chief point of the discussion here is that existentialism is basically a European movement and as such it does not and cannot reflect the thrust of the American religious mentality. It is not, in other words, an apt vehicle for engaging young Americans in the process of religious growth and information.[15]

If American students today are not by nature speculative Greeks or philosophical existentialists, how best can they be described? What is that elusive thing known as the American style or the American approach to life?

Any account of today's students as authentic Americans must seriously consider the descriptions and analyses of the American scene produced in this country. This would indicate that it is necessary to probe deeply into American philosophy and particularly into the uniquely American philosophical point of view known as pragmatism. Unfortunately, pragmatism does not enjoy an esteemed reputation in American intellectual and academic circles, and many commentators upon the American scene have been hesitant even to use the word for fear of gross misunderstanding. The Jesuit philosopher, Robert Roth, perhaps, has best expressed such hesitation:

> I would almost like to call the American approach pragmatic and practical, except that in the eyes of many Americans and almost all Europeans, the American bent for the pragmatic and practical reduces him to a tinkerer with gadgets who views things and situations in terms of their "cash-value" and for whom the value of an object depends on whether it works.[16]

Nevertheless, I sincerely believe that the best way of describing the present generation of Americans would be to say that they are authentic pragmatists in the richest and deepest meaning of that word. This statement obviously requires some clarification.

John E. Smith has characterized the American mentality by delineating three major elements:

> There are three dominant or focal beliefs through which our

---

[15]James Sellers, "The Almost Chosen People: A Theological Approach to American Society" in *The Journal of Religion* 45 (October, 1965):271.

[16]Robert J. Roth, *American Religious Philosophy* (New York: Harcourt, Brace and World, 1967), p. 20.

philosophic spirit can be articulated. First, the belief that think-ing is primarily an activity in response to a concrete situation and that this activity is aimed at solving problems. Second, the be-lief that ideas and theories must have a "cutting edge" or must make a difference in the conduct of people who hold them and in the situations in which they live. Third, the belief that the earth can be civilized and obstacles to progress overcome by the application of knowledge.[17]

I would like to take each of these beliefs and show how they apply to contemporary Americans. This will be followed by a consideration of their catechetical consequences.

The first belief is that thinking occurs in response to a con-crete situation and is aimed at problem-solving. This belief is easily verifiable as an integral part of the American mentality. In 1957 the Soviet Union launched Sputnik I, and the universal response of the American people was to think out and actively create the most far-reaching program of space exploration imaginable. Within a very short time, the American educational establishment looked deeply into its conscience and proposed a crash program of science education, the effects of which are still evident in American schools. But each of these occurrences generated other situations which in turn begot more thinking and more programs of action so that the one concrete situation of 1957 has been responsible for a real revolution—material, social, and academic—in the United States.

The thought and action generated by the advent of the space age has been condemned or praised by the present adult gen-eration. This is because the adults of today can remember what it was like before Sputnik I, and they, therefore, have some basis of comparison upon which to form their judgments. It is important for educators, and especially for religious educators, to reflect upon the fact that today's students do not have this basis of comparison. The world to which they are accustomed is a world of technological innovation. These students had

---

[17]John E. Smith, *The Spirit of American Philosophy* (New York: Ox-ford University Press, 1966), p. 188.

barely reached the so-called age of reason at the time of Sputnik I, and they have grown up with one spectacular scientific triumph after another. Whether we like it or not, thinking as a response to a concrete situation and as the effort to overcome a specific problem has been a part of the "now generation's" environmental condition since the time they were first able to perceive their environment.

Secondly, the American approach to reality is characterized by the belief that the ideas and theories a person holds must make a difference in the conduct of that person and in the situation in which he lives. Americans traditionally have stood up for what they believed in; to be sure, the outstanding mark of an authentic American hero is the man who not only expresses his beliefs but acts upon these beliefs with every power at his command. The controversy which raged so acutely in the United States during the McCarthy presidential nomination campaign of 1968 on the question of the war in Vietnam is a classic example of this characteristic. The "hawks" believed that armed conflict, although not always the most desirable situation, is at times a necessary means of preserving the very basic American belief in freedom from tyranny. Armed conflict, after all, was the means used by the colonists to insure democratic freedom in the United States at the birth of this nation. The "doves," for their part, were highly expressive and active in regard to what they consider a more fundamental American belief, namely that freedom in a democracy must include the right of each individual to dissent from the stated policies of political leaders. Both groups, however, appeared to be living up to their natural "Americanness" because, "ever since the days of Jonathan Edwards action has been taken as the chief clue to the sincerity of the individual. Willingness to act upon a belief, especially one involving risk, meant that a person took seriously what he professed to believe."[18]

The third typically American belief holds that the world can

---

[18]*Ibid.*, p. 194.

become better and obstacles to progress overcome through the application of knowledge. This belief more or less follows from the first two, and also it can be verified easily by an analysis of contemporary American society. Only since the early 1960's have the American people been aware of the presence of real poverty in the midst of the most affluent country the world has ever known. The revelation of poverty's existence sent a shock wave throughout the nation, and in typical American fashion, the response was to create massive programs of aid and development in order to produce a better America. Even the title of these programs, the "War on Poverty," indicates the American's deep-rooted belief that the worst evils can be overcome by the practical application of the resources available. The use of the metaphor "war" is important, for it manifests the conviction that a day of total and ultimate victory can be achieved, in which the forces of evil are conquered definitively by the forces of good. Just as the United States has never lost a shooting war, so there is the implicit assumption that she will not lose the War on Poverty.

All of these basic American beliefs, then, find their concretization in contemporary American society. They are still characteristics of Americans and, therefore, should be seen as characteristics of young Americans today. Paul Van Buren, the Death-of-God theologian, has attempted to summarize these and other aspects of the American mentality by claiming that the typical American has "a rough-hewn, man-in-the-street, general, technological Western approach to life, somewhat empirical, somewhat pragmatic, somewhat relativistic, somewhat naturalistic, but also somewhat aesthetic and somewhat personalistic."[19]

TOWARD A RESOLUTION OF THE TENSION BETWEEN SCHOOL AND RELIGION CLASS

It seems to me that these American beliefs are extremely im-

---

[19]Paul Van Buren, "Christian Education: Post Mortem Dei," in *Religious Education* 60 (January-February, 1965):5.

portant for the catechetical movement and especially for the problem outlined at the start of this chapter. A tension can exist between the religious education program and the daily regime of a school. This tension has developed from two sources. On the one hand, there has been progress in religious and secular education leading to a deep and abiding concern for the healthy formation of the individual human person. On the other hand, existing discrepancies between theory and practice cannot be tolerated by the present generation because young people today have been weaned on a steady diet of basic American approaches to life and life-problems.

What options are open to Catholic school personnel which take into account all of the factors making up this complex situation? There are basically three life-styles a school-as-institution can adopt. It can operate under authoritarianism, anarchy, or community. By way of conclusion, I will take each of these in turn and relate them to the new religion and the American metaphysical stance.

An authoritarian school is directed by one person or a small group of persons whose function is to control all of the nonteaching activities of the school environment. In itself a strictly authoritarian school is not necessarily an evil thing. However, since the nonteaching activities of a school do affect the conduct and actions of everyone in the school, it would seem that the authoritarian school is of little value in contemporary American society. This is especially true if teachers insist upon the development of human dignity as a goal of education. Human dignity presupposes human freedom, and such freedom is difficult to reconcile with the purely authoritarian style. From the point of view of the American mentality, moreover, the authoritarian mode seems contrary to the fundamental American belief that a person's ideas must make a difference in the way that person lives. Under an authoritarian regime, both students and teachers are asked to perform opposite to this belief. They are asked to conduct their lives according to someone else's ideas and theories, even if they themselves have not personally assimilated these ideas. In effect this is asking the school community to give up a part of itself, to somehow become less American, and such a request makes as much sense as asking a black man to become less black.

But if an authoritarian regime seems out of place on the American educational scene, so does anarchy. An anarchical school operates under the belief that no authority, control, or regime is necessary for the educational enterprise. Each group or faction within the school should be allowed to do its "own thing." Fortunately this kind of school "organization" has been rare in the United States, although some doomsday citizens seem to believe that current student rebellions are representative of a desire for total anarchy on the part of the young. Such feelings have even been confirmed by some school officials. For example, a university president, who resigned in the late 1960's, stated publicly that he "left law practice to become an educator, not a policeman. Now every university president has to be a policeman. There are little groups that are determined to destroy. They don't want solutions, just confrontation."[20] Statements and feelings such as these are, hopefully, extremely exaggerated, not to say simply inaccurate. But if a true anarchical school did exist in the United States, it definitely would go against the grain of the American mentality by denying the belief that obstacles can be overcome and progress made through the rational application of knowledge. An anarchical school, by definition, does not apply rationally knowledge to the problems and tensions shared by the entire school community.

The third basic form of school organization is one which revolves around the formation of an authentic community. In this setup every faction within the school has the opportunity to participate in the total life of the institution. Obviously, such

---

[20]Elvis J. Stahr, as quoted in "Academe's Exhausted Executives," *Time* 99 (September 27, 1968):55.

an organization of the school respects to a high degree both the progress in the teaching of religion and the American mentality outlined earlier. It also recognizes, as Robert Roth has pointed out, that "what is central to the development of American thought and experience is the recognition of the importance of involvement in the environment."[21]

Community, then, within the school structure is the only way of easing the theory-practice gap, while at the same time insuring fidelity to the American approach to life. The biggest problem, of course, is that community is not something one creates overnight. While this is true, and it is equally true that school officials, teachers, and students must all struggle, perhaps painfully at times, through the process of becoming a community, the creation of lasting community in the school is not impossible. It is only impossible if any one faction of the school remains self-seeking, fearful, or genuinely antagonistic to the idea that a school should be a community.

CONCLUSION

Many Catholic school officials, teachers, and students are not adverse to the creation of a Christian community among themselves. Many, however, have expressed an inability in regard to the steps necessary for the formation of community. I would suggest here that everyone take seriously the three basic characteristics of the American mentality treated in this chapter. They can be the starting point for real progress toward community first, by reflecting or thinking clearly about the concrete situation of a particular school for the purpose of solving the problems of that school, and second, by pinpointing ideas and theories which really do make a difference in the life-situation of the school. Such a procedure can be successful to the extent that everyone involved actually does believe that their common problems can be solved and life made better through the communal application of their collective knowledge and insights.

---

[21]Roth, *American Religious Philosophy*, p. 19.

2 The Learning of Attitudes, Values and Beliefs

Jeffrey Keefe

A song in the Rogers and Hammerstein musical, *South Pacific,* has lyrics which run:

> You've got to be taught, before it's too late
> Before you are six or seven or eight,
> To hate all the people your relatives hate,
> You've got to be carefully taught.

Rogers and Hammerstein are talking—or singing—about the formation of prejudice. They make the point that it is not innate; it is acquired. Prejudice must be acquired at a young age. And it is acquired through family influences.

With some modifications psychological research supports these conclusions, not only for prejudice, but for attitudes in general. If one considers character as the complex of attitudes or habitual reaction tendencies which *characterize* a person, then the acquisition of prejudice provides a paradigm of much characterological formation. Character—an individual's motivating attitudes and the values which form them—has its foundations in early life. This simply rephrases the wisdom of the human experience found in adages; for example, "As the tree is bent so shall it grow." St. Ignatius Loyola has been credited with the claim that if he could educate a child until six years of age he could promise a Christian for life. Psychological research and clinical experience sometimes correct but generally confirm the wisdom of proverb, folklore, and anecdote. In addition, however, the researcher and the clinical psychologist supply perspective and delineation for such general truths, as well as furnish insight into the dynamic processes which occur between and within people.

A painstaking longitudinal empirical study of Midwestern youths concluded that a child's pattern of motivating attitudes is strongly set by age ten and relatively stable thereafter.[1] Marc Oraison, the French priest-psychiatrist, explained that the emotional experiences of the first seven or eight years condition an individual's whole future life.[2] Adler said that the style of life is set at four or five. And Sigmund Freud moved the foundations of character back to age three.[3] While one may draw oversimplified and fatalistic conclusions from such research findings and clinical inference (which will be treated in some detail subsequently), both do confirm that early childhood familial history is prepotent in establishing values and developing attitudes.

Attitudes and values are terms of everyday vocabulary—familiar abstractions which we all understand in approximately the same way. Therefore, we have little difficulty in communicating about these terms in ordinary conversation. But, as with many things very familiar to us, we find ourselves hardput to define them. Moreover, these and other terms that enter such discussions—terms like motive, standard, trait, or interest—are difficult to tease apart because they tend to merge with one another in our interchangeable usage of them.

The Nature and Formation of Attitudes

A helpful approach toward understanding attitudes is to consider how they are formed. One of the ways the human mind

[1]Ralph F. Peck and Robert J. Havighurst, *The Psychology of Character Development* (New York: Wiley, 1960).

[2]Marc Oraison, *Love or Constraint* (New York, Kenedy, 1959).

[3]Sigmund Freud, *Three Essays on the Theory of Sexuality,* standard edition, vol. 7 (London: Hogarth, 1953).

has for dealing with its tremendous input of information is generalization. There is a great economy to this process because we simply could not function if we dealt with each datum of experience separately, just as we could not walk if we consciously averted to each neuromuscular movement and adjustment. So we generalize, we categorize, we develop rules of thumb to cover many cases. When we perceive Notre Dame, we might classify it as "university" or "football powerhouse"; we might categorize Rockefeller as "politician" or "wealthy man." A speeding car might be assigned to mental categories such as "fun" or "dangerous." Categorization is an implicit statement of fact, opinion, or belief.

We can witness the process of categorizing in young children who are just learning to speak. To the two-and-a-half year old, every animal is "doggie," and to the three year old, every uniformed man is a policeman. As a child grows, he revises and refines his categories in order to organize his experience more accurately. Refinement of categories is one of the aims of education, for it gives precision to one's beliefs, and hones rules-of-thumb into sophisticated scientific law.

When I was a seminarian, I was in the sacristy of my home parish, and a young girl about seven years old came to the sacristy and asked, "Father, please bless my rosary." I told her that I was sorry, but since I was not a priest, I could not bless the rosary. But I gave the reassurance that Father would be along soon. The young girl looked at me rather quizzically and said, *"Sister,* when will Father be here?" By this categorization she was expressing one of her beliefs: people in black robes are priests or sisters. She was trying to formulate a rule-of-thumb or a law, but in doing so she oversimplified the world of black-robed people and then assimilated one object too many to her category of nun—this nonpriest in a black robe. She was trying to make her experience consistent.

As adults we often classify as loosely as this girl and with less amusing results. We oversimplify our world and assign, for example, not black-robed but black-skinned people to a single category. We type, and we stereotype. Prizefighters are expected to be burly and dull-witted, women to be poor drivers, and people who advocate academic freedom or liberalized social legislation to be Communists. The tendency to overgeneralize, to assimilate to a class, to be simplistic, to get along with as few categories as possible, is one of the root conditions for erroneous beliefs and intolerant attitudes. We have such a strong need for lawfulness and consistency to regulate our lives, to make predictions, and insure our security, that we often impose regularity when it does not exist. Thus one hears that "Negroes are lawless," "Puerto Ricans are lazy," and—more recently—"bishops are lackadasical."

Our understanding of our experience is not limited to cognitive elements, however. In addition to perceiving some objects and abstracting and knowing them under rather neutral prosaic headlines such as "animal," "policeman," or "nun," there is also an evaluative dimension in much of our organization of experience. Research has indicated that "good/bad" is a basic dimension of meaning. This finding was replicated in studies carried out in a wide variety of languages and cultural areas.[4]

To return to the little girl with the rosary, we do not know her evaluation of sisters. But we know, for example, the evaluation of sisters expressed by Perry Smith, one of the partner-murderers in Truman Capote's *In Cold Blood*.[5] Smith's evaluation of nuns was extremely negative; as a child in an orphanage he had been beaten by them for bedwetting. On the other hand, Robert Louis Stevenson's evaluation of nuns was highly positive; he had witnessed their heroic tenderness among the lepers at Molokai. In brief Smith and Stevenson had organized attitudes toward sisters because their knowledge about them was merged with a feeling about them. Attitudes are

---

[4] Charles E. Osgood, "Studies on the Generality of Effective Meaning Systems," *American Psychologist* 17 (January, 1962):10-28.

[5] Truman Capote, *In Cold Blood* (New York: Random House, 1966).

"stored cognitions which have some positive or negative associations."[6]

Structurally an attitude has first, a cognitive component composed of the thoughts—sometimes beliefs—about the object of the attitude, and second, an affective component, which are the feelings toward the object. In addition attitudes may have a behavioral component. Perry Smith's behavioral component was to avoid nuns and by generalization to avoid priests and religion as well. Robert Louis Stevenson's behavioral component was to write a poem of encomium to the nuns at Molokai.[7]

An attitude, then, is an organizer of experience; in it we join a cognitive and affective element, and by it we are predisposed or conditioned to respond in a particular way to any number of class of objects. Gordon Allport's classical definition states that an attitude is "a mental and neural state of readiness organized through experience, exerting a directive and dynamic influence upon the individual's responses to all objects or situations with which it is related."[8] When an attitude is activated, we react in an affective as well as effective manner. Attitudes combine dynamic processes, such as emotion and striving, with cognitive processes, such as thought and memory.

The Nature and Formation of Values

The affective component of an attitude is sparked by evaluation. What, then, is a value? "Value" is a term which is already a definition; it is one of those primary concepts which define themselves, as does "existence," for example. Values are conceptions of the desirable; an object or symbol or idea is a value if we conceive of it as desirable. Values are rather inclusive goals. Some values are radicated in basic physiological needs,

---

[6] Theodore M. Newcomb, Ralph H. Turner, and P. E. Converse, *Social Psychology* (New York: Holt, Rinehart & Winston, 1965), p. 40.

[7] Robert L. Stevenson, "To Mother Maryanne," in *Collected Poems* (London: Rupert Hart-Davis, 1950), p. 266.

[8] Gordon Allport, "The Historical Background of Modern Social Psychology," in Gardner Lindzey, editor, *Handbook of Social Psychology*, 2 vols. (Cambridge, Mass.: Addison—Wesley, 1954), 1:3-57.

comfort and safety, for example. Other values are hallmarks of the mature person, for instance, love and productiveness.[9] Independence, responsibility, courage, honesty: these are values we all subscribe to explicitly or implicitly in greater or lesser degree.

Values are more general than attitudes. Attitudes are limited to a fairly specific class of objects (such as Negroes) or to an abstraction (such as foreign aid), while values on the other hand encompass generalities.

The value which a person holds formalizes and directs his attitude toward an object. One man's central value is personal freedom, while another's is law and order. These two men will have quite different attitudes toward collegian riots, or legislation on obscenity, or gun control laws. It is the value which gives rise to the dynamic, affective quality of an attitude. Depending on our particular value, we see a person or a class or an abstraction as something good, which attracts us, or something evil, which we are prompted to avoid. An attitude makes one ready, set to go. An attitude is an underlying predisposition that serves as a potential for action.[10]

The Place of Childhood

Earlier in this chapter, it was stated that clinical experience and research generally confirm the human consensus regarding the acquisition of attitudes and values. A person without any psychological sophistication would list the sources of values and attitudes as follows: the general culture in which one lives, his social class, his group memberships, and his family life, especially early family life. And probably he would give greater weight to successively closer and earlier influences. We must add one more source of attitudes, namely, oneself. For if atti-

---

[9]Erich Fromm, *Man for Himself* (New York: Holt, Rinehart & Winston, 1947).

[10]John D. Campbell, "Studies in Attitude Formation: The Development of Health Orientations," in Carolyn Sherif and Muzafer Sherif, editors, *Attitude, Ego-Involvement and Change* (New York: Wiley, 1967).

tudes are functions of values, surely one's dominant value is his own self-image.[11]

Child development studies have confirmed this general outline of sources and provided considerable insight regarding the processes at work. Freud's monumental contribution was to point our attention to the earlier stages of personality development, to the prehistory of life prior to the periods which conscious memory records.[12] In hindsight this approach makes eminent sense. For if values and attitudes have substantial affective components, we might have suspected that the origin of some attitudes, at least, would occur during preintellectual life, since emotional life precedes intellectual life.

Clinical research from Bowlby,[13] Spitz,[14] and Bettleheim,[15] to mention only major names among many studies, provides strong evidence that one's basic evaluation of self, and one's basic outlook toward others, have their *prefiguration* in infant experience. Satisfaction of the physiological and, even more important, of the affectional needs of the infant communicates to him that the world is after all a satisfying place and lays the groundwork for what Erik Erikson calls basic trust.[16] Excessive deprivation of the affectional needs of the infant leads to lack of hope, depression, and even death.[17] Nursing is now seen by the clinical psychologist as much more than a nutritive, physiological experience. It is the primary interpersonal relationship, and, therefore, optimally is a *mutual* relationship in which the infant is not simply a passive recipient, but by his response gives satisfaction to the mother. One only need witness a nursing

[11]Gordon Allport, *The Nature of Prejudice* (Cambridge, Mass.: Addison, Wesley, 1954).

[12]Freud, *Three Essays on the Theory of Sexuality.*

[13]J. Bowlby, "The Nature of the Child's Tie to His Mother," *International Journal of Psychoanalysis* 39 (1958):1-23.

[14]René Spitz, *The First Year of Life* (New York: Norton, 1965).

[15]Bruno Bettleheim, *The Empty Fortress* (New York: Free Press, 1967).

[16]Erik Erikson, *Childhood and Society,* second edition (New York: Norton, 1964).

[17]Spitz, *The First Year of Life.*

mother and child to sense the emotional interplay, and clinical studies indicate that the affective tone can be quite enduring, whether it be a secure or anxious note. Bruno Bettleheim speaks of mutuality as an activity wherein two persons engage in an action from separate personal needs, leading to a relief of tension and the emotional satisfaction of both.[18] From the mutuality experienced in nursing, an infant develops a primitive sense of mastery as well as trust, and a sense of autonomy in that he can influence his environment. This prefigured sense of mastery will grow more definite through successful toleration by the child of the first major frustrating demands made on him, for example, in toilet training. When this realistic demand is carried out with the joyful communication that the child is acquiring control of himself, that *he* has accomplished a task mutually pleasing to himself and his mother, his embryonic *sense* of autonomy develops. When toilet training is carried out as the demand of a controlling and seemingly gigantic parent, his sense of autonomy suffers an embryonic lesion. He begins to feel that he is controlled by outer forces in a world which is insensitive to his contributions. All this is not, to be sure, an intellectual or even conscious evaluation, nor an emotional experience as an older child or adult might experience. Marc Oraison labels it a "confused prefiguration"; it is an amorphous condition of gratification or tension, an inchoate feeling which develops into more defined emotion, and forms the base of attitudes gradually developed through further experiences.[19]

The religion teacher who is concerned with developing religious values and attitudes and genuine religious behavior may wonder what relevance these empirical research studies possibly can have for his work, which, after all, is not with infants. These studies are cited to lay the groundwork for two major conclusions. First, self-evaluation and attitudes toward the environment have their origins in early life, earlier than ever

---

[18]Bettleheim, *The Empty Fortress.*
[19]Oraison, *Love or Constraint.*

before suspected. From self-evaluation and attitudes toward others, the self-concept develops. (It should be remembered that the self-concept is the basic frame of reference for later perception, evaluations, and attitude formation). Second, these values and attitudes are mediated by interpersonal relationships. Gordon Allport expressed it clearly: attitudes are more caught than taught. The acquisition of values and attitudes is contingent on the relationship involved between teacher and learner, rather than on the roles of transmitter and receiver.[20]

A substantial number of empirical research studies have explored differences in the backgrounds of young persons who show a highly mature system of values and motivating attitudes, as compared to those youths whose value and attitude system was judged immature or even antisocial. These studies have covered a wide age range, from five-year-olds to college-age subjects. They have employed a variety of assessment procedures: behavioral histories, teacher's reports and ratings, ratings of interviews with parents and the subjects of the studies themselves, ratings on home visits, projective testing, case conferences using multiple criteria, sociometric measures, and experimental situations where subjects could be observed without their knowledge, and in which they had the opportunity to cheat on some assigned task. The rationale of these studies is that behavior reflects values and motivating attitudes, and that guilt is a sign of internalized norms. A striking feature of these studies is their consistency of results. Many confirm one another; others add new insights to fill out a dovetailing cluster of conclusions.

The Development of Conscience

One of the few longitudinal studies in the literature, that of Peck and Havighurst, followed its subjects intensively from age ten to sixteen.[21] This study concluded that there are five charac-

---

[20]Allport, *The Nature of Prejudice*.
[21]Peck and Havighurst, *The Psychology of Character Development*.

ter types, each successively more socialized. Expressed another way, there are five successively more mature levels of conscience development. The descriptive categories of these investigators, confirmed by the professional and nonprofessional assessments of their subjects, show an amazing parallel to the successive levels of cognitive maturity of moral judgment found by Kohlberg.[22] Kohlberg's cross-cultural studies led him to a theory of invariant sequence in conscience development, a sequence linked with cognitive development from age three upward.

Peck and Havighurst differentiated groups of adolescents whose conscience was stunted or fixed at various levels of development, as well as a group of youths who had developed a mature value system. The most primitive character types in Peck and Havighurst's "Prairie City" study manifested amoral and expedient characters, described independently by Kohlberg as the stage of premoral conscience. Such individuals guide their behavior principally on the aim to avoid punishment or, on a slightly higher plane, to gain a reward. These two stages of conscience development are rather typical for all children of three through seven years of age.[23] But some adolescents and even adults show no further development of conscience.[24]

The next level of conscience development, according to Kohlberg, reflects incipient interpersonal values. On this second level, the individual is motivated by his search for the approval of others, or by his aim to placate authority.[25] Peck and Havighurst identified similar character types and labeled them conforming and irrational-conscientious respectively. The conformist is an imitator of others, rather than a self-directing agent. His norms are largely external, and his reaction to his

---

[22]Lawrence Kohlberg, "Development of Moral Character and Moral Ideology," in Martin Hoffman and Lois Hoffman, editors, *Review of Child Development Research*, 2 vols. (New York: Russell Sage Foundation, 1964), 1.

[23]*Ibid.*

[24]Fromm, *Man for Himself;* Peck and Havighurst, *The Psychology of Character Development.*

[25]Kohlberg, "Development of Moral Character and Moral Ideology."

own failures regarding these norms is shame—the embarrassment that others know of his failure. The irrational-conscientious person does internalize the code of his parents and superiors, and he experiences self-reproach or true guilt should he fail to live up to the code. But he is immature in that he tends to unquestioning and blind observance to the law as he sees it, and for this reason his conscientiousness is considered to have irrational elements.[26] Kohlberg found that conventional moral judgments, that is, morality in order to gain approval or avoid censure, was typical of latency in children from eight to twelve years of age.[27] However, older persons also may have developed only to this intermediate level of conscience.

Finally, the highest level of conscience development is the morality of self-accepted principles, a considered conformity on the basis on reasoned inquiry, wherein the individual sees that the highest value is not the law itself, but the purpose it serves. Peck and Havighurst called those who gave evidence of this level of psychosocial development the rational-altruistic character type.[28] Kohlberg maintained that mature moral judgment requires the understanding of principles and their application, a cognitive operation which does not develop until early adolescence.[29]

The Place of Family Life

Most salient to the concern of this chapter is that each character type of the "Prairie City" study revealed its own specific pattern of family life. The amoral subject typically experienced family relationships marked by chaotic inconsistency and even active rejection. The hallmark of the expedient subjects' family was usually overpermissiveness, but sometimes severe autocratic control. The thematic discipline in the families of conformers and overly conscientious persons ranged from benign to severe

[26]Peck and Havighurst, *The Psychology of Character Development*.
[27]Kohlberg, "Development of Moral Character and Moral Ideology."
[28]Peck and Havighurst, *The Psychology of Character Development*.
[29]Kohlberg, "Development of Moral Character and Moral Ideology."

autocratic control respectively. The rationally altruistic subject was the product of a home with the most clear-cut family pattern: consistency, strong trust, affection, democratic structure, a child-centered but not child-dominated home. Peck and Havighurst concluded that the character of their subjects proved to be almost a direct reproduction of the way in which their parents treated them.[30]

None of the subjects in the Peck and Havighurst study were in open conflict with society. A study of adolescents who displayed a history of antisocial, aggressive, or malignantly sexual behavior was carried out by Bandura and Walters.[31] They matched two groups of adolescents in order to investigate the factors that differentiated delinquents from normal, socialized, teenage boys. The investigators matched subjects from the gamut of socioeconomic levels, with a concentration of subjects from lower middle-class families in which the breadwinner was a skilled laborer or white collar worker of minor status. All the boys of the study were from intact homes. All were white and Protestant.

Comparison of the child-training practices and family interrelationships indicated that in early life the delinquent boys had received considerably less affection from their fathers than had the nondelinquent boys. Among the delinquent boys, their mothers' response to early-life dependency behavior was inconsistent. The sons, therefore, received little satisfaction of their basic dependency need for parental interest, attention, and approval. Such experience provided little incentive to sacrifice self-gratification for conformity to parental demands and prohibitions, and later, to those of the larger society. Moreover, their early negative experience left these sons anxious about any dependency relationship as they grew older. As adolescents the delinquents demonstrated an almost pathological nonde-

---

[30]Peck and Havighurst, *The Psychology of Character Development.*
[31]Albert Bandura and Richard Walters, *Adolescent Aggression* (New York: Ronald, 1959).

pendence. They decided to be too "tough" to be hurt.

Mothers of the boys who later showed poor social values made less demands on their sons than did the mothers of normal boys, whereas the fathers of the aggressive boys tended to set more restrictions. But the hostility of these fathers gave poor example; their behavior contradicted the norms they set, and their lack of affiliative interaction with their sons provided the boys with little basis for positive identification with their father. Thus there was little prospect for internalization of parental norms. The aggression of the delinquent boys, spawned by the physical punishment from their fathers and the frustration of their dependency needs, was displaced to other authority figures, particularly to teachers. These boys showed almost no guilt in projective tests or interview data. They had a history of low resistance to temptation. Similarly in another study, data from collegians who cheated in an experimental test situation revealed that lack of internalized norms as well as lack of guilt was correlated with a nonaffectionate and punitive posture by their fathers when the subjects were younger.[32]

In the Bandura and Walters study, inconsistency was also illustrated in parental handling of the aggression in the sons who later became delinquent.[33] The parents actually encouraged aggressive behavior outside the home, but they took extreme suppressive measures in the home. The fathers, especially, were intolerant of any display of anger aimed at themselves.

A contrary picture developed from the data on parental practices in the control group of normal, nondelinquent adolescents during their childhood. Both parents were warm toward their sons; the fathers took a more affectionate interest. Discipline, while generally more restrictive, also was more consistent and employed more appeals to reason. As adolescents these boys gave evidence of stronger guilt feelings and a higher degree

---

[32]Donald W. MacKinnon, "Violations of Prohibitions," in Henry A. Murray, editor, *Explorations in Personality* (New York: Oxford University Press, 1938), pp. 491-501.

[33]Bandura and Walters, *Adolescent Aggression.*

of identification with their fathers. Internalized guilt reactions in children regularly have been shown to be correlated with psychological rather than physical types of discipline, and with parental warmth rather than parental hostility, rejection, and physical punitiveness.[34]

Even in the worst environments—broken families and severely deteriorated neighborhoods having high delinquency rates— some boys run afoul of the law and some do not. There is a startling difference in the early disciplinary and familial relationships experienced by such delinquent and nondelinquent boys, despite the substandard neighborhood. When maternal discipline (the father often being absent) is consistent and reasonable in the boy's eyes, when supervision by a responsible adult is constant, and when the family is democratic and cohesive, there is only a three percent chance that a son will become involved in delinquency, as against an eighty-five percent chance when these conditions are markedly absent.[35]

Keeping in mind the danger of simplified categorization, these studies allowed for overall classification of the climate of a home as love-oriented or power-asserted.[36] The love-oriented home is one in which the final goal is the growth of the child to equality with his parents and a responsible freedom of adulthood. It is a home in which parents use praise as a reward and where punishment is lenient and unlikely to be physical. The

[34]Wesley Allinsmith and Thomas C. Greening, "Guilt Over Anger as Predicted From Parental Discipline," *American Psychologist* 10 (August, 1955):320; Robert R. Sears, Eleanor E. Maccoby, and Harry Levin, *Patterns of Child Rearing* (Evanston, Ill.: Peterson, 1957); Justin Aronfreed, "The Nature, Variety and Social Patterning of Moral Response to Transgression," *Journal of Abnormal and Social Psychology* 63 (September 1961):223-240.

[35]Sheldon Glueck and Eleanor Glueck, *Predicting Delinquency and Crime* (Cambridge, Mass.: Harvard University Press, 1959); Maude Craig and Selma Glick, *A Manual of Procedures for Application of the Glueck Prediction Table* (New York: New York City Youth Board, 1964).

[36]Wesley Becker, "Consequences of Different Kinds of Parental Disciplines," in Hoffman and Hoffman, *Review of Child Development Research,* 1:169-208.

approach to regulations is through reason rather than *fiat*. Children are helped to understand what is expected of them and are given explanations of the consequences of failure to observe a rule. It is a permissive home in the sense that childishness is tolerated in children. Corrections are made but instant adulthood is not expected. Although the parents allow the child to share in democratic discussions and give him increased latitude in making decisions as he grows older, they firmly maintain their prerogative of making the final decision if they believe it necessary. It is a warm home in that the parents show their affection, and trust their children.

Children from love-oriented homes typically reflected strong consciences—defined operationally as the tendency to confess wrongdoing, to apologize, and to make restitution. The older youth resisted temptations to cheat because of internalized standards. By the time he reaches mid-adolescence, a mature youth's moral code is based increasingly on a considered conformity; that is, he has reasoned out his standards, rather than blindly having accepted them. He is rated high in honesty, responsibility, moral courage, and kindness by his teachers and peers. The dynamics of development of mature values and attitudes appear to have been that the love relationship with parents was sufficient incentive for the child's early acceptance of their values and norms, thereby making more severe forms of discipline unnecessary. In addition his parents' use of reason gave the child a gradual understanding of values and at the same time provided him with a model of self-control.

The power-asserted home is one where discipline serves the end of establishing who is in charge. Physical punishment is used, and at times shouting, abrupt commands, and verbal threats are employed to enforce rules. Displays of aggression by a child or childish sexual curiosity are swiftly suppressed. Regulations and restrictions are many, and enforcement is unbending.

It is more difficult to generalize about children from power-oriented homes, since restrictiveness can be benign or it may be a covert expression of parental hostility. However, it can be said that children from restrictive homes typically show fixation of conscience development at some immature level.[37] Children from power-asserted homes are likely either to react fearfully after wrongdoing, or just the opposite, to react with a challenging aggressiveness. As youths they may be rigidly conformist and thereby placate the superior, or they may be callous and experience little internal discomfort over transgressions. The differing patterns of behavior seem to hinge on the presence or lack of affection shown by the restrictive parents. In restrictive homes where there is warmth, children are likely to be submissive and dependent, and inhibit anger, a condition which makes one prone to project his repressed hostilities onto some scapegoat minority in prejudice.[38] Where there is a lack of warmth in a home, there is little incentive for internalization of values and norms by a child and little evidence of guilt in adolescence.[39] One of the safest inferences drawn from these studies is that parental love and consistency appear to be the two crucial factors in the internalization of socialized value systems as the child grows toward adulthood.[40]

A child identifies with his parents and introjects their values. This process can be most easily understood in terms of learning theory. The child is totally dependent on parents for all his needs. He must maintain his parents' love, or, if unfortunately the parents are not particularly warm, he must ward off their displeasure. He accomplishes this by conforming to their values and directives, and thereby he receives one or more rewards: the satisfaction of parental love and approval; the reduction of his fear of losing their love; the reduction of anxiety over threatened

[37]Peck and Havighurst, *The Psychology of Character Development;* Kohlberg, "Development of Moral Character and Moral Ideology."

[38]Allport, *The Nature of Prejudice.*

[39]Bandura and Walters, *Adolescent Aggression.*

[40]Robert R. Sears, "The Growth of Conscience," in Ira Iscoe and Harold Stevenson, editors, *Personality Development in Children* (Austin, Texas: University of Texas Press, 1960), pp. 90-111.

punishment. As a result conforming behavior is reinforced, and gradually it becomes a habitual response pattern. If the child does not conform, if he misbehaves, then he is ignored or receives some punishment, be it withdrawal of love or some physical pain. Punishment tends to inhibit future misbehavior; being ignored tends to extinguish the annoying response.[41] In other words, the child identifies with his parents by adopting their values both explicitly stated and implicitly contained in the standards of behavior they require.

As part of this identification process, the child also picks up subtle cues of what parents do and do not like. Children are hypersensitive to the affective tone of things parents do and say. They sense the confident, calm, friendly tone when parents speak of "our kind" and the anxious or hostile tone when they speak of "those others."

Probably everyone who deals with children has had the experience of some three-year old saying in irritation, "You big stupid!" The child surely could not define the word, "stupid," but somewhere, probably at home, he has picked up the affect attached to the word in parental usage. This phenomenon, that words sometimes are expressive before they are denotative,[42] is a contributory factor in the development of attitudes. Words like "wop" or "nigger" are charged emotionally, and later when cognitive elements are added, children absorb the negative valence already in the word. Thus a child has "caught" an attitude, prefabricated so to speak. Conversely, a reverent, or a pleasant, or any positive affect can be picked up by the child prior to his conception of the word or thing to which it is attached. The child absorbs a sense of awe and reverence in church before he has any well-defined conception of what church is.

Everyone goes through a similiar development. As preschoolers and through the years to junior high school, youths are conformists of a sort; the source of their values is principally

---

[41]Bandura and Walters, *Adolescent Aggression*.
[42]Allport, *The Nature of Prejudice*.

in another person, the parent. But with the advent of adolescence, the main prop of one's value system is knocked out from under him. Until teenage the principal incentive for adopting a value system has been the satisfaction of the child's dependency needs. The adolescent is no longer totally dependent on his parents; moreover, the inherent dynamic of adolescence requires that he break away from parents and establish his own independent identity. In addition, his value system is exposed to his own intellectual awakening and the pressures of instinctual reawakening. Until now his value system was a means to an end, namely, parental nurturance and approval; this end is losing its importance and potency as the adolescent becomes an independent agent. A major task of the adolescent, therefore, is to develop from this predominantly other-directed status to self-direction. His value system, which was a means, must become an end. What was largely conformist morality must become autonomous if maturity is to be attained.[43]

New props are needed. Formerly, parental love and approval reinforced values. Now self-esteem will reinforce them. The re-examination and reformation of an adolescent's value system will be in terms of his self-concept. One's values say: "This is the kind of person I intend to be." The reinforcement of one's self-concept—its reward—will be the adolescent's self-fulfillment rather than the feedback of parental approval, though in a good relationship this latter aspect remains to some extent. Although this sounds like a move toward egocentricity, it must be noted that human self-fulfillment includes socialized goals, the growth and development of others as well as self. In optimal conditions a person grows to accept basic Christian values not because they are commanded, but because they are good, and because they are in accord with the growth-potential of his human nature.

[43]Gordon Allport, "Values and Our Youth," in *Teachers College Record* 63 (December, 1961):211-219; Carl Rogers, "Toward a Modern Approach to Values," in *Journal of Abnormal and Social Psychology* 68 (February, 1964):160-167.

The Place of the Peer-Group

A few words about peer-group influence on attitudes and values are in order. The adage is: "Birds of a feather flock together." But in our thinking and policy-making we often rephrase it to "Flocking together feathers the birds." One of the few longitudinal studies in which children were followed intimately from latency to mid-teenage, concluded that peer-group influence seldom changes the value system which a boy or girl has absorbed in the family.[44] In the last analysis, parents control or allow membership in peer-groups. The family influence has primacy, and the conclusion of this empirical research study was that peer-groups reinforce or crystallize tendencies already present in a youngster. Studies indicate that the adolescent boy seeks out a peer-group with his general values and interests even if it means leaving his neighborhood to find it.[45] This is not to say that group membership has no influence; the more fundamental consideration is that the strength of peer-group influence depends on the prior family history of the youth. If a child's home situation has been one in which his early needs for affection, interest, and attention were severely neglected, then the child, and especially the adolescent, will be willing to conform to almost any group norms to satisfy these dependency needs, which he now shifts from parents to transitional peer-groups.

IMPLICATIONS FOR TEACHING RELIGION

An overview of the psychological research literature on the development of attitudes and values allows for some general conclusions, or more accurately in some cases, general inferences for religious instruction programs. These findings are presented to stimulate critical appraisal of approaches long taken for granted. I do not intend to give any cookbook suggestions. My role is that of consulting psychologist, not catechist.

---

[44]Peck and Havighurst, *The Psychology of Character Development.*
[45]Glueck and Glueck, *Predicting Delinquency and Crime.*

However, present practice and innovative experiment should be appraised with awareness of the psychological research findings and insights into personality dynamics involved in the formation of values and attitudes. On the other hand, there is always a danger of imbalance in extrapolating a total dynamics of the human person. Selective scholarship, choosing studies to validate a prior position, is not scholarship at all.

Parental Interaction

The first and most general conclusion is that an individual's fundamental values and attitudes are developed in early years through interaction with parents. This process has substantial affective, often unconscious components; one's motivational value system is not simply a body of cognitive beliefs. Therefore, educational programs undertaken to foster values and attitudes must recognize that their formation, consolidation, and maturation is an interpersonal experience, not simply a transmission of knowledge from one generation to another. Cognitive approaches to attitude formation will have little effect when affective components and catalytic interpersonal influences are ignored.

In value and attitude formation, the medium is also a message. The medium is the catechist's own interpersonal attitude toward the student. The message as received by the student will range from "he respects me; I am worthwhile," to "he is controlling me; I am a robot." (Admittedly, a student can misperceive, since any message is filtered through his own prior attitudes.) The former message allows the student the freedom essential to autonomous choice. The latter message impels the student to reject proposed values in order to protect his own integrity. The ultimate internalization and self-acceptance of mature values will be conditional upon the affective climate of the catechetical situation as love-oriented, that is, as trustful, democratic, and consistent. A study carried out in the Catholic secondary schools of the Archdiocese of New Orleans revealed that students who felt that their relationship to God had improved during the preceding year tended to perceive their religion teachers as approachable, enthusiastic, and willing to devote class time to relevant discussion.[46]

Parent-Child Relationship

A second implication arises from the finding that the parent-child relationship is the initial and crucial factor in attitude and value formation. Peck and Havighurst estimated that other agencies, such as school and church, can match no more than one-tenth of parental influence.[47] A study of the orthodoxy and church involvement among Lutheran college students found no difference on the basis of parochial and nonparochial elementary school attendance. But when the same students were divided on the basis of high and low religious home background, significant differences appeared in the expected direction.[48] Presently, Catholic schooling systematically deals with the child only, and thereby focuses on one-half of a dynamic, interacting system. Successful education in values and attitudes must enlighten and enlist parents, as well as deal with children. Seminars for parents and parents-to-be on the psychology of character formation and the paramount importance of pre-school years should increase greatly the effectiveness of the religious education process.

Stability of Early-Formed Attitudes and Values

Thirdly, attitudes and values formed in childhood tend to be stable. Attitudes are actually habits, an organized kind of psychological functioning which provides economy of functioning. They join cognitive and affective elements into a habitual

---

[46]L. Tooley and Victorine Thiry, "The Teaching of Religion in Catholic Secondary Schools of the Archdiocese of New Orleans," 1967, mimeograph.

[47]Peck and Havighurst, *The Psychology of Character Development.*

[48]Daniel J. Mueller, "Effects and Effectiveness of Parochial Elementary Schools: An Empirical Study, in *Review of Religious Research* 9 (Fall, 1967):48-51.

reaction tendency. The degree of stability of an attitude will depend on the intensity of the affect integrated into the attitude, and/or the service the attitude provides a person.[49]

Some attitudes arise by the extension to associated objects of feelings connected with satisfying or unsatisfying experiences. Examples of such affective associations are nostalgia toward the campus where one went to school, the place of one's honeymoon, or conversely, a certain discomfort upon entering a hospital or dentist's office. Associative attitudes will be strong if the originating emotional experience was strong, or if the experience was repeated.

Other attitudes are functional; they do something for the person. The teenager has a strong positive attitude toward the automobile, for it gives him a sense of status, power, and emancipation. The teenager is more ego-involved with the automobile than, for example, the mature adult, for whom the car is mainly a means of transportation.

Prejudice provides an illustration of how an attitude may be associative or functional. Some people display prejudice simply because it is a custom in the group or culture in which they were raised. For others, however, prejudice serves an intrapsychic purpose; it makes them feel superior, and provides a scapegoat for the projection of one's own unacceptable impulses. Associative prejudice is much less resistant to change than functional prejudice.[50] This distinction and conclusion hold for attitudes in general, positive as well as negative. If one's religious values are associative, they may not hold up as one's associations change in life. But if they are functional—expressions of one's concept of oneself—they will manifest endurance.

Religion teachers need to be aware that every attitude tends to stability, and that its affective component gives an attitude

---

[49]Daniel Katz and Ezra Stotland, "A Preliminary Statement to a Theory of Attitude Structure and Change," in Sigmund Koch, editor, *Psychology: A Study of Science,* 6 vols. (New York: McGraw-Hill, 1959—1963), 3:423-475.
[50]Allport, *The Nature of Prejudice.*

both its strength and stability. When basic values and attitudes developed in the early homelife are wholesome, in general harmony with Christian norms, a cognitive approach by teachers will reinforce the attitude structure. But when there is a conflict between values and attitudes presented by the catechist and those of the youth, a cognitive approach creates tension in the student which the youth reduces by selective perception, distortion, or compartmentalization. Attempts to change attitudes through an instructional, cognitive approach are almost always unsuccessful. The evaluative and affective components must be dealt with before behavior will be altered; however under some conditions, such as role-playing, compliance forced by circumstances, or minimal pressure, a behavioral change can effect attitude change.

Research indicated that role-playing in which subjects treated Negro housing problems brought a positive change in attitudes of white people toward Negroes. It is noteworthy that this change did not occur in those subjects of the study who were highly defensive. This difference in results can be explained in terms of associative and functional attitudes. Other studies show that the majority of persons who lived in housing projects which subsequently became integrated,[51] and who had to work with Negroes,[52] or who attended schools which became integrated,[53] developed more favorable attitudes toward this miniority group.

These remarks on attitude forms and attitude change are only samplings of the findings of social psychology. Hopefully, they are sufficient to show the need for more sophisticated approaches to religious attitude formation and change than

[51]Martin Deutsch and Mary E. Collins, *Interracial Housing and a Psychological Evaluation of a Social Experiment* (Minneapolis: University of Minnesota Press, 1951).

[52]John Harding and Russell Hogrefe, "Attitudes of White Department Store Employees Toward Negro Co-workers," in *Journal of Social Issues* 8 (January, 1952):18-28.

[53]Kenneth Clark, "Desegregation, an Appraisal of the Evidence," in *Journal of Abnormal and Social Psychology* 9 (April, 1953):230-233.

the traditional classroom method. The few empirical research studies noted here make the point also that total permissiveness is not essential for developing attitudes. Firm and prudent insistence on certain standards of behavior can develop positive attitudes or lessen negative attitudes if these latter are not deeply ingrained in the defensive functions of personality.

Generalizability of Research on Attitudes and Values

A fourth point is that studies in human psychological development allow for generalizations about variation in attitude and value formation in successive periods of childhood. It is during the preschool years that basic values and attitudes are formed. During latency—by age ten—they are consolidated. During adolescence they are reformed. It is not until early adolescence that cognitive development has progressed sufficiently so that values and principles can be comprehended. Moreover, the adolescent restructures his identity during this period and looks for meaning in life. Values and norms received from significant adults are reassessed, and are made one's own, or modified, or rejected. Adolescence is the time when imposed values are changed to accepted values. Of all the school years, adolescence is the period during which the psychologically sophisticated mentor of youth will have the deepest influence on the congealing value system of youth by his deft response to adolescent crises of identity, emancipation, heterosexuality, and conscience.

Financial pressures and personnel shortages are forcing the Catholic school system to consider how most effectively to invest its resources. The solution of the dilemma of what to retain, what reluctantly to drop, and how to revise the religious education program must take into consideration psychological findings in character formation, that is, the learning of values and attitudes.

CONCLUSION

These findings on the interpersonal mediation of values and

attitudes have implications for the individual teacher. Teachers must try to be ever more aware of their own *affective* contribution to the teaching situation. Is the teacher motivated to see the child grow to autonomous adulthood, or does he or she tend to dominate, to make his superior status an end instead of a means? In other words, is he love-oriented or power-oriented? Moreover, let it not be thought that love and power orientation are opposite poles, for there is still further extension of this spectrum which is overpermissiveness. Therefore, another self-examination is in order. Is the teacher one who compromises, waters down the Christian value system, and appeases his students because he does not want to endanger the gratification of his own affiliative needs by incurring their disapproval? The student, especially the adolescent, will object, contest, deride, and debate. Teachers, as well as parents, may retreat from their own convictions in the face of the adolescent's argumentativeness. They must remember that such adolescent behavior is only partially an authentic search for truth. It is also his somewhat petulant declaration of independence. And it is a test the adolescent applies to the convictions of the adult who tries to hand down the accrued wisdom of age and experience. The adolescent objects and complains, but always with the silent hope that amid his world of changing body, mercurial emotions, fluctuating drives, and unsteady values, he will find some model who reassures him of stability, an adult who believes, a model who is not a reed shaken by the wind.

3 The *Teaching* of Religion

James Michael Lee

"I don't care if it rains or freezes
Long as I got my plastic Jesus
Up on the dashboard of my car"
—*Cool Hand Luke*

Most people would agree, at least provisionally, that teaching is causing another person to learn something. Now there are three principal elements embodied in this concept of teaching: the teacher, the learner, and the act by which the learner is taught. Central to these three, and indeed running through each, is the emphasis on the learner. As Thomas Aquinas observed, the student is the primary proximate cause of learning, *with the teacher being the secondary extrinsic proximate cause.*[1]

Put in another way, this means that teaching can be adequately described and defined basically in terms of learning. The degree of "teaching" which occurs in a given lesson is determined by the degree of learning which takes place. In terms of durational context, teaching is circumscribed not only by what learning takes place at the actual moment of teaching, but also by how much of that learning is later retained and acted upon directly or indirectly.

The overall importance of the preceding paragraph is that

---

[1] Thomas Aquinas, *De Veritate,* q. II.

it recasts into operational terms the purely notional or conceptual approach to teaching delineated in the opening paragraph. This operationalizing of the term "teaching" is of paramount importance for religion teachers, since it radicates the teacher and his act into the dynamic, existential world where learning is really done. Further, this operationalizing throws into bold relief the essential nature and real difficulty of the task of religious education. For as J. Donald Butler concluded, "Studies in the psychology of learning have been most helpful in showing how complex the learning process is. If religious educators take [empirical research] studies in learning seriously, they will recognize at least by implication that religious nurture is by no means a simple task."[2]

THE NATURE OF TEACHING

Theories and Models of Teaching

Specialists in religious instruction have a rather clearcut concept of the nature of teaching religion. Typical of the descriptive definitions of teaching religion, as given by the specialists, are "imparting the Christian message";[3] "proclaiming the message";[4] "heralding the Good News";[5] and "presentation of the faith."[6]

Speculatively, this conception of teaching is based on the *transmission theory* which postulates that teaching consists in the transmission of a given message from the teacher to the student. The more intact this message is received by the student,

---

[2]J. Donald Butler, "Religious Education," *Encyclopedia of Educational Research,* 3d edition (New York: Macmillan, 1960), p. 1151.

[3]Johannes Hofinger, *Imparting the Christian Message* (Notre Dame, Indiana: University of Notre Dame Press, 1961).

[4]Marcel van Caster, *The Structure of Catechetics,* translated by Edward J. Dirkswager, Jr., Olga Guedetarian, and Nicolas Smith (New York: Herder and Herder, 1965), pp. 185-187.

[5]Johannes Hofinger, *The Art of Teaching Christian Doctrine: The Good News And Its Proclamation,* 2d edition (Notre Dame, Indiana: University of Notre Dame Press, 1962), p. 17.

[6]José Calle, "Prophetical Pastoral Theology," in Johannes Hofinger and Theodore C. Stone, editors, *Pastoral Catechetics* (New York: Herder and Herder, 1964), p. 201.

the better the teaching is. The passionate devotion of specialists in religious instruction to the transmission theory can be illustrated in a recent attempt by one such specialist to transmute transmission from the methodological sphere into the realm of theology.[7]

Historically, adherence to the transmission theory is due probably to the particular attachment which Catholics always seemed to have for teacher-centered, highly directive education. The teaching method of the medieval universities (institutions which were, after all, a Catholic creation) was the lecture. Subsequently, the Jesuits, who have served as models for many religious institutes engaged in teaching, developed their system of "prelection," which is a form of the lecture method. The lecture and the prelection are still widely used in seminaries, particularly in the cycle courses in theology. In religion classes on the sub-collegiate level, "telling," that is, little lectures followed by questions from the students, came into vogue. Since the doctrinal content of the message had to be presented clearly in order to avoid the learning of heresy, the development of lessons by the pupils was frowned upon. Candidates for the priesthood and sisterhood are typically subject to a spiritual director whose directive advisement is regarded by ecclesiastical authorities as the will of God vis-a-vis the student listener. The lecture, the prelection, telling, and spiritual direction—all concretizations of the transmission theory—constitute a large bulk of the educational methodological *Weltanschauung* of the majority of the functionaries in religious education, namely, the priests and the sisters.

The transmission theory of religious instruction has so many weaknesses as to make it a blunt and ineffective tool for religious instruction. Its main defects are psychological and methodological. The transmission theory posits the univocity of learning. Yet there are few philosophers who deny that learning is by

---

[7]Alfonso M. Nebreda, "The Theological Problem of Transmission," *Lumen Vitae* 20 (June, 1965):309-324.

analogy; certainly the Thomistic school holds the analogy of learning at the very center of its principles of psychology.[8] The transmission theory assumes a materialistic view of man in that knowledge, attitudes, values, and the like can be transfused from one person to another much like blood is transfused. The transmission theory takes the learner out of the center of the teaching-learning process, something against which virtually every philosopher from Socrates to Dewey has protested, and something which the behavioral sciences have shown to be psychologically impossible. The transmission theory confines teaching within overly narrow parameters: the verbal, the conceptual, the product. Finally, and especially relevant to our own day, the transmission theory unduly restricts the freedom of the learner to explore and to experience: the teacher rather than the student becomes both the *terminus a quo* and the *terminus ad quem*.

In short the transmission theory is based on the preaching model. Thus Domenico Grasso clearly makes catechesis, or religious instruction, a mode of preaching:

> What the term "catechesis" fails to express is that religious instruction is not simply a communication of ideas, but rather the transmission of facts and actions that are intended to become principles of thought and moral conduct. But this deficiency resides in the nature of preaching itself, of which catechesis is merely one form. For this, too, the term "preaching" is preferable to any other for describing the phenomenon of the transmission of the message.[9]

If religious instruction is to be optimally effective and to come of age, it will have to be radicated in the teaching model. Of its very nature, the teaching model does not center itself

---

[8]See, for example, Tad Guzie, *The Analogy of Learning: An Essay Toward a Thomistic Psychology of Learning* (New York: Sheed & Ward, 1960).

[9]Domenico Grasso, *Proclaiming God's Message: A Study in the Theology of Preaching* (Notre Dame, Indiana: University of Notre Dame Press, 1965), p. 247.

in the teacher or in the content (as does the transmission theory and the preaching model) but rather in the learner. Teaching, as has already been shown, is basically a function of learning.

Possibly the most effective and most fruitful type of teaching model bases itself on the *structuring theory.* Briefly defined this theory suggests that teaching consists in the deliberate, conscious structuring of a learning situation so that the desired learning outcomes are effected. "Structuring the learning situation" means that the various physical, emotional, socially climatological, and product-process elements of a lesson are so arranged that they tend to effect the desired learning outcomes. This concept of "structuring the learning situation" is by no means easy to understand unless one has had first-hand experience in doing it or in seeing it done. Consequently, it might be helpful to give an example. Like all examples, the one which I shall give does not illustrate perfectly the concept which I am attempting to elucidate. Despite this defect, however, I hope the example will serve to give an indication of some of the elements involved in the structured learning situation approach to the teaching of religion.

In order to grasp the force of the example, it might be advantageous for the reader to pause a few moments and pose the following problem to himself: I wish to teach third-grade elementary school children that no man is an island, and that they need each other in order to develop into fully functioning persons. In other words, brotherhood is not simply an arbitrary command of God, but rather it flows from man's very nature as a human being.

How would the reader teach a lesson so that this learning objective is achieved? Some transmission theorists would doubtless suggest that a little talk on the brotherhood of man under the fatherhood of God, reinforced perhaps by some audio-visual materials, would do the job. Other transmissionists might propose that the pupils listen to a story from the bible which illustrates how all men are brothers. Some of the European catechetical specialists might suggest that a little analysis of family life would help the students attain the desired learning objective. But an educational experiment conducted in an elementary school offers one example of how a pedagogical structuralist dealt with the problem in a pilot school.

The teacher waited for a bright sunny May morning. When this day came, the teacher proceeded with class as usual, except that she made the first hour of class deliberately dull, in order that, by so doing, the children would be especially receptive to a change in both physical and psychological environment. Then the teacher asked the little children if they would like to listen to a story. With much glee and excitement, the boys and girls eagerly told the teacher that they wanted very much to hear the story. The teacher proposed that they move to another classroom where it was more sunny and cheerful. The pupils welcomed this suggestion.

Unknown to the pupils, the chairs and tables in the new classroom, while looking exactly like those in their own room, were actually much heavier—in fact, they were so heavy that no one child by himself could lift a chair or a table. When the teacher arrived with her pupils in the new room, she again asked them if they would like to hear the story which she had told them was very interesting and exciting. By this time the boys' and girls' curiosity and anticipation for the story had reached a very intense state. The teacher then asked the children to bring their chairs and tables closer to her in a particularly pleasant and cheerfully decorated part of the room. The children, wishing so much to hear the story right away, attempted immediately to move the furniture as they had been asked to do. The weight of each chair and table was so great, however, that the children were unable to move the furniture.

The teacher waited judiciously for a few moments, then clapped her hands for attention and said in an invitational tone of voice, "Hurry up, children, or we will miss the story." The pupils attempted again to move the furniture, but without success. The teacher spoke not a single word. Suddenly some of the boys and girls teamed up to help one another move the chairs and tables to the section of the room which the teacher had indicated. The other children, observing that this was a successful way to operate, also began freely and spontaneously to cooperate with each other to move the rest of the furniture. When everything was in place, the teacher began the story.

The lesson, which was essentially nonverbal, was of course not the story at all, but rather structuring the learning situation so that the students would *of their own accord* cooperate in sharing each other's burden in attaining a desired objective. In this way the children learned first-hand and in the concrete the importance of mutual cooperation and brotherhood. The story, which was a biblical story of brotherhood, served to reinforce the lesson which had already been learned, to insert the overt religious dimension into the Christian act of sharing which they had already done.

Some persons might believe that structuring the learning situation constitutes undue manipulation by the teacher and therefore takes away freedom from the students. Actually, however, quite the reverse is the case. Lecturing, telling, reciting, teacher-directed questions, and other teacher-centered pedagogical devices constitute the ultimate in the deprivation of student freedom, for in these situations the students are encased in an extremely narrow range of free acting. In other words, in the traditional teacher-centered, transmission approach, the students are free solely to react in a certain way clearly delineated by the teacher, or not to react; to listen or not to listen. The teacher is the total source of control.

In the structuring approach, on the other hand, the student has much more freedom to act in a variety of ways. It is true that the situation is carefully structured so as to induce certain behavioral changes. But after all, consciously leading the student to specified and desirable learning outcomes constitutes the essential ingredient of teaching. The structured kind of learning

situation advocated here, while focused, nonetheless is sufficiently broad to allow and indeed to promote a wide variety
of student response. The transmission theory perceives the
classroom as a broadcasting studio in which the teacher (transmitter) sends his message to the students (receivers). The
structuring theory, in contrast, perceives the classroom as a
learning laboratory in which the students act, interact, and react
toward the development of personalized and meaningful learning
outcomes. The transmission theorists almost never speak of
teacher-student planning of the lessons whereas such planning
typically is advocated by the structuring theorists,[10] surely an
indication of which of the approaches provides the students
with optimum freedom.

It is in the learning laboratory, which is the classroom, that the
student can interact and can encounter things, situations, and
other persons with his whole self, past and present. It is this
whole *engagement* which is so important for a religion class,
for God speaks most fully to students through an individual's
complex interaction with the widest possible types of persons
and things. It is rather arrogant—and rather unscriptural too—
for a religion teacher to assume that the best and perhaps the
only way for God to speak to students is through the teacher.
Gabriel Moran puts it nicely when he observes:

> Catechetical writers are afraid to take seriously their own state-
> ments that God speaks to the student in the religion lesson. The
> result is that the student's own history is simply added to the
> scheme of past events or else the past is constantly "applied"
> to the present. The student's participation in the history, how-
> ever, should not be tacked on at the end. It should rather be the
> starting point and the locus of all historical reflection.[11]

Much of the mediocrity in the teaching of religion stems from

---

[10]See, for example, James Michael Lee, *Principles and Methods of
Secondary Education* (New York: McGraw-Hill Catholic Series in Education, 1963), pp. 269-285.

[11]Gabriel Moran, *Catechesis of Revelation* (New York: Herder and
Herder, 1966), p. 46.

the fact that it relies so heavily on second-hand experience.

In addition to the theological reason which Gabriel Moran advances for an experience-based, student-centered axis of religious instruction, there are powerful psychological reasons which can be adduced. In this connection it might be well to remember that transfer of learning is at the base not only of religious instruction but indeed of all types of classroom instruction. To be sure the *raison d'être* of classroom instruction is that those things learned in the school setting will be transferred to situations outside the confines of the school.[12] As applied to teaching strategy, the principal finding of the celebrated empirical research study conducted by G. M. Haslerud and Shirley Meyers should be cited: "Independently derived principles are more transferable than those given."[13] The transmission theory of religious instruction, of course, is based on presenting or giving facts and principles while the structuring theory is rooted in the creation of a planned learning situation which is so structured that the students will discover these principles by and for themselves.[14]

The transmission theory tends to result—though not necessarily so—in religious instruction which is heavily fact-oriented rather than principle-oriented. In contrast, the structuring theory, by virtue of the fact that it places students in a first-hand experience situation, tends to be principle-oriented. Jack Kittell's review of the pertinent empirical research plus his own investigation concluded that principles are much more easily transferable than are facts.[15] It is to be hoped that religion teachers

[12]For a reasonably comprehensive overview of transfer of learning, see Henry C. Ellis, *The Transfer of Learning* (New York: Macmillan, 1965).

[13]G. M. Haslerud and Shirley Meyers, "The Transfer Value of Given and Individually Derived Principles," in *Journal of Educational Psychology* 49 (December, 1958):297.

[14]Of interest here is that Thomas Aquinas teaches that learning by discovery is superior to learning by instruction, that is, by precept. Cf. Thomas Aquinas, *De Veritate,* q. II.

[15]Jack E. Kittell, "An Experimental Study of the Effect of External Direction during Learning on Transfer and Retention of Principles," in *Journal of Educational Psychology* 48 (November, 1957):404.

are unanimous in their agreement with Bert Kersh's review of the pertinent empirical research investigations which concluded that "the hypothesis that learning through independent discovery is superior to learning by rote" is supported by the research.[16]

Strategies of Teaching

It should be underscored that the point at issue here is not a simple one of specific teaching methods, but far more globally, one of pedagogical strategy. In terms of basic, overall strategy, what is being proposed in this chapter is a pedagogy which is student-centered rather than teacher-centered, which is product as well as process-oriented rather than solely product-oriented, which is experience-oriented rather than verbally oriented, which is affective-oriented rather than exclusively cognitive-oriented. These orientations will be discussed later on in this chapter. In any event the goal of the overall strategy of religious instruction must be a behavioral outcome in terms of the student's life. To be effective, the religion teacher should structure his teaching strategy in terms of learning experiences rather than in terms of content to be taught. In Benjamin Bloom's words, "We must find ways of penetrating beyond the labels of teaching method (e.g., lecture, demonstration, discussion, team teaching) and move to a more precise definition of what takes place in the learning situation."[17]

The foregoing is not adduced to deprecate the religion teacher's attention to teaching methods, but rather to radicate these methods with the more global thrust of pedagogical strategy. Thus, for example, the specific teaching methodology of role playing is of great worth because as a specific methodology it concretizes in a very full way the structuring theory and

---

[16]Bert Y. Kersh, "The Adequacy of Meaning as an Explanation for the Superiority of Learning by Independent Discovery," in *Journal of Educational Psychology* 49 (October, 1958):282.

[17]Benjamin S. Bloom, "Testing Cognitive Ability and Achievement," in N. L. Gage, editor, *Handbook of Research on Teaching* (Chicago: Rand McNally, 1963), p. 388.

the student-centered, process-oriented, and affective-thrusted pedagogical strategy as well.[18]

I have talked to religion teachers and to Catholic school officials who believe that neither global pedagogical strategies nor particular teaching methodologies are of any great significance in religion class. These persons claim that what is of primary importance in a classroom situation is the degree to which the student can identify with the teacher. In this view the teacher, through the medium of his or her own person serves as an ideal or role model and in so doing causes the students to become like the teacher because of admiration or liking. However, as Lee Cronbach has pointed out, to say that a student learns by imitation and that the way to teach is therefore to set a good example, oversimplifies.[19] Imitation—or identification, to use the technical term—is selective. No student imitates every action he observes. Even those he does imitate he might place into a different behavioral context so that the result may hardly resemble that of the model. Nevitt Sanford relates the story of a two-year old child, initially terrified by a puppy dog, was within a few hours crawling about, barking and threatening to bite people.[20] This is not to deny that identification does go on in the school setting. Rather, it is to realize that identification may be good or bad and in any event that the learning outcome is chancy. And the nature of teaching

[18]Role-playing is an unrehearsed dramatization of a problem in which the members of a class, without scripts, extemporaneously portray how they would react in a given situation. Arthur Jacobs' doctoral study on role-playing emphasized the fact that a unique contribution of this methodology is that it literally brings to life intellectual, emotional, and attitudinal learnings in a concrete real-life situation in a way that few if any other learning devices can. See Arthur J. Jacobs, "Role Playing as an Educational Method," unpublished doctoral project, Teachers College, Columbia University, New York, 1951, pp. 73-75. See also James Michael Lee, *Principles and Methods of Secondary Education*, pp. 314-315; Alan Klein, *Role Playing in Leadership Training and Group Problem Solving* (New York: Association Press, 1956).
[19]Lee J. Cronbach, *Educational Psychology*, 2d edition (New York: Harcourt, Brace, and World, 1963), pp. 424-435.
[20]Nevitt Sanford, "The Dynamics of Identification," in *Psychological Review* 62 (March, 1955):106-118.

is that it consciously and deliberatively causes a specified learning outcome, reducing the element of chance to the lowest possible level.

While a teacher as model is not in himself the teaching act per se, nonetheless the teacher as model can serve fruitfully as a motivation for learning desired educational outcomes. But even here, discretion and caution should be the watchwords. Typically the teacher in a religion class is a priest or a religious, and as such hardly serves as an ideal model of Christian living for the vast majority of boys and girls who must work out their Christian existences as laymen in the secular sphere. This problem is all the more compounded for religion teachers who work in Catholic schools or in CCD centers located in the inner city. Priests and religious appear to come predominantly from the middle-middle or lower-middle socioeconomic class of society,[21] as do also those lay teachers who might be teaching religion in those milieux.[22] Surely such teachers, personifying middle-class mentalities, values, and goals, are hardly suitable as role models for the slum or semislum child.

Indeed, this pervasive middle-class value structure carries over into teaching materials, a not surprising finding in that most teaching materials are composed primarily by teachers or teaching specialists. According to Irvin Child and associates, stories in readers typically portray children receiving rewards when they carry out the ideas of the authorities; however, when the children act independently they are likely to get into difficulty. Acquiring knowledge by asking superiors is depicted as the correct procedure. (These superiors always seem to be readily able to supply the answers.) However, if the child in the story sets out to discover things on his own, he not uncom-

---

[21]See Joseph H. Fichter, *Religion As an Occupation* (Notre Dame, Indiana: University of Notre Dame Press, 1961), pp. 59-87.

[22]W. W. Charters, Jr., "The Social Background of Teaching," in N. L. Gage, editor, *Handbook of Research on Teaching*, pp. 718-721. While the data reported by Charters deal with public school teachers, it seems safe to extrapolate it to lay teachers in Catholic schools.

monly receives punishment. When the child sees no solution in a difficult task, he receives assistance by appealing to adults. The readers typically neglect to provide models of peers assisting each other to complete a project.[23]

In religion class in Catholic schools and in CCD programs, models should be appropriate to the students' actual existential situation, and also should reflect a proper emphasis. This has not always been the case. Thus a study by Robert Morocco showed that sixty-two percent of the students of the Catholic secondary schools studied chose as their primary ideal a religious personage—although it is interesting to note that the most frequently mentioned names were Fulton Sheen and the Blessed Mother, with Jesus named by only nine students.[24] It shall be remembered that the vast majority of students in religion classes will remain in the lay state. Hence an undue emphasis on clerical and religious models is unwarranted; actually, the paramount or exclusive depiction of clerical and religious models may imply to the student that sanctity is somehow the special preserve of those who have a religious vocation.

Religious Instruction as Behavior Modification

What this chapter has thus far been leading up to, what it will reinforce in divers ways, is the following: *the religion teacher fundamentally is a professional specialist in the modification of student behavior as it affects his religious life.*

Education itself is a system of complex, planned, purposive, and interrelated learning experiences which bring about desirable changes in students. These changes are all measured and assessed behaviorally: increase in cognitive skills, in emotional maturity, in affective development, in physical growth, and in

---

[23]Irvin L. Child, Elmer H. Potter, and Estelle M. Levine, "Children's Textbooks and Personality Development: An Exploration in the Social Psychology of Education," *Psychological Monographs*, 60, no. 3, 1946.

[24]Robert R. Morocco, "A Study of the Ideals Expressed by a Selected Group of Parochial and Public School Students," unpublished master's thesis, The Catholic University of America, 1947.

religious education, these four are interpenetrated by—I do not say added on to—Christological charity.[25] Society erects and maintains schools in order to insure that each of its young develops his potential both for himself and for the common weal. Naturally every society defines "desirable changes in students" in terms of its own value structure, since one of the cardinal aims of the school is to act as a purposeful agent for the socialization of the child into that society. Catholic schools and CCD programs equally aim to produce desirable changes in their students (becoming more Christlike) and so act as an agent of socialization into the society of the Church (which is different, of course, from ecclesiastical society). The role of the Catholic religion teacher, then, is first, to be clear on which behavioral changes are desirable and within his scope, and second, to be skilled in the use of pedagogical strategies and methodologies to effect these behavioral modifications.

In one sense all of one's experiences are educational since whatever a person experiences in one way or another modifies his behavior, however slightly. But educational experiences provided by the school or CCD program differ most significantly from educational experiences found in ordinary life in that the former represent a deliberately structured, consciously planned set of expanding and reinforcing experiences which are intended to have a more intense and powerful effect than do ordinary life experiences in changing the individual in a given direction. These school experiences, like ordinary life experiences, revolve around subject *products,* as well as around the cognitive, affective, volitional, physical, and religious *processes.*

From this vantage point, it is possible to more fully perceive the essential nature of the religion teacher as a specialist in the modification of behavior along religious lines. The religion teacher can be called a teacher only because he or she has the

---

[25]Charity of the Christological sort, by definition, includes faith. To Thomas Aquinas charity is, of course, the "form" of all the virtues.

technical competence or process expertness[26] which is indispensable to effect the modification of behavior. To illustrate by way of analogy, the physiologist possesses expert *knowledge* of the nature and functioning of the material aspects of the human organism, but it is the physician-surgeon who possesses the *technical competence or process expertness* necessary to perform an appendectomy. This technical competence or process expertness of the physician does not deny the fact or the importance of his possessing a high-level knowledge of physiology. In the words of Walter Doyle, "his primary concern as physician in learning physiology is not necessarily to advance the frontiers of knowledge in this science. Rather, as physician, he is charged with the application of the findings of physiology to promote human physical development. Hence competence in physiology as such constitutes only a part of the defining competence of a professional physician. His essential competence lies in the processes involved in the application of the knowledge of physiology to promote health in the patient."[27]

The principle underlying the analogy of physiologist-physician can now be applied to the distinction between the theologian and the teacher of religion. The theologian is one who is competent in the content of the science or study of God. His task is to inquire into the nature and workings of God, and if possible to advance knowledge in this field. The religion teacher, on the other hand, besides possessing a knowledge of the science of theology, must also possess the technical competence or process expertness to so structure the learning situation that the student's behavior is modified along religious lines; that is, that the students learn religion. Thus the Committee on Articulation —Religion of the National Catholic Educational Association

---

[26]This particular terminology is borrowed from Walter Doyle's rather thorough analysis of the teacher as professional. See Walter Doyle, "A Professional Model for the Authority of the Teacher in the Educational Enterprise," unpublished doctoral dissertation, University of Notre Dame, 1967, especially p. 123.

[27]*Ibid.* I have substituted the word "physiology" throughout this quote for the word "biology" which appears in the original Walter Doyle text.

recommended that "Catechists should have a master's degree in religious education or be working toward this degree. An equivalent degree in theology, while it may prove beneficial, would not and should not be considered a substitute for graduate work in the field of religious education and catechetics."[28]

As has been shown earlier in this chapter, optimum behavior modification is effected not through the transmission of the message, but by structuring the total learning situation so that it is induced. The skill required of religion teachers to so structure the learning situation belongs to the domain of technical competence or process expertness. John Dewey phrased it this way:

> A primary responsibility of educators is that they not only be aware of the general principle of the shaping of actual experience by environing conditions, but that they also recognize in the concrete what surroundings are conducive to having experiences that lead to growth. Above all, they should know how to utilize the surroundings, physical and social, that exist so as to extract from them all that they have to contribute to building up experiences that are worthwhile.[29]

Teaching religion, then, must be radicated in concrete specific behavioral goals in terms of the students' lives. To structure the learning situation means nothing more than to carefully and systematically architect the lesson and, indeed, the entire course to insure that specific behavioral outcomes are achieved. To do this effectively is not to erect—as has been done ad nauseam—general statements of aims or goals of the religion class, but to delineate with some measure of precision just what particularized behavioral outcomes are to be worked for. Thus, the development of faith or growth in the love of God is so broad and general in aim as to provide little direction for the ascer-

[28]Committee on Articulation—Religion, National Catholic Educational Association, "A Report," in *Bulletin of the National Catholic Educational Association* 61 (February, 1965):25.

[29]John Dewey, *Experience and Education* (New York: Macmillan, 1938), p. 35.

taining of appropriate learning experiences. In contrast, an objective such as the ability to relate the principles of distributive justice to the civil rights question is more specific and begins (but only begins) to give teachers and students some direction with regard both to the subject *product* and to the cognitive, affective, volitional, physical, and religious *processes* which the student is expected to develop. Secular educationists and educators have developed two rather admirable sets of pyramidal taxonomies of educational objectives, one for the cognitive domain[30] and another for the affective domain.[31] These taxonomies clearly delineate the various specific elements which comprise each level. What is urgently needed in religious instruction is the development of a taxonomy of educational objectives in the religious domain to replace the torrent of platitudinous goals for religious instruction which seem to emanate from every quarter.

Laws of Learning

If in general teaching is a function of learning, and if specifically teaching is the effecting of a modification in the student's behavior, then it is incumbent upon the teacher to radicate his teaching in the laws of learning. Teaching is a science as well as an art. The teacher as a practical scientist who as such possesses technical competence or process expertness must therefore shape his lessons so that they are "plugged into" the learner. Part of the teacher's competence, to be sure, is a knowledge of the "subject matter"; but another indispensable part of his professional competence is the conscious implementation of the psychological laws governing the way in which the student learns. Without the latter the religion teacher is technically incompetent and quite likely an ineffective teacher.

---

[30]Benjamin S. Bloom, et al., *Taxonomy of Educational Objectives: Handbook I, Cognitive Domain* (New York: McKay, 1956).

[31]David R. Kratwohl, Benjamin S. Bloom, and Bertram B. Masia, *Taxonomy of Educational Objectives: Handbook II, Affective Domain* (New York: McKay, 1964).

Now this might seem quite obvious, but in fact it is almost universally overlooked by the bulk of contemporary catechetical writers. Two examples from a pair of the more widely recognized catechetical writers will serve to illustrate this point. The first of these two men, a gifted and perceptive man, writes as follows:

> Indeed, it can be said that only a morality based upon an historical, personal, social revelation can preserve us from a "situation ethic." Nothing is more certain to lead to arbitrariness and lawlessness than the maintenance of an abstract and impersonal system of moral precepts. Not coming to grips with the real world, it must inevitably result in leaving men to make decisions on a subjective basis.[32]

This statement, viewed operationally in terms of the way in which a person acquires moral learnings, is a statement of a principle of learning. Consequently one would expect that as support for his contention this catechetical writer would cite a psychologist or an empirical investigation. But instead he cites theologians, Karl Rahner and Louis Monden.

To compound the error, there is a host of empirical studies which seem to indicate that the catechetical writer, however buttressed he might be by theologians, simply is not correct in his assertion that religion as a revelation-centered entity is the best way (and I might even add, the necessary way) to produce religious behavior in the students. Research investigations such as those of Robert Friederichs,[33] Hugh Hartshorne and Mark May,[34] Pleasant Hightower,[35] Clifford Kirkpatrick,[36] William

---

[32]Moran, *Catechesis of Revelation*, p. 101.

[33]Robert W. Friederichs, "Alter versus Ego: An Exploratory Assessment of Altruism," in *American Sociological Review* 25 (August, 1960): 496-508.

[34]Hugh Hartshorne and Mark A. May, *Studies in Deceit* (New York: Macmillan, 1928).

[35]Pleasant R. Hightower, *Biblical Information in Relation to Character* (Iowa City, Iowa: State University of Iowa, 1930).

[36]Clifford Kirkpatrick, "Religion and Humanitarianism: A Study of Institutional Implications," in *Psychological Monographs*, 63 (1949): 1-23.

Kvaraceus,[37] and George Mursell[38] have found that religionism (membership in a particular religion) has no pivotal relationship with ethical behavior, humanitarianism, altruism, and non-delinquency.[39] Unless this catechetical writer were willing to assert that the morality of these religionists was not at all centered in revelation, his assertion seems to have floundered upon the rocks of the available psychological evidence. To be sure an empirical investigation by Russell Middleton and Snell Putney[40] of normative standards and behavior patterns of religionist and skeptic (nonreligionist) college students concluded first that religionists were more likely to believe in traditional (that is, non-situation-ethic) ascetic standards than were the skeptics, but the two groups did not differ in the degree to which they believed in the elements of common social morality. Second, religionists and skeptics did not differ in the degree to which they lived up to the norms which they professed. Third, the two groups reported the same degree of violations of conventional social morality.

A second example of the ignoring of the laws of learning by a leading catechetical writer appears in a book written by one of the older, well-established specialists in religious instruction.[41] In a chapter entitled "The Right Ordering of Catechetical Material," this writer goes to great lengths in discussing

---

[37]William C. Kvaraceus, "Delinquent Behavior and Church Attendance," in *Sociology and Social Research* 38 (March-April, 1944):284-289.

[38]George R. Mursell, "A Study of Religious Training as a Sociological Factor in Delinquency," unpublished doctoral dissertation, The Ohio State University, 1930.

[39]I am speaking here of ethical or moral behavior in general. Several studies have found that religionists tended to violate *certain* specific moral standards less than nonreligionists. As might be expected, for example, religionists violated traditional sexual mores less than did nonreligionists. (On this last point, see also Alfred C. Kinsey, et al., *Sexual Behavior in the Human Male* [Philadelphia: Saunders, 1948]; and Alfred C. Kinsey, et al., *Sexual Behavior in the Human Female* [Philadelphia: Saunders, 1953].)

[40]Russell Middleton and Snell Putney, "Religion, Normative Standards, and Behavior," in *Sociometry* 35 (June, 1962):141-152.

[41]Hofinger, *Imparting the Christian Message*, pp. 51-61.

the best way to arrange the scope, sequence, and continuity of the "presentation" of religion to children at different grade levels in the Catholic school. His three touchstones for arriving at this best way seem to be: (1) to work toward perfecting—while still keeping the basic curricular principles intact—the arrangement of material as found in the Roman Catechism, (2) through an examination of the order of "presentation" used by the Apostles, (3) as refined by the insights of kerygmatic theology. Yet his chapter reveals a rather appalling ignorance of, or at least a woeful neglect of the psychological laws of learning of the findings of relevant empirical research studies. It is all well and good to bring the apostolic sequence and the kerygmatic dimension into play; however, unless the religion curriculum utilizes the laws of learning as a key starting point, the curriculum never will be rooted in reality. (As a side note, scope, sequence, and continuity properly belong to that subdivision of educational science called "curriculum"; yet the catechetical writer did not indicate, by either text or citations, that he was integrating the findings of curriculum science into his order of "presentation."[42])

A scientific law is a statement of an order or relation of phenomena which as far as it is known, is invariable under the specified conditions. Scientific laws, then, express generalized regularities. And as May Brodbeck has observed, "a generalization is such by virtue of its form, stating that all things having a certain character also have another, or whenever we have the first then we also have the second."[43] Conversely, a fact is actually an instance of a law, something which has great significance to the religion teacher when assessing the value of the laws of learning in his daily professional activities. Laws of learning are important because without them explanations and predictions about human learning would not be possible.

---

[42]For a brief overview of these curricular concepts, see Lee, *Principles and Methods of Secondary Education*, pp. 208-210.

[43]May Brodbeck, "Logic and Scientific Method in Research on Teaching" in Gage, editor, *Handbook of Research on Teaching*, p. 56.

In order to ascertain whether laws of learning (or any other kinds of scientific laws) are valid, they must have been proven by the appropriate empirical research. Armchair philosophizing about the nature of learning can be helpful in providing clues to the behavioral scientist in evolving laws of learning from a welter of individual phenomena about him. But philosophizing about laws of learning does nothing to construct or validate them. Thus the individual religion teacher, observing that telling Johnny to be good does not necessarily cause him to be good, develops empirically his own "negative" law of learning that cognitive presentation does not of itself yield volitional behavior. This represents an empirical approach—however unsophisticated—to the development of a law of learning. Adherence to this law helps the teacher to see other than cognitive teaching strategies when trying to get the student to learn volitional behavior.

There are many theories of explanations of the laws of learning. Ernest Hilgard and Gordon Bower have classified learning theories into two principal schools: the stimulus-response theory, represented by such psychologists as Thorndike, Skinner, Hull, and the cognitive theory represented by such psychologists as Köhler, Lewin, and Wertheimer.[44] For the purposes of this chapter, a consideration of the theories of learning is not as important as the effect that the laws of learning ought to have on the religion teacher in the classroom.[45] In the classroom encounter, the teacher who bases his activities on the empirically established laws of learning runs a much better chance of effecting desired learning outcomes in the students than the teacher who is either ignorant of these laws or who fails to operationalize them.

---

[44]Ernest R. Hilgard and Gordon H. Bower, *Theories of Learning,* 3d edition (New York: Appleton-Century-Crofts, 1966).

[45]For a treatment of the relation of the theories of learning to the task of instruction, see National Society for the Study of Education, *Theories of Learning and Instruction,* Sixty-third Yearbook, Part I (Chicago: University of Chicago Press, 1964).

THE TEACHING ACT

There is more involved in the teaching act than a group of students seated in a classroom with someone standing in front "teaching." Rather, there is a series of interlocking components in the teaching act. It is the purpose of this section to explore quite briefly several of the essential constituents of the teaching act.

Product and Process

Viewed in terms of the makeup of learning outcomes, there are two kinds of content, namely, product and process. Product content refers to the particularized, static, and usually "tangible"[46] content. To illustrate: in the example two times two equal four, the product content is four. If the student gains the content "four" as a solution to this problem, he has learned a product content. Process content refers to a generalized, dynamic, and usually "intangible" content. In our example of two times two equals four, the process content is the getting of the four, and the ability to arrive at four again when another like mathematical problem comes to him.

It is important to note that content is not identical with product. Indeed, the identification of product with content is a mistake into which many religion teachers seem to fall. The same is true of the catechetical writers who identify product with message. In reality both product and process are contents and messages—different kinds of contents and messages, but contents and messages indeed. This is one of the most important points made in this entire chapter, and until religion teachers and especially catechetical writers grasp it, there can be no genuine breakthrough in the teaching of religion.

As a matter of fact, it would appear that process content is a much more important learning outcome than is product content. Product outcomes are particularized and, consequently

---

[46]Tangible here does not mean concrete; rather, it means a specified content which can be pinpointed.

can be transferred only to identical situations. Because of their
generalized nature, process outcomes are readily transferable.
The product outcomes in the mathematical problems two times
two, three times one, five times three, and four times four are:
four, three, fifteen, and sixteen respectively. These results hold
true only when the numbers in the problems are exactly the
same. But the process outcome, skill in multiplying, can be
generalized far beyond these specific examples to all other
arithmetical multiplication problems involving integers.

One of the key process outcomes for a religion class is that
of attitude formation. Attitude change and development are
not effected by the cumulative addition of product contents,
so that their sum produces attitude change; rather, it is the
develop*ing*, the grow*ing*, the chang*ing* which are decisive in
the genesis and transformation of attitudes, values, and beliefs.

Perhaps a brief consideration of the nature and development
of attitudes might illumine the point made above. An attitude
is a relatively permanent disposition or personality-set toward
someone or something. It always involves a preconceived
judgment and emotion about the object together with a pre-
prepared reaction toward it. Attitudes condition virtually all
learning. As Gordon Allport has observed, "Attitudes will determine for each individual what he will see and hear, what he will
think and what he will do."[47] The differences in rate and amount
of learning among the students in a religion class are often due
as much to their individual attitudes as to their intelligence or
other personality factors. An empirical investigation by Jerome
Levine and Gardner Murphy in which students of similar intelligence but with different attitudes were given controversial
material to read concluded that if the opinion expressed in
the material is in agreement with the opinion of the reader,
the reader will remember it better and longer than if the opinion

[47]Gordon W. Allport, "Attitudes," in Carl Murchison, editor, *A Handbook of Social Psychology* (Worcester, Massachusetts: Clark University
Press, 1935), p. 806.

expressed in the material disagrees with that of the reader.[48]

Attitudes, of course, can be changed. One of the functions of education, and particularly of religious education, is to effect a change in attitudes. But unless the teacher orients his instruction around and toward process outcomes as well as (and to a certain extent more than) around and toward product outcomes, student attitudes will not be purposively changed. This requires religion teachers and particularly catechetical writers to redirect their efforts toward process-rooted behavioral outcomes. Teaching for a knowledge of the doctrinal elements of Christianity is one thing, but teaching to directly develop a living Christianity is quite another.

Cognitive and Affective

There are, to be sure, several interrelated and intersecting domains of life in which a person works out his existence. Benjamin Bloom and his associates have identified three separate and distinct domains: the cognitive, the affective, and the psychomotor. Catholic educationists and educators would probably add a fourth domain, the religious. Indeed, I would hope that Christian catechetical specialists would soon develop a taxonomy of educational objectives for the religious domain.

The *Taxonomy of Educational Objectives: Cognitive Domain* classifies the cognitive, that is, the intellectual domain, into six specific and distinct categories. From lower to higher intellectual processes, these categories are knowledge, comprehension, application, analysis, synthesis, and evaluation.[49] The affective domain—much more difficult to classify than the cognitive domain—customarily includes such elements as responsiveness, openness, attitudes, values, and beliefs.[50]

---

[48]Jerome M. Levine and Gardner Murphy, "The Learning and Forgetting of Controversial Material," in *Journal of Abnormal and Social Psychology* 38 (October, 1943):507-517.

[49]Bloom et al., *Taxonomy of Educational Objectives: Handbook I, Cognitive Domain.*

[50]Krathwohl, Bloom, and Masia, *Taxonomy of Educational Objectives: Handbook II, Affective Domain*; George G. Stern, "Measuring Noncognitive Variables in Research on Teaching," in Gage, *Handbook of Research on Teaching*, p. 407.

It is immediately apparent that the teaching of religion ought to be focussed on the affective domain. This is not to negate the great importance of the cognitive domain; rather, it is to assert that in terms of religious instruction, the cognitive is a tool—indeed, an indispensable tool, but a tool nonetheless—in the achieving of affective learning outcomes in the students.

Notwithstanding, it would appear that focus on affective learning objectives is not typical of religion classes, of catechetical writers, or of Catholic educators in general. In the high school religion classes which I have observed, there was seldom if ever any deliberate teaching for affective outcomes. Very few catechetical writers have addressed themselves in any sort of systematic, scholarly fashion to the question of pedagogical strategies for achieving affective outcomes. Nor have Catholic educators given due attention to this vital matter.

The importance of bringing about affective outcomes in religion class can be demonstrated by the findings of an empirical research investigation in which penitentiary inmates and college students were asked to rank the ten commandments in order of importance to themselves. The results indicated a high degree of similarity in the conclusion of both groups.[51]

It might well be that a one-sided concentration on cognitive outcomes and the concomitant neglect of affective outcomes on the part of Catholic schoolmen have resulted in the possible failure of American Catholic schools to be truly distinctive from their government school counterparts. Thus, for example, a national research investigation comparing Catholic students attending Catholic schools with matched Catholic students attending government schools discovered that in terms of the practice of the virtue of charity (identified by the investigators as constituting "the essence of Christianity"), there was no noticeable difference between the two groups of students.[52] The in-

---

[51] Ray Mars Simpson, "Attitudes Toward the Ten Commandments," *Journal of Social Psychology* 4 (May, 1933):223-230.

[52] Andrew M. Greeley and Peter H. Rossi, *The Education of Catholic Americans* (Chicago: Aldine, 1966), pp. 66-67. Interestingly, the first group seemed to be higher than the second in rate of attendance at religious services.

vestigators concluded: "All we can say is that if the Catholic schools are turning out people who are more diligent in the practice of love of neighbor, the fact is not confirmed by the evidence available to us."[53]

It is possible to hypothesize as to the causes of the neglect of the affective domain in Catholic schools whose officials so stoutly assert to parents that the most distinctive characteristic of the Catholic schools is its heavy emphasis on the religious and affective domains. Perhaps the notion of "affective detachment" which forms a deep part of both traditional ascetical theology and of the formation programs in seminaries, and particularly in novitiates, has had its conditioning effect on the priest and sister in the classroom.[54] Perhaps too, there is an unconscious transferral, especially by those teachers not deeply grounded in theological science, of the theological concept "Word" to the cognitive domain. Perhaps too, it is due to the residue of the emphasis placed on the intellectual by Thomas Aquinas—or perhaps more accurately by the authors of Scholastic manuals which purported to follow Aquinas—whose philosophical principles pervade most seminary and novitiate training programs.[55]

But even within the cognitive domain itself, the school's almost exclusive emphasis on the intellectual seems to be too narrowly encased. This is to say that in the school's current concepts, the parameters of the cognitive domain seem excessively restrictive. Let us take the entire question of creativity as illustrative of this point. Research by Jacob Getzels and

---

[53]*Ibid.*, p. 67.

[54]On this point, see Fichter, *Religion As an Occupation*, p. 194.

[55]In another book, I wrote: ". . . like Aristotle, Thomas Aquinas emphasized that man's highest faculty, and hence the mode by which he most resembles God, is his intellect (*Eth.* X). Moreover, for Aristotle and Aquinas, the highest intellectual activity is not in the practical intellect, but in the speculative. The Beatific Vision is first and fundamentally an intellectual activity, an encounter of the speculative intellect of man with God." James Michael Lee, *The Purpose of Catholic Schooling* (Dayton, Ohio: Geo. A. Pflaum and the National Catholic Educational Association, 1968), p. 32.

Philip Jackson indicated that in their sample, the overwhelming percentage of creative children were not found within the top quintile of children ranked according to IQ scores.[56] E. Paul Torrance presented data which indicated that in his sample, the use of the Wechsler Intelligence Scale for Children to determine giftedness would have excluded seventy percent of the children placing in the upper twenty percent on creativity measures.[57] It might well be that as it is perceived today, intelligence—which the school tends to equate with the cognitive domain—is in large measure an invention of Western culture. It might well be that another culture, for example, Indian or Eastern culture, has ways of assessing intelligence which are more in congruence with creativity.[58] One might wonder as to the degree to which religion teachers operationalize the cognitive domain of intelligence to the consequent neglect of the creative dimension.

Verbal and Nonverbal

Gerard Sloyan once observed that "The better framed the statements of divine truth are in the order of human thought, the more imperiled will the reality of the encounter be."[59] Despite the importance of this concept, catechetical writers still discuss the importance of "presenting" the message, or are seeking ways—all of them verbal—to more efficaciously "impart" the Good News. Doubtless the great devotion to the verbal on the part of the vast majority of religion teachers and catechetical writers is a natural outgrowth of their commitment to the product outcome and to the cognitive domains. But whatever

---

[56]Jacob W. Getzels and Philip W. Jackson, *Creativity and Intelligence: Explorations with Gifted Students* (New York: Wiley, 1962).

[57]E. Paul Torrance, "Explorations in Creative Thinking in the Early School Years: A Progress Report," in Calvin W. Taylor, editor, *The 1959 University of Utah Conference on the Identification of Creative Scientific Talent* (Salt Lake City, Utah: University of Utah Press, 1959), pp. 58-71.

[58]See, for example, Sarvepalli Radhakrishnan, *An Idealist View of Life,* revised edition (London: Allen, 1937).

[59]Gerard S. Sloyan, "What Should Children's Catechisms Be Like?", in Hofinger and Stone, *Pastoral Catechetics,* p. 35.

the cause, few general pedagogical strategies are more at variance with the development of well-rounded religious outcomes than is the heavy reliance on the verbal mode of teaching.

To move from the prevailing almost exclusive stress on the verbal to the nonverbal requires several progressive stages, each of which the religion teacher might well try out for himself. The first stage is the moving from the heavy teacher-centered pattern of classroom verbal behavior to a more student-centered pattern, from lecturing (whether overt or covert) to discussion. That the vast majority of religion teachers still use one form or another of lecture or telling can be confirmed by a visit to the religion class of most Catholic schools. Indeed, books on education authored by prominent catechetical writers and/or by influential Catholic educators seem to lend support to this kind of teaching. Thus, for example, not too long ago Robert Henle, a nationally famous priest-educator wrote a dialogue which he felt illustrated the ideal question and answer pattern in a Catholic school.[60] This dialogue was consciously rooted in Henle's conception of a Catholic philosophy of education as specifically applied to classroom methodology, since his exposition appeared as an article of a planned collection of writings, each of which advocates a different philosophy of education. In this ideal dialogue in a model Catholic school, the sister teaching the class used 286 words in her questions. The total number of words used by the students in all their responses was eight.

Genuine discussion—where the students can verbalize more than the teacher—has been shown to be superior to the lecture and telling methods in effecting attitude formation and change in students. Reviews of the pertinent empirical research by George Stern[61] and by myself[62] have indicated that while both

---

[60]Robert J. Henle, "Roman Catholic View of Education," in Philip Phenix, editor, *Philosophies of Education* (New York: Wiley, 1961), pp. 81-82.

[61]Stern, in *Handbook of Research on Teaching*, p. 427.

[62]Lee, *Principles and Methods of Secondary Education*, p. 299.

methods had fairly equal effect in terms of the student's learning of factual material, the discussion method proved superior to the lecture technique in effecting attitude development and change.

The second stage in moving toward a nonverbal teaching strategy is the use of methodologies which revolve around a goodly portion of nonverbal material. This is done by utilizing specific teaching techniques which have as the most essential—but by no means the sole—ingredient, the experiential dimension, particularly affective experiences. The role-playing methodology discussed earlier in this chapter is an especially useful teaching device in this second stage.

The third and final stage consists in utilizing teaching methodologies which are primarily nonverbal in nature. Naturally verbalization will enter the classroom situation, but this will not be part of the essence of the learning experience itself; rather, it will be each students' verbalized expression of what he felt and innerly perceived during the experience. Sensitivity-awareness methodologies provide a representative example of this third stage.[63]

Perhaps it might be helpful to illustrate these three pedagogical stages. Let us suppose that the learning outcome desired by the teacher and the students is the acquiring of a deeper Christian attitude toward Negroes. A lecture on social justice or on man's inhumanity to man is clearly inadequate. In terms of the three methodological stages just outlined, a class discussion should have some specific attitudinal objective, for example, deeper insight into the dynamics of the Negro's plight in a white and therefore non-Negro oriented society. Negro students, key civil rights leaders and typical poor Negroes from the community should be brought into the religion class to participate appropriately at pivotal points of learning.

---

[63]See William C. Schutz, *Joy* (New York: Grove, 1967); William C. Schutz, *TTIRO: A Three Dimensional Theory of Interpersonal Behavior* (New York: Holt, Rinehart & Winston, 1958); also Frederick Perls, et al., *Gestalt Therapy* (New York: Dell, 1962).

The second stage might involve a role-playing situation. The teacher-student lesson planning committee can set up a problem situation which induces a deeper experiential understanding of and affective feeling for the Negro in white America. Such a role-playing lesson might deal with a situation involving a white Catholic girl in the parish who has fallen in love with a Negro Catholic boy. Roles might include the girl's mother, the girl, the boy, the boy's mother, the president of the Rosary Society who was born and raised in the deep South, and the parish priest.

The third stage would involve sensitivity awareness sessions which revolve around *feeling* and innerly perceiving what it is to be black. Such sensitivity sessions might consist in such learning situations as will directly promote the student's self-awareness and self-feelings of a black body, of the situation of this black body in social space, and the personality consequences of both black body and of black-body-in-social-space. The techniques of sensitivity training as they are customarily employed in depth in group counseling and in group therapy can, if properly adapted by the trained teacher, be of great assistance to the religion teacher.[64] These techniques, used in conjunction with other nonverbal teaching strategies, should, of course, be used to effect instructional goals and not counseling-type objectives.

The lecture technique is the implementation of the transmission theory of teaching. The three pedagogical stages, on the other hand, represent the concretization of the teaching model. Each of the three stages represents a progressive evolution toward the total structured situation which at once provides for the greatest student freedom and the greatest experiential structure.

---

[64]Implementation of the three pedagogical stages in the classroom situation requires, obviously, that the religion teacher be well trained in pedagogical *process* skills. Extended treatment of this point falls outside the scope of this chapter.

Person and Content

In the heyday of progressive education the pedagogical war cry was "we teach children, not subject matter." With the passing of this truism into the realm of cliché, the essential validity of the war cry unhappily has been lost on many of today's generation of teachers. In terms of religious instruction it might be well to refocus on the pregnancy of this maxim.

If religion teachers are product-oriented, do they not focus on the subject matter rather than on the learner? If religion teachers are cognitive-oriented, is not the emphasis being placed on the subject matter instead of on the learner? If religion teachers stress the verbal, is not the subject matter, especially in its verbal formulations, given priority over the learner? Conversely, does not a radication in process, in the affective, in the nonverbal-experiential place the emphasis where it belongs, in the learner inside rather than in the subject outside?

Do not the three pedagogical stages take both as their starting point and as their line of development the primacy of the learner?

From the psychological point of view there is no subject matter apart from the learner who is acquiring this subject matter. Indeed, the learner's phenomenal field, his need-structure, and even his socioeconomic background will substantially modify the very subject matter itself, to say nothing of the use to which he will put this subject matter.[65] That learning occurs after the manner of the learner is a rather familiar—and pedagogically useful—Thomistic dictum.

All of this dramatizes the necessity for broad teacher-pupil planning of the religion course, from the elementary level through college. To be sure, the extent of the religion teachers' genuine commitment to person-oriented instruction as distinct from subject-oriented instruction can in no small way be assessed by the degree to which he makes use of teacher-student

---

[65]On this point, see Lee, *Principles and Methods of Secondary Education,* pp. 144-183.

planning. This, of course, does not mean that there will be no rigorous learning of subject content; rather this subject content will no longer be radicated in itself, but in the ongoing psychodynamics of the learner himself. In the final analysis, the chief practical reason for joint teacher-student planning is that such a procedure will cause the students to learn more, to retain more, and to utilize to a greater degree what they have learned.

Teacher-control and Student-control

From the viewpoint of pedagogical dynamics, the classroom represents an interaction of teacher with students. In the superior classrooms, this pattern is always shifting. Educational science carries this concept to a deeper level, and reveals how the flow of this interaction is basically a mode of communication control. In the professional literature, teachers who exercise exclusive or even heavy communication control in the classroom are called "traditional" or "autocratic," while teachers who purposively structure the learning situation so that the students share substantially in the communication control are termed "progressive" or "democratic."[66]

There has been veritably an enormous amount of research done in the educational, psychological, and sociological sciences on the effects of autocratic versus democratic communication flow in classrooms and in other social situations. Thus, for example, Kurt Lewin reported on an empirical investigation which separated a democratic classroom and an autocratic classroom for comparison. The study concluded, among other things, that as far as the child-to-child relationship was concerned, "there was about thirty times as much hostile domination in the autocracy as in the democracy, more demands for attention and much more hostile criticism; whereas in the democratic atmosphere cooperation and praise of the other

---

[66]These terms as used by educational scientists form a descriptive nomenclature, and are not intended to denote or connote a pejorative or eulogistic sense.

fellow was much more frequent."[67]

It is well known that traditional, autocratic teachers tend to be more punitive than are progressive, democratic teachers. An investigation by Jacob Kounin and Paul Gump revealed that pupils who have punitive teachers "manifest more aggression in their misconducts, are more unsettled and conflicted about their misconducts in school, and are less concerned with learning and school-unique values" than pupils who have nonpunitive teachers.[68]

Progressive, democratic communication control tends to be superior to the traditional approach in effecting desirable behavioral outcomes in students. Thus George Stern's review of the pertinent empirical research studies concluded that regardless of whether the investigator was concerned with attitudes toward a cultural outgroup, toward other participants in the class, or toward the self, the results of the studies generally have indicated that progressive instruction facilitates a shift in the students in the direction of a more favorable, acceptable behavior than does traditional instruction.[69]

Rather poignant in this connection is the report of the psychologist Kurt Lewin concerning his own inner feelings upon observing children during their first day in a traditional-type classroom situation: "There have been few experiences for me as impressive as seeing the expression on children's faces change during the first day of autocracy. The friendly, open, and cooperative group, full of life, became within a short half-hour a rather apathetic-looking gathering without initiative."[70]

Perhaps this traditional pattern of teacher behavior in which

---

[67]Kurt Lewin, "Experiments in Social Space," in *Harvard Educational Review* 9 (January, 1939):27.

[68]Jacob S. Kounin and Paul V. Gump, "The Comparative Influences of Punitive and Nonpunitive Teachers upon Children's Conceptions of Misconduct," in *Journal of Educational Psychology* 52 (February, 1961): 49.

[69]Stern, in *Handbook of Research on Teaching,* p. 427; see also D. Pumpinatzi and I. Zwetschken, *Herzkontakt und Unterfluss* (Lisbon: Algarve, 1968).

[70]Lewin, "Experiments in Social Space," p. 31.

the teacher tends to heavily dominate, if not actually exclusively control the flow of communication in the classroom emanates from the traditional concept of the teacher's role. I use the term "role" here in its technical sense: a set of expectancies which a person, or set of persons have about another not because that other is who he is as a person but rather because that other is encased in a certain role. Operationally defined the teacher as teacher (not as Father Morawitz, the human being) performs certain acts which the students observe and then organize into a perceptual whole, a role. On the basis of this perception of the actions of the teacher, the students form a generalized set of expectancies for the future actions of the teacher. The students then tentatively act out a set of behaviors in accordance with their perceptual set. The teacher, observing the students performing these behaviors, in turn acts in those ways which tend to flow from the position reciprocal to the acts of the students. Through such interaction both the students and the teacher learn and congeal their roles.

Because the role of teacher has been handed down from generation to generation, and indeed, from older students to younger ones within the same generation, the students enter the classroom with a preconceived perception of teacher role. (This is probably not true for children first entering school; nonetheless, it is not too long before these tots learn the teacher role.) In religion class this concept of teacher role is reinforced by the culturally-accreted authoritarian symbol of the priest's or sister's garb, and by their distinctive title of "Father" or "Sister." The typical Catholic perception of the religion teacher's role, then, is that of a person who stands up in front of the class "presenting" and "imparting" the truths of the Catholic religion.

In an interesting empirical research study, Arno Bellack and his associates investigated the verbal interaction of the teacher and the pupils. The results confirm the concept of role discussed above. Utilizing gaming theory as his experimental framework, Bellack found a relatively consistent set of "moves" which belonged to the teacher and a set which belonged to the students —primarily because the teacher was the teacher and the students were the students. In other words, certain "moves" were expected of the teacher because he was the teacher. Bellack found that the teacher was the most active player in the game. The teacher made the most moves, spoke most frequently, and his speeches were longest. The pupil's primary role, on the other hand, was that of respondent; indeed two-thirds of his "moves" were those of responding. His responses tended to be primarily in terms of statements of facts and explanations of them. Students tended to evaluate little except by way of reporting what others, such as public officials, had said. Students tended only very infrequently to present evaluations of the facts in terms of what these facts meant in their own personal lives, or how they evaluated these facts in terms of their own values.[71]

In short, Arno Bellack found that in the class sessions he investigated, the teacher tended to rely most heavily on the traditional role of teacher and hence utilized the recitation type of methodology.

Teachers of all kinds, including religion teachers, tend to assert with vigor that their classrooms are progressive and not traditional. Yet it is the opinion of many educationists and other professional observers of teacher classroom behavior that the typical teacher tends to be more or less traditional, whether he believes so or not.[72]

If religious instruction is to come of age, it must pass out of the level of heavy or exclusive teacher control. Only in this way can the teaching of religion be radicated in process, in the affective domain, in the non-verbal-experiential. The introduction of genuine teacher-pupil planning is one way for the religion teacher to move away from the traditional form of

---

[71] Arno A. Bellack, et al., *The Language of the Classroom* (New York: Teachers College Press, 1966).

[72] Norman E. Wallen and Robert M. W. Travers, "Analysis and Investigation of Teaching Methods," in N. L. Gage, editor, *Handbook of Research on Teaching*, pp. 468-470.

heavy teacher-control. The use of verbal interaction instruments to assess systematically the patterns of verbal communication also provides a splendid initial assistance to the teacher in seeing his classroom behavior as it really is, not as he imagines it to be.[73]

Social Climate

Every organism, including the human organism, is in large measure conditioned in its growth and development by the ecological milieu in which it is situated. It is axiomatic—and with good reason—that the person's prime ecological milieu, namely, the family, exercises an enormous formative influence on the developing person. The atmosphere in the social setting that is the family acts at once as an envelope and a vector in the formation of the child's self-system. Thus, for example, empirical research has indicated that the less restrictive and protective the parents are, the more likely will be the independent achievement of the children.[74]

The school too—especially the classroom—forms one of the most important ecologies affecting the growth and development of the child and the youth. The classroom, as Jacob Getzels and Herbert Thelen have taken pains to point out, is itself a social system, and a rather unique social system at that.[75] Thus from the human development point of view, there is a vast difference between the one-to-one relationship which characterizes the tutorial setting and the one-to-many and many-to-many relationship which characterizes the classroom milieu.

---

[73]One such instrument is that developed by Ned Flanders and his students. See Ned A. Flanders, *Interaction Analysis in the Classroom: A Manual for Observers,* revised edition (Ann Arbor, Michigan: School of Education, University of Michigan, 1966).

[74]Bernard Berelson and Gary Steiner, *Human Behavior: An Inventory of Scientific Findings* (New York: Harcourt, Brace, and World, 1964), p. 81.

[75]Jacob W. Getzels and Herbert A. Thelen, "The Classroom Group as a Unique Social System," in National Society for the Study of Education, *The Dynamics of Instructional Groups,* Fifty-ninth Yearbook, Part II (Chicago: University of Chicago Press, 1960), pp. 53-82.

Indeed this difference is much more clearly etched in the affective domain than in the cognitive domain. After all, virtually every behavioral scientist, no matter what his theoretical orientation, will agree that attitudes and values are socially formed. The social climate of the classroom, therefore, is correlated significantly with attitude formation in the students. On the other hand, the amount of cognitive gain in the classroom seems largely unaffected by the social climate of the classroom.[76]

Since the attitudes and the value system of the teacher play the major role in the resultant social climate in the classroom, there has been a goodly amount of research done on this pivotal problem. Further, instruments have been devised to assess the teacher's attitudes particularly as they relate to a prediction of his human relations abilities and to the degree of his authoritarianism. The most celebrated instrument to assess the former is the Minnesota Teacher Attitude Inventory (MTAI),[77] while the California F Scale[78] remains one of the best exemplars of the latter.

From what has been said thus far in this section, it is obvious that the nature and thrust of the social climate in the religion class are of paramount importance in achieving desired outcomes in the learners. Perhaps diocesan and religious-institute school officials might well use the MTAI or the California F Scale in screening out persons whose rankings in interpersonal skills are so low and whose scores in authoritarian traits are so high as to preclude their ever establishing in their classrooms that type of social climate so essential for a well-rounded religion class. Certainly these school officials might give serious thought to planning extensive and intensive inservice workshops for their teachers of religion so that they might improve their interper-

[76]Stern, in *Handbook of Research on Teaching*, pp. 426-429.

[77]Walter W. Cook, Carroll H. Leeds, and Robert Callis, *The Minnesota Teacher Attitude Inventory* (New York: Psychological Corporation, 1951).

[78]T. W. Adorno, et al., *The Authoritarian Personality* (New York: Harper, 1950).

sonal skills and more consciously create in their classrooms that type of social climate most productive of the desired outcomes.

CONCLUSION

Perhaps more things were omitted from this chapter than were included in it, but the goal of this chapter was to give the reader an inkling of the complexity of the act that is the *teaching* of religion. In the welter of all that currently is being written about the importance of relating the kerygma and the new theology to religious instruction, it is regrettable that a very careful consideration of the *teaching* of religion is somehow relegated to the background. One may possess all the insights gleaned from the new theology, and all the conviction of the kerygma, but if one does not possess the technical competence or process expertness requisite for an effective teacher, then the religion class will not achieve the desired behavioral outcomes in the students. *Teaching* religion is far more complex than standing in front of the class "presenting" or "imparting" the Good News. The sooner religious instruction sheds the simplistic mantle of "presenting" and "imparting," the sooner it will mature and come of age. In short, the teacher of religion must move away from the preaching model and into the realm of the teaching model.

4 Biblical Pedagogics

Didier Piveteau

Introduction

We all know that catechetics should be biblical in one way or
another since faith, as the Dogmatic Constitution on Divine
Revelation of the Second Vatican Council has suggested, is the
assent of man's spirit and heart to God's revelation, of which
the bible is a privileged expression. Yet it is true that there
are special reasons in our days to scrutinize what is meant
exactly by biblical pedagogics.* On the one hand, we are just
now gathering the fruit of the tremendous amount of work
done during the past twenty years in Catholic circles on the
bible itself, both from the point of view of content and the
literary genres, and also from the point of view of the relationship between bible and tradition (a study which culminated in
the teaching of Vatican II on the long-disputed question of the
two sources).[1] And on the other hand, the progress achieved
in the domain of catechetics, due especially to the insights of
the social and behavioral sciences, has enabled us at present

---

*Editors' Note: The term "biblical pedagogics" was first coined by the
senior editor of this volume (Professor Lee) to denote the bible as a
pedagogical form and a pedagogical tool. The bible, in this context, is
viewed as a connected thematic series of events by which God historically
catechized his people.

[1]Gabriel Moran, *Scripture and Tradition* (New York: Herder and
Herder, 1963).

to perceive more clearly the essence of the tradition of faith. One of the insights furnished by the social and behavioral sciences is a shift of emphasis from the old duality of content and methods to another dual terminology, namely the catechist and the one whose attitudes should be changed. Consequently, those changes and precisions which have been made recently cast radically new light on the two terms that make up the substance of this chapter: bible and catechetics. Indeed, the relationship between the bible and catechetics is, I suggest, quite different than was the case only a half dozen years ago. It is fitting therefore to examine what is currently understood by biblical pedagogics. This analysis will enable us to pass judgment on the validity of the catechist's everyday teaching methodology, as well as on the reliability of the catechetical materials which are furnished for the use of religion teachers.

The treatment I have chosen for my analysis of biblical pedagogics is a historical one, which will turn out to be somewhat Thomistic. It may be said that chronologically biblical pedagogics has gone through three different stages during the past twenty years, each one representing progress over the preceding one. But these divisions do not belong only to the past; they still coexist in current practice, so that even now they constitute three different levels. The fact that I shall point out the weaknesses of the first two, specifying, as does Aquinas, what true biblical pedagogics is not, does not mean that we should come to the third level through the negation of the first two. Rather, by subsuming them, by recapitulating them in order to advance to the third stage, we shall attain a true concept and an overall vision of biblical pedagogics in our time.

THE BIBLE AS FORM

The first prescribed way for the catechist to look on the bible is to consider it as a form. This form, which is basically a mode of transmission, is language. Viewed solely from the perspective of language, the bible has been regarded in terms of the three essential elements comprising language, namely, vocabulary, syntax, and rhetoric. The common denominator of these three categories is a quantitative approach to the use of the bible. This has led catechists and apologists (who, after all, form one type of catechist) to believe that the conversion of the world is a direct function of the number of biblical quotations they make or of the number of biblical books they distribute, independent of the quality of explication or transmission which is attained. Catechists who regard biblical form in terms of any or all of the linguistic elements mentioned above tend to share a static, solid, subhuman conception of language. Indeed, this conception implies that language can exist in books, dictionaries, or grammars independently of the *hic et nunc* situation in which these linguistic elements are used. Yet, it is precisely this *hic et nunc* situation which makes even the most simple word—such as the "yes" I might answer to some question another person poses—a unique moment of our history and the history of the world.

The three essential elements of language—vocabulary, syntax, and rhetoric—differ in practice according to the relative stress each places on a different aspect of the language.

Vocabulary

Catechists who stress the vocabulary element of biblical linguistic form tend to possess an artistic or aesthetic mentality. These catechists, whether in pictorial art or in words, think it absolutely necessary to address children or students in terms of the good shepherd, the mustard seed, and all the other imagery that fills both the old and the new testament. I must confess I am reminded of this attitude when I see on the exterior walls of the University of Notre Dame's massive library building the carefully chosen expressions of certain biblical symbols and themes: "the holy mountain," "the tree of life," "the star of David," "the burning bush," and so forth. This mentality can also be found in holy cards, in the illustrations of some catechetical books, or in the new-style songs which have been inspired by the psalms and which are intended to promote both the piety of youth and the homiletic style of preachers.

I maintain that stress on the vocabulary element of biblical linguistic form is wrong on two counts. First, this emphasis is based on an outmoded concept of language. This antiquated view of language, characteristic of the schooldays of the older generation, took as a pedagogical principle the assumption that the more words a student knows from a list, the better he is prepared to understand and speak a language. Yet, now we know that biblical terms and symbols will never introduce a student to the depth of biblical communication. Second, at the root of the vocabulary-oriented mentality lies the assumption that the bible has been inspired in the very words found in the biblical text. The implication here is that to be a Christian, it is first necessary to become a Jew—a position difficult to maintain when one considers how Peter abandoned his decision to have the Gentiles circumcised because of the action of the Spirit on Cornelius. To state the case bluntly: we do not have to circumcise our language to become a fully contemporary Christian.

Syntax

Catechists who stress the syntax element of biblical linguistic form, cognizant that language is composed not only of words but also of patterns and structures, attempt to find in the bible examples of ready-made catechetical reasonings or homilies. Their need arises from their experience of how difficult it is in a catechetical lesson to bridge the gap between the beginning of the class, when the students are attentive, and the moment when the lesson starts to revolve around God and other divine topics. Confronted daily with this pedagogical problem, these religion teachers recall that the gospels and epistles are echoes of the first preachings and teachings of apostolic times; thus encouraged, these catechists resort to the patterns of speech used by the early Christians. Using this approach as a pedagogical springboard, certain catechetical writers[2] have discovered four different modes of preaching, all biblical, and all claiming to have the adequate answer to the problems confronting contemporary catechetics. The first mode, the "Matthew method," is quite rational, and aims at giving proof from the scripture itself. (Matthew frequently resorted to the expression: "because it is written in the scriptures.") The second mode, the "John method," is highly symbolic in its approach. (John frequently employed the double connotation of symbols such as water, light, the road, birth, life, to help his readers to pass from the daily world to the world of the spirit.) The third mode, the "Luke method," is the beatitudinal kind of catechesis. (Luke frequently resorts to the beatitude pattern of reasoning, showing that Christ's revelation stands in the line— though with a difference—of Christian aspirations.) The fourth and final mode, the "Paul method," is more radical and rooted in the personal encounter of Jesus with man. (Paul knew only one thing: Christ and Christ crucified—a scandal to the Jews and a folly to the Gentiles. Paul did not care for reasoning, for symbols, or for human values; indeed, on the one and only occasion he altered his encounter method and utilized another approach, namely with the Greeks on the top of Acropolis, he met with a dismal catechetical failure.)

The fact that there have been at least these four structures of gospel catechetics should already indicate that teaching, even in early times, was dependent on human conditions, and not just the pure "transmission" of a solid and untouchable bulk of words and expressions. The lessons were different according to whether they were given to Greeks or to Romans, to Jews or to Gentiles, to converts or to pagans. Consequently,

---

[2]Jacques Audinet, *Forming the Faith of Adolescents* (New York: Herder and Herder, 1968).

rather than copying narrowly the procedures of the past as so many stereotypes, contemporary catechists ought to employ the basic *hic et nunc* situational emphasis found in gospel catechetics. If we are to use gospel approaches in contemporary catechetics, as I think indeed we should, it is because they are permanent possibilities of human thinking rather than because they are in the bible. Further, if there are other pedagogical dimensions which are not used in the bible, catechists should feel free to use them. Failure to understand this is to reduce communication to language, to shrink personal exchange to sets of words. This kind of attitude would be pedagogically unfortunate, particularly in the light of James Michael Lee's analysis of the nature of the teaching process found in Chapter III of this volume.

Rhetoric

The third group of catechists stress the element of rhetoric in biblical linguistic form. These catechists view the bible as a resource book of teaching techniques. They see the bible pedagogically as a rhetoric, a series of judgments or proofs. Religion teachers in this category are the modern representatives of that permanent temptation which threatens the wise use of the bible, namely concordism. The best-known form of concordism emerged in the nineteenth century when biblical scholars, confronted with the onslaughts of the natural scientists, tried to reconcile the sacred text with the findings of natural science. These biblical scholars went to considerable effort to dovetail Genesis with geological epochs, with the migration of races, and with the origin of species. This "reconciliation mentality" is obsolete and has all but disappeared from the ranks of pure biblical scholarship. Yet today, a more subtle variety of reconciliationism is emerging, primarily among religion teachers who still do not know the nature and structure of the bible. The modern type of concordism is that which establishes close links between the bible and the new sciences of our time, which are much less physics or astronomy than the social sciences such as anthropology, psychology, and sociology.[3] There are religion teachers and catechetical specialists, therefore, who will turn to the bible to find in it theories of education, or theories of prayer for men of our time, or theories about politics, and so on. In their eyes we should not be afraid to embrace new sociological theories, such as community living, or contemporary political theories like the art and science of revolution, or emerging psychological theories as long as we can find references, though too often merely verbal, in the bible.

Critique of the Bible-as-Form Approach

Thus far in this chapter, I have discussed the threefold manner in which some catechists have approached biblical linguistic form, namely, from the viewpoint of vocabulary, syntax, and rhetoric. Of course, it is obvious that these three approaches are not devoid of all pedagogical value, and hence, there is no reason why religion teachers should not utilize them if they are consistent with the science of teaching-learning and if they prove to be pedagogically efficient. After all, these three approaches were pedagogically useful in the Middle Ages—although, it should be remembered that during that era society was much less urbanized, and the city was not yet secular. To be sure, the Middle Ages were quite close to the agrarian civilization of the bible. During the medieval period, the stained glass windows in the cathedrals were the only religion textbooks in use. But times have changed, and the Middle Ages are gone. Nowadays, our experience teaches us that the old threefold catechetical approach to biblical linguistic form simply does not work. The message does not reach the hearers who live in an entirely different cultural world from the Middle Ages; consequently, religion teachers should not be surprised at peda-

[3]Eric Butterworth, *Discover the Power Within You: A Guide to the Unexplored Depths Within Based on the Actual Teaching of Jesus* (New York: Harper & Row, 1968).

gogical failure.

At this juncture two observations are in order. First, the old threefold approach to biblical linguistic form does not affect the structure of catechesis itself, the sequence of information given, or the scope of the various parts treated. The backbone of this outmoded threefold approach to biblical pedagogics is taken from outside the biblical world; these pedagogics are clothed in biblical outfits. In this old approach, the bible is used as a byproduct, as a resource treasure for examples or for illustrations, as a sugarcoating that will help students swallow the more intellectual theological diet. This kind of biblical pedagogics remains on the margin of biblical significance, a fact which explains why so many older biblical textbooks or biblical pedagogics are content with merely enunciating some verse from the bible or with simply recounting biblical anecdotes in order to motivate students and keep them aware.

Second, this old kind of biblical pedagogics is nothing more than a mode of the transmission theory of teaching, which James Michael Lee correctly condemned in Chapter III of this book. The old type of biblical pedagogics centers only on what Lee termed "product content." It is centered around words or phrases, and does not take into account the two terms of communication, namely, the teacher who talks and also listens, and the students who listen and also talk. The old kind of biblical pedagogics is basically a form of pedagogical spoonfeeding, but it is not even good spoonfeeding, since it both neglects concrete biblical information and fails to teach for attitudes and value systems. It believes that words can foster faith, a well-known type of error called magic. Curiously enough, in many cases this pseudobiblical approach runs counter to the traditional vision of knowledge propounded by Christianity. We all know that Christian knowledge is motivated by faith: *fides quaerens intellectum.* No tricks, no gimmicks, no artificial incentives can take the place of the essential motivation of faith. After all, man's contact with the bible is best exemplified by the model of human encounter in which revelation follows recognition. It is because a young man is attracted by an attractive girl that he wants to know more about her. I do not think that lecturing about a girl, giving details about her background, her tastes, her acquaintances, has ever inflamed any young man's heart with love.[4] The old type of biblical pedagogics reverses the traditional formula of *fides quaerens intellectum* by teaching as though knowledge precedes faith. There are thousands of biblical words and analogies. Yet, it is patently foolish to assert that, as if by magic, faith will emerge sooner or later from these words or analogies themselves. Such a pedagogical approach is simply hopeless and, indeed, antibiblical.

THE BIBLE AS CONTENT

The first major catechetical approach to the bible is to regard it as form, while the second is to view it as content. To be sure, content constitutes the other aspect of language besides form. Content is not simply vocabulary, rhetoric, or syntax, but more: it is meaning, with at least an apparent objective core of which the words and figures of speech are just the expression. Those religion teachers who perceive the bible principally as content have a more unifying vision of the bible than those who see the bible primarily as form. They do not slice the bible into small bits—verses or books—but instead look upon the bible as a whole, and attempt to find the underlying central message, the unifying doctrine that pervades the whole.

There have been two main practical consequences of viewing the bible primarily as content. The first is the application to contemporary catechetics of the findings of the new biblical scholarship. One of these key findings is that the content of most of the new testament is built around small structures of speech representing the first announcement of the good news.

---

[4] Alfonso Nebreda, *Kerygma in Crisis* (Chicago: Loyola University Press, 1965), p. 50.

This kerygma revealed the salvation of mankind through Jesus, who was conceived of the Holy Ghost, who was born of the Blessed Virgin Mary, who preached the kingdom and the fatherhood of God, who was crucified, who died, and whom the disciples saw risen from the dead in full glory at the right hand of the Father. The application to catechetics of this finding of the new biblical scholarship largely explains the success of the kerygmatic approach in the decade following the Second World War, an approach which demanded that each lesson both reactivates the presentation of the call to conversion and also seeks the student's response to this challenge of God.

The second main practical consequence of viewing the bible primarily as content is that this same kerygma became, so to speak, the summary of the whole bible. As a result Christianity was reduced not so much to a philosophy or to an ethical code, but to history. The content of the bible became the history of salvation. Therefore, to teach biblical catechesis was to present the history of God's concern for humanity through the choice of a people, with whom he established a covenant and to whom he gave the promises destined to all men, in somewhat the same way as the Hebrews did under the tents in the desert, passing on the memory of the great deeds that God had achieved for their ancestors, those great deeds being the sign of greater things to come in eschatological times.

This emphasis on the bible-as-content, therefore, resulted in a blossoming of textbooks built around salvation history. This salvation history approach in turn led the students to such a satiety that in the high school where I taught in the early 1960's the sophomores founded an anti-Abraham club because they refused to hear any more about this biblical person. For preadolescents the salvation history approach has a less deleterious effect, since this age group is known for its interest in time and history on the one hand, and for its ability to understand attitudes when they are embodied in heroes (this age group has been characterized as the age of hero-worship).

Catechetical specialists, therefore, have issued for preadolescents curricula and material presenting the history of salvation as reflected in the consciousness of the main figures of the bible.[5]

How is this concept of the bible-as-content to be regarded? It is obvious, first of all, that this approach has been commonly in use throughout the history of the church, as long ago as apostolic times, as can be seen from the first epistle of St. Peter. When St. Augustine, answering the letter of his deacon Deogratias in his *De Catechizandis Rudibus*, wishes to give an example of biblical pedagogics, he spontaneously adopts the salvation history approach. So does the *Didaché*, as well as the epistles of St. Ignatius of Antioch. If, therefore, a biblical pedagogic centered on the bible-as-content is utilized with skill, and if it is used in a more general context, which aims at building attitudes, there is no reason why this approach should not be employed. One should be aware, however, of the limitations and dangers of interest in the bible-as-content approach.

Critique of the Bible-as-Content Approach

The first danger is that the resulting type of catechesis will find it difficult for the students to become really concerned with that portion of time which is called *now* and which is the only one in which their attitudes and values can be exercised, the only moment to which they can give a personal response. The bible-as-content approach tends, on the one hand, to overemphasize the importance of the past: catechesis then becomes a part of apologetics or exegesis. (The maleffects of this danger are illustrated in those so-called biblical clubs which emphasize purely historical culture and information and which are not radicated in the dynamics of learning.) On the other hand, the bible-as-content approach tends to overemphasize the influence of the future in an attempt to show that, like the prevailing trends of twentieth-century philosophy, Christianity has nothing

---

[5]Jacques Bournique, *Pédagogie des Héroes* (Paris: Mame-Fayard, 1966).

to fear from the modern myth of "the sense of history." Cate-chesis then becomes another type of Marxism, aiming at one or another eschatology, but completely foreign to the formation of new attitudes in the here-and-now situation. We must remem-ber that in patristic times, this historical catechesis was given in connection with the reception of sacraments; it was the means of actualizing in the *hodie* of the liturgy those things which tend in the classroom milieu to be purely historical.

The major problem in this connection is to bring students to a deeply felt concern with the history of salvation, to bring them to an adequate understanding of relevance to their present lives of Abraham, Moses, the kings, and the prophets. Short of this, religion teachers just play with words and do not even introduce students to the world of catechetics. But to bring students to these goals requires a continuing process of maturity and growth; it is not at all the result of telling over and over again the stories of the old and new testaments. To allow the student to be introduced to the history of salvation, he must be able to give personal, individual meaning to events occurring to him throughout life; he must be led to interiorize such biblical happenings as war and peace, life and death, success and failure. When the student's own level of maturity enables him to exer-cise such specific human activity, then he can feel challenged by the Christ event, his claim to resurrection and lordship. The student then can identify himself with the meaning Jesus has given to man's life, when on the cross he trusted the Father to the end and jumped into his death, assured that this would be the gateway to another richer existence. To be reached by the history of salvation is, for the student, to accept his own life as modelled and shaped according to the same personal dynamics as those of Jesus. The implications of this for biblical pedagogics are obvious. The best religion teachers can do as catechists is to structure the educational variables in such a way as to attain this necessary attitude of conferring meaning. To catechize basically is to create a pedagogical milieu which facilitates that kind of growth without which the student cannot even know what people talk about when they speak of salvation history.

The second major danger in the bible-as-content approach is the resultant overvaluation of kerygma. It is common knowledge that the kerygmatic route has not produced all the results which were expected of it by Josef Jungmann and his followers. Hyperemphasis on salvation history seems to be an inevitable consequence of the kerygmatic approach. As Alfonso Nebreda has aptly pointed out:

> All over Europe I have heard former students say that they need more help. I am convinced that everywhere, not only in missiology and catechesis but also in the whole pastoral field of the Church we must restudy our whole approach to pre- paring people for the kerygmatic message. In this task of pre- paring for the kerygma, apologetics has an important role. In fact it is essential to the kerygmatic approach.[6]

Let us not be misled with the reference to apologetics in this Nebreda quote. The term "apologetics" has had a bad connota- tion in the past. The type of apologetics Nebreda pleads for is nothing more than the essentially biblical patience of God, who always met people at the point of their development. It has always struck me as rather odd that catechetical specialists and religion teachers have so frequently forgotten that Jesus *is* the kerygma, the good news, the mystery of God. But Jesus did not come before his way had been paved by persons such as the prophets, and by experiences such as war, exile, destruction of the temple, and so forth. The student has to be in the state of expecting salvation if the coming of the Savior is to have any meaning. He has to be made aware of the possibility of news in his life if we wish him to be attentive to the proclamation of the good news. Once again, catechetists are sent back to a much deeper and different understanding of the bible than merely

---

[6]Nebreda, *Kerygma in Crisis*, p. 49.

content or form.

The third major danger in the bible-as-content approach is that this type of biblical pedagogics almost inevitably tends to be solely concerned with words, and even a very superficial use of words at that. This type of biblical pedagogics results in a monologue on the part of the teacher with just an occasional agreement on the part of the student. The religion teacher's message runs the risk of being primarily journalistic. The characteristic of journalism is that it does not deal with history but with stories, because it sticks to what is most exterior in events, and because it presents them like a mosaic without any real inner relationship. The only underlying unifying theme in a front page of a typical newspaper is emotion. Similarly, the catechist runs the risk of seeking unity from purely emotional expressions such as: "Look, students, how great God is to perform such wonders, how kind, and merciful he is to take care of mankind." Further, journalism does not relate the events which are narrated to the inner life and developmental state of the readers. It circulates information, not experience. It brings the readers something from the outside; it seldom or never reveals the secret life of a community. It is obvious that this journalistic mode is not biblical. Indeed, it is foreign to the nature of Christianity.

In order to clarify the point I have made in the preceding paragraph, let me utilize a supposition and a comparison. Let us suppose that through some cataclysm all Christians on earth were destroyed. Our biblical books would remain, though, on the shelves of our library. Could nonbelievers, unfamiliar with Jesus, come to faith through the reading of these books? My answer is no. If we suppose, on the contrary, that all biblical books happened to be destroyed, but the Christian community managed to survive, could there be new people brought to faith? The answer is not to be doubted and is affirmative. This should not surprise us. This hypothetical situation is analogous to a science-fiction supposition according to which all males perished.

Could the remaining women give birth to babies even if all the books about sex and gynecology were preserved? The answer is no. But if the hypothetical question were reversed, so that if all those books of gynecology and biology were destroyed but that there remained on earth men and women, then surely new babies would be born. The basic point is that faith is primarily a work of the living, and the word of God is the judgment passed at each generation on the history of each and every person to redeem that history and save it from despair.[7] This is the way in which the bible was written: the prophets interpreted unique situations which the Jews were undergoing, for example, the crossing of the Red Sea. In like manner, the religion teacher, who is a kind of prophet for those in his charge, should try to read faith afresh in his students' lives.[8]

In short, an overly narrow kerygmatic practice or salvation history system is not biblical at all. In this connection it is sufficient to recall that the kerygma offered by Peter and the one offered by Paul were widely different. Both kerygmas, of course, presented the good news of Jesus Christ, but on quite different axes. For Peter the death and resurrection of the Lord constituted the fulfillment of all the prophecies that had been the hope of the Jews for centuries. For Paul the same event provided the answer to the deepest cravings and aspirations buried in the human heart. What all this means is that the bible itself has been written in a dialogic situation, that it did not ignore the persons involved and that therefore the theory of biblical language either as form or as content is inadequate to be the basis of biblical pedagogics.

THE BIBLE AS COMMUNICATION

It is my belief that communication theory, rather than the bible-as-form or the bible-as-content, should form the basis

---

[7] Moran, *Scripture and Tradition*, p. 23.
[8] The catechetical training program in the graduate department of education at the University of Notre Dame—unique in all the world because it is social-science-oriented—has a formal course entitled "Prophetic Role of Religious Instruction."

and the axis of biblical pedagogics. Before discussing this in detail, however, I should like to make several prior remarks, which should be of assistance in better understanding my thesis.

I believe it is rather important to assess, with some degree of exactitude, the contemporary significance of what the literature frequently refers to as "the catechesis of the early church fathers." This patristic catechesis is at once a difficulty and a help for illuminating the nature of contemporary biblical pedagogics. It is a difficulty because since the early church fathers belonged to practically the same environment as Jesus—their anthropology was that of a rural pastoral type of society—they did not alter substantially the type of catechesis found in the Acts or in the epistles. There was obviously no need for a change in catechetical approach or style. Yet, there is the danger that some religion teachers might therefore believe that catechetics has a built-in stability which should not be greatly improved or altered. On the other hand, patristic catechesis provides a help to contemporary catechesis because the early church fathers did make certain changes in catechetical style and approach from the Acts and the epistles. Small though these alterations were, they do exist and can be traced. Naturally, the early church fathers still preached the kergyma; yet, they did find new words, new symbols, new expressions, new comparisons, new experiences, as compared to the Acts or the epistles. Let us take, for example, the comparison of Christians to little fishes at the beginning of Tertullian's *De Baptismo*. Tertullian was not satisfied with merely repeating the words of the holy writings. As was typical of the early fathers, his was a work of translation, the translation of an experience he had actually felt, and which his dialogue with the preceding generation had helped him elucidate and name. To be sure, this elucidation, this naming, is done in a way relevant to the time of the early fathers, as, for example, through the use of a dialogue form so as to engage the concern of the younger generation. The catechetical practice of the early church fathers, therefore, reveals that what is primary is the community of the people (in whose midst Jesus stands according to his promise) who voice their religious experience and their faith and their hope in Christ risen from the dead. During the nineteenth century, religion teachers seem to have had difficulty ingesting the patristic approach to catechetics principally because of the formulation of the two sources, which some people thought had been defined by the Council of Trent. Since Vatican II, however, this difficulty should have been wiped away.[9]

There is another point worth dwelling on for a moment, namely, the tense of the verbs we use when speaking about the word of God. Perhaps religion teachers have insisted too much on the grammatical form: "God *has spoken*" or "God *has saved*" as if God's action, which is outside of human temporal categories, is regarded as being in the past. Yet, it is exact to say "God *now speaks*" and "God *now saves*." (Of course, in the past God used men for the channels of his action, but this temporality was the temporality of those men and not a temporality of God.) Curiously enough, we have no difficulty in accepting the present tense concerning redemption, since we believe in the actual saving power of the sacraments and since we believe we can, through our lives, now participate in the act of salvation without diminishing the value of the unique source of salvation, namely Jesus Christ. But since salvation is achieved by the word of God, is it not true that God speaks now in my own existence and that I can cooperate in its formulation? The history of salvation is not only the history of the chosen people then, but also the history of my own existence into which meaning should flow and where the word of God should echo.

Catechetics therefore appears to be essentially a relationship from one person to another under a prophetic light, the purpose being to have the disciple enter the history of salvation by

---

[9]Gabriel Moran, *Catechesis of Revelation* (New York: Herder and Herder, 1966); also his *Theology of Revelation* (New York: Herder and Herder, 1966); and his *Scripture and Tradition*.

acknowledging Christ as the sole master of his life. Can cate-chetics be said to be a mode of training? To a certain extent, I believe so. But in one great respect I do differ from this view-point. A theory of learning holds it is possible to create life-experience in a school setting for a group of people. No doubt a great deal of catechetical learning can be achieved in that way. But communication theory holds that true authenticity lies in the situation which springs spontaneously from the history of the human destiny of each subject. A religion teacher—how-ever pedagogically skilled he may be—cannot create a truly authentic experience for the learner. Further, a situation which is created for a group is obtained at the expense of robbing what is unique in each individual. The bigger the group the truer this becomes. The catechetical format of the teaching-learning specialists can be pedagogically fruitful only when the class is composed of a small group which comes to community life through a long-shared experience. Otherwise this form of pedagogy can lead only to building very superficial behaviors such as those used with mice in laboratories for validating the laws of learning. In his chapter James Michael Lee, a teaching-learning specialist who has advanced the structuring approach to religious instruction, suggested that the basic pedagogical device was to create structures of behavior and learning situa-tions. That is correct. However, it should be noticed that Jesus utilized this structuring form of pedagogy chiefly with a group of twelve people, who were linked together by frequent spells of common life. Indeed, on occasion, when communication became very personal and intimate, he would reduce the group size to three, as in the transfiguration. Sometimes Jesus would reduce the number to a one-to-one situation, as he did at least twice with Peter, for example, after he created a motivating situation including the possibility of sin and betrayal, and at the seashore after the resurrection. What I am suggesting is that the ultimate implications of communication theory go further than the teaching-learning theory in that, for example, it indicates that there are moments when catechesis should become individual.

What, then, is the essence of communication as opposed to language? Marshall MacLuhan provides a helpful guide in this regard. To the author of *Understanding Media,* the medium is the message. But it is important to note that the message is not words, not content; rather, the message is an attitude. In terms of the biblical pedagogics, the message is not the good shepherd or the prodigal son but rather the careful search of Jesus' meaning *to us,* the hope we can have in him. If the message is not words, then it is obvious that it cannot be conveyed by words, even if these words are taken from the bible. As Gabriel Moran says: "Holy Scripture used as the source of the new content will inevitably become a rigidly systematized body of data. This will happen because Scripture cannot be true to itself unless it points beyond itself."[10] What communication theory suggests to biblical pedagogics is that, in terms of human discourse, the religion teacher can be very biblical without uttering a word from the bible. There is a way of saying "Good morning, John" which is an authentic projection of the long-experienced attitude of God towards men and which is very biblical. Yet, a teacher can pour tons of biblical material over the heads of the students in such a way that he negates all the essence of the bible itself. The teacher who in the old days said "Johnny, I want you to copy twenty times our Lord is a good shepherd" has used a medium which literally slaughtered the message. Is the present practice of catechists so far from this caricature?

Some Central Biblical Themes

What is the central message of the bible which religion teachers should communicate to their students? Naturally, a religion teacher cannot find it solely by himself. He finds it in constant

---

[10]Moran, *Vision and Tactics* (New York: Herder and Herder, 1968), p. 64.

dialogue with others and with reference to what the preceding generations have told us about it. Thus Gabriel Moran tells us "the total, fleshy, social life of her people is what the church calls tradition and it is there that God's revelation is to be found."[11] Seen in this perspective, biblical pedagogics can be divided for the sake of analysis into three basic themes. These themes or messages cannot be conveyed through words but have to be discovered by the students through the medium of human relationships.

The first basic message or theme of biblical pedagogics is that of freedom. This theme recurs all through the old and new testaments, and, indeed, forms the core of Christianity. It is to the freedom of man that the covenant is offered. The Lord's propositions are always introduced by the words: "If you will." But why, then, do most students experience difficulties in fully realizing this message of freedom? Why is it that for most of them, the Lord is like a barrier, a border, rather than the one who wants to set them free? The answer is that students seldom had as religion teachers persons who treated them in a way which would induce students to perceive such a message. The catechists have the message, but there is no medium to convey it. The structure defeats the purpose. Students had as teachers authoritarians, who believed that the students' freedom should be curtailed as much as possible, or they encountered teachers who were merely lax and who never proposed challenges to and goals for their freedom. What all this indicates is that the Catholic school can be a wonderful reinforcement to the religion class; on the other hand, the Catholic school, if it is operated in an authoritarian manner—more suitable to surface efficiency than to true education—can create a medium which will destroy the very message it is supposed to engender.

A second basic biblical message is that of salvation. The bible is the multifold history of salvation brought to men. Consequently, the Christian is a person whose fundamental creed

---

[11]*Ibid.*, p. 26.

can be expressed as follows: "I believe that Jesus is risen from the dead. I have faith that this resurrection is the promise of my own, and that one day I shall rise and see my God. And I believe that this magnificent glory already flows in my life and the grace I have now is the warrant of the glory that will be. I already have one foot set in heaven. My work is to set the other one." This is a message, but how can it be conveyed? I suggest there are two conditions necessary to convey this message. First, the religion teachers whom the students encounter should themselves appear to be saved. The worst indictment on Christianity was made by Nietzsche when he reproached Christians with the fact that they do not *look* saved. A sad saint is a very inadequate medium indeed to evoke in the student's mind the notion of salvation. Second, both the school and the religion teachers must perform actions of salvation on a purely human basis if they want their message to make sense to the students. And here again it is obvious that some Catholic schools, by the way they are operated, are the exact negation of the essence and thrust of biblical pedagogics. If a Catholic school simply judges a student on the basis of academic standards alone, and if it is more interested in the regulations of the school than in the unique destiny of that student, how can he feel that the message of Christianity is salvation? How can he make sense out of this contradiction: "We do not love you really as you are, Johnny. But believe us, God loves you."

Finally, the bible tells us about God as long-enduring. God is always present, and the whole history of his relationships with man shows how he respects both the *Zeitgeist* and the tempo of evolution. Religion teachers cannot be adequate media of the Lord, therefore, unless they, too, are respectful of time and of the delays of each destiny. Religion teachers ought to abandon their impatience for the immediate, ought to renounce the quest for quick and massive results that too often characterize their pedagogy.

Conclusion

Biblical pedagogics cannot be achieved by biblical methods, or by biblical textbooks, or by biblical exposés. It can be realized only by biblical men and women, that is, by religion teachers who can read God's actions in our present day life and formulate it in an authentic dialogue with their brethren—the students.

5 Liturgical Pedagogics

Christopher Kiesling

The New Catechetical Approach

In the late 1960's, two surveys of catechetical texts and programs appeared in a national review of books.[1] Very discernible in these overviews is a shift in approach. The earlier catechetical materials rooted revelation in salvation history reported in the bible, celebrated in the liturgy, interpreted in the teaching of the church, and witnessed in Christian living. These materials aimed at forming in a person a dynamic faith and an intimate relationship to Christ, chiefly by providing an understanding largely of the past, that is, the wonderful works of God in Israel, Jesus Christ, and the primitive church recorded in the bible. A person's own present experience of self, of the world, and of society was viewed as secondary, as something which should be modified as a result of applying to it what was learned about the past.

The new texts and programs approach revelation through present personal experience. It is believed that in personal experience of self, of society, and of the world, God-in-Christ reveals himself and his designs for mankind and for creation,

---

[1] Sheila Moriarity, "Catechetics—Present and Future," in *Herder Book Supplement* (Spring, 1968), pp. 3-14; also her "Catechetics for the *Now* Generation," in *ibid.*, pp. 19-26.

and invites men to communion and cooperation with him.[2] Present personal experience is not merely a motivational device to capture attention so that instruction about the past can be given; nor is it something to be looked at after the real work concerning the past has been done. In the new approach, present personal experience is the heart of catechetical concern.[3]

The important illustration in the catechetical textbook is no longer Jesus healing a sick man, but a contemporary doctor transplanting a heart. Catechizing strives to help a person see God-in-Christ working and speaking to him in the doctor's care for his fellowman. The hope is that the student will go on to discern God-in-Christ working and speaking elsewhere in his experience, and will respond to God's presence by cooperating with his creative and redemptive activity; or, if the student discerns the absence of God and his activity in some area of life which he experiences, he will endeavor to bring God and his saving action into it.

Nature of Liturgical Pedagogics*

My concern in this chapter must follow this same shift of attention to present personal experience. We can successfully

---

[2]Gabriel Moran's *The Theology of Revelation* (New York: Herder and Herder, 1966) elaborates the theological basis for this supposition.

[3]It should be noted that by "experience" I do not mean purely subjective feelings of an elevating and inspiring kind, nor subjective intuitions with transcendent but very vague content. Experience is obviously subjective, for it is a subject or person who experiences. But experience is *of something;* experience has objective content, and normally a very definite content, however difficult it may be to conceptualize, describe, and define this content in words. The new approach of catechetics seeks God-in-Christ in objective reality, but objective reality as it is encountered by a person in his daily life and as it includes himself, his acts of knowing, and his affective states.

Editors' Note: The senior editor of this volume (Professor Lee) first coined the term "liturgical pedagogics" to denote the liturgy as a pedagogical form and tool. In this context the liturgy is viewed as the way in which the church officially and formally catechizes her people as a community. In the social-science-oriented graduate school program in religious instruction in the department of education at the University of Notre Dame, there is a formal course entitled "Liturgical Pedagogics."

educate people liturgically only if they are provided with opportunities to participate in liturgical celebrations which speak to them in terms of self, of society, and of the world as experienced by them. If we consider the possible forms of liturgical pedagogics, we will see that the crucial problem consists in actual liturgical celebration which is relevant and instructive.

By the term "liturgical pedagogics" we can signify three things: (1) catechetics insofar as it explicitly prepares a person *theoretically* for mature liturgical worship; (2) catechetics insofar as it explicitly prepares a person *practically* for mature liturgical worship; and (3) liturgical worship as a means employed by catechetics to form a mature Christian. Let me explain in more detail.

Catechetics is the complex of factors and activities which aim at developing mature Christians in fulfillment of Christ's mandate to announce the Gospel to all men.[4] It includes more than intellectual instruction. It involves leading a person to a Christian style of living. Christian life includes, as one of its components, participation in liturgical worship, and it includes both confessing faith in Jesus Christ and serving neighbor by corporal and spiritual works of mercy. Catechesis, therefore, must prepare a person for mature liturgical worship even as it prepares him to confess faith in Christ and to serve his neighbor in need. Liturgical pedagogics can refer to catechetics precisely insofar as it explicitly prepares a person for liturgical worship.

Catechetics can prepare a person explicitly for liturgical worship theoretically and practically. It prepares for liturgy *theoretically* by imparting knowledge about the nature of the liturgy, the meaning of its rites, the origin and development of the liturgy, the impact which the liturgy ought to have on

---

[4]Johannes Hofinger, "Program of the Catechetical Apostolate," in Johannes Hofinger, editor, *Teaching All Nations,* translated by Clifford Howell (New York: Herder and Herder, 1961), pp. 394-405.

life, and so forth. This preparation is directed to the intellect. However, it should also embrace affective knowledge and emotional sensitivity by providing—through poetry, art, drama, and nonliturgical worship—emotional experiences and cognitive insights analogous to those which can be experienced in liturgical worship, namely, awe before the mysterious, fear before the frailty of human existence, and so on. People can be prepared for the liturgy by information-type knowledge about the liturgy, and experience-type knowledge about the kind of experience they may expect in worship. Characteristic of all this preparation is that it does not take place in actual liturgical worship, but rather prior to it and outside of it.

Catechetics can prepare people for liturgy *practically* by engaging them in meaningful and instructive liturgical worship. Practical preparation provides people with liturgical worship which is an attractive human experience, which ties in with and enriches experience of self, society, and the world. This kind of preparation may result in little information about the liturgy compared to the results of theoretical preparation, but it provides experiential knowledge of the liturgy as a recognized value in life worth seeking and experiencing.

Liturgical pedagogics can refer thirdly, to the liturgy itself as a pedagogical instrument used to lead to the goal of catechetics itself, namely, the mature Christian life in response to the good news. Liturgical pedagogics in this third sense coincides with liturgical pedagogics in the sense of practical catechesis for liturgy, insofar as both refer to actual liturgical worship. They differ insofar as the purpose of liturgical worship in practical catechesis is preparation for further liturgical worship, while the purpose of liturgical worship as an instrument of catechetics is maturity of Christian life as a whole. The distinction is made mainly for the sake of understanding the problem of liturgical pedagogics.

Attempting now to pinpoint the problem of liturgical pedagogics, we can say first, that the crucial problem is not the use of the liturgy as a means or instrument for achieving the goal of catechetics itself. This is indeed a problem, but not the supremely critical problem. The use of the liturgy by catechetics to form mature Christians presupposes that people are able to understand the liturgy, appreciate it, and draw profit from it. No sensible educator uses a means beyond the capacity of his pupils. The rites and texts of our present liturgy, however, are culturally foreign and, hence, obscure in meaning for people today. A reformed liturgy will still contain some elements of this sort, because the mystery of Christ celebrated in the liturgy involves a particular historical person, event, and milieu. Religious worship itself, moreover, is a unique kind of experience, unlike other components of human experience. The presumption is, therefore, that people cannot understand well, appreciate fully, and profit greatly from the liturgy without help. Liturgical pedagogics in the sense of using the liturgy to form mature Christians presupposes for effectiveness liturgical pedagogics in the sense of catechetical preparation for liturgy.

The crucial problem of liturgical pedagogics is not *theoretical* catechetical preparation for liturgical worship. There is, of course, a multiplicity of problems in this area. Christians ought to be well-informed about the liturgy according to their age and level of maturity. The liturgy is, after all, a part of their Christian heritage and a major factor in their Christian life. Experiential knowledge through the arts about the general kind of experience which liturgy involves is obviously helpful for fruitful liturgical participation. How catechists can most effectively impart this theoretical preparation raises a host of problems regarding program, syllabus, and method. Nevertheless, this theoretical catechetical preparation is not the most critical problem of liturgical pedagogics.

The decisively crucial problem of liturgical pedagogics is *practical* catechetical preparation for liturgy by providing people with relevant and instructive liturgical worship. By relevant, meaningful, or significant liturgical worship, I mean liturgy which can be readily recognized as saying something about self, society, and the world of one's experience. By instructive, educative, or formative liturgical worship, I mean liturgy which, because it has relevance, meaning, or significance, makes faith operative in personal experience, offers an interpretation of experience, provides direction for life, and shapes attitudes with regard to self, society, and the world. Without this sort of liturgy, theoretical catechetical preparation remains sterile knowledge; and liturgy as an instrument for forming mature Christians is inefficient.[5] The critical question which we must consider, then, is what must be done to provide meaningful and formative liturgical worship for those entrusted to our catechetical care. To provide this kind of liturgical worship, something must be done *to* the liturgy, *with* the liturgy, and *about* the liturgy.

Catechetical Renewal to *the Liturgy*

First, something must be done *to* the liturgy. The "official" liturgical rites and texts of the church must be reformed. Ultimately the only agency which can effect this reform is the college of bishops with their head, the pope. Practically speaking, given the present legislation, this means the Sacred Congregation of Rites and the *Consilium* for the implementation of the Second Vatican Council's *Constitution on the Sacred Liturgy*. But this reform concerns us, the People of God, for the liturgy is our worship. The liturgy belongs to the church, and the church is the whole body of believers, not the hierarchy alone, nor the pope alone, nor any Roman congregation or committee. Therefore, *we* must think about what kind of reform is needed, and apply legitimate political pressure to move authorities to take the action for which they bear particular responsibility.

---

[5] I am not questioning the *ex opere operato* efficacy of the sacraments, but rather the efficiency with which that efficacy can operate in a poorly celebrated and irrelevant liturgy.

When we say that this reform, that is, this new composition, of the liturgy of the church can be made only by the college of bishops with their head, the pope, according to the apparatus canonically established for this purpose, we are saying only this: that the liturgy of the church, the worship which even those outside the church can point to as the "official" worship of the church, can be fixed only by the legitimate authority in this particular social entity where the church is. I am not suggesting that the clergy and faithful can exercise no initiative of any kind at all in the celebration of the liturgy. I shall discuss shortly what this initiative is. At this point I simply wish to note that when I suggest only the official authorities in the church can make new legislation reforming the liturgy, I am not asserting that this is equivalent to saying that laity and clergy become legalists and do nothing except what is prescribed explicitly by law. It is one thing to recognize a place for authority and its legislation in the church and in Christian life, and quite another thing to say that the only authentic ecclesial and Christian activity is that which is prescribed somewhere in print.

Catechists should be familiar with what already has been done to the liturgy. Many important documents have come forth since the *Constitution on the Sacred Liturgy.* The Sacred Congregation of Rites and the *Consilium* have issued two instructions for the implementation of the constitution on the liturgy, one on September 26, 1964, and the other on May 4, 1967; an instruction on music in the liturgy, March 5, 1967; and another instruction on eucharistic worship, May 25, 1967. The American Bishops' Committee on the Liturgy published an important statement on "The Place of Music in Eucharistic Celebrations" in its January, 1968, *Newsletter.*[6]

These documents contain a maturing new theology of the liturgy, with a corresponding new spirit and attitude in regard

---

[6] All these documents are available from the United States Catholic Conference, 1312 Massachusetts Ave., N. W., Washington, D.C. 20005.

to the liturgy, as well as legislation embodying that theology, spirit, and attitude. Catechists should be familiar with all of this so that they can take advantage of the reforms which have been made and can instruct those who are ignorant about the reformed liturgy which already exists. It is disheartening as well as annoying to hear people complaining about an outmoded liturgy and then proceeding to celebrate the liturgy in the old way or in an inferior way of their own devising, when legislation already exists providing explicitly or implicitly for a new way of celebrating which makes sense and at the same time remains integrated with tradition and the universal church.

If we are convinced that certain reforms should be made in the liturgy, we should act maturely about this conviction. To pout, to be cynical, to dismiss the hierarchy and existing legislation as irrelevant, and to go ahead with a coterie of like-minded people to celebrate one's own liturgy is childish and politically unrealistic. The church has its human, social, institutional, or structural aspect (which is to be distinguished from bureaucracy or officialism) to which the liturgy pertains. Factors of the human, social, institutional order are handled by political action. Political action involves different points of view confronting each other: dialogue, debate, tension, hard-feelings, fights, campaigning for issues, gathering popular support, and finally obtaining appropriate legislation. All of this requires hard and long work, courage, and patience.

One must learn to apply to the life of the church what one takes for granted in the life of one's country. The citizen who thinks welfare legislation for the poor ought to be reformed is acting childishly if he pouts about it, becomes cynical, dismisses Congress and its legislation as irrelevant, and emigrates to Sweden. He runs away from the problem rather than doing something about it. The "official" liturgy of the universal church and of the local churches which comprise it, together with the liturgical worship of future generations are now at stake. If religion teachers and catechetical specialists are convinced that the liturgy needs reform, then with courage and patience they ought to undertake the long, arduous labor and the personal inconveniences, discomforts, failures, and disappointments required to accomplish this reform. This is truly service to our fellowmen.

Catechists can do something *to* the liturgy, then, by implementing the reformed liturgy we now have, by thinking about the kind of reform that is needed, and by taking political action to bring about appropriate legislation. But catechists can also do something *with* the liturgy.

Catechetical Renewal with *the Liturgy*

When I suggest that we can do something with the liturgy, I do not mean experimentation. There are several reasons for saying this. First of all, experimentation with the liturgy—if we take the word "experiment" in its strict sense—means testing a particular preplanned pattern of worship in controlled circumstances and gathering data about its effectiveness. Experimentation in this strict sense is reserved to the Vatican and is authorized only by the *Consilium* for the implementation of the *Constitution on the Sacred Liturgy*. Not even episcopal conferences can undertake it without prior permission from Rome. Under present legislation there is the ever-present presupposition that the rites to be experimented with have been prepared and officially approved prior to celebration. Such experimentation is meant to lead eventually to something being done *to* the liturgy of the Church, as I discussed earlier. I suggest that we do not wish to be involved in experimentation in this sense. It is complicated, slow, and involves much drudgery.

I am suggesting that we should not speak about experimentation with the liturgy even in a loose sense. People are not going to distinguish the two senses. If word goes out that we are experimenting with the liturgy, a response will come quickly from the bishop declaring that no one has the right to experiment with the liturgy, and that whatever is being done should be stopped. Thus, needed imaginative implementation of present rites will be choked off when such implementation should not be asphyxiated and need not be.

Besides, the very word "experiment" is loaded with connotations of uncertainty, nonpermanence, newness. If we are thinking of every liturgical celebration as an experiment, soon interest and value will be attached more to what novelties are introduced in successive celebrations than to how well the participants worshiped God, grew in mutual love, and gained insight and inspiration for mature Christian life and service.

In the final analysis, religion teachers and catechetical specialists really are not interested in experimenting. Rather, they are interested in meaningful and instructive liturgical worship. They are interested in liturgy which is a "humanly attractive experience" and a "genuinely human faith-experience," to use the words of the Bishops' Committee on the Liturgy.[7] Let us therefore avoid confusion, tension, and a frivolous mentality by talking about and concentrating our energies on good liturgical worship, and leave experimentation to those whose business it is.

The most obvious thing catechists can do *with* the liturgy is implement in a human, personal, communicative manner the new rubrics which have been provided. Very often these new rubrics are followed without any liturgical sense, without any understanding of why they have been introduced. Unfortunately, even many of the younger generation have not bothered to learn the new rubrics; they are indifferent toward liturgical legislation. They complain about the poverty of liturgical rites, when, in fact, they do not know what these rites are today and what alternatives are provided to make the liturgy meaningful. Priests alone are not at fault; laity and religious are hesitant to step forward, to speak out, to enter into the celebration in a human way. Lectors often read the lessons

---

[7] "The Place of Music in Eucharistic Celebrations," *Newsletter*, January, 1968.

so poorly that they may as well be reading them in Latin. We still have a long way to go to implement well, in a truly human, communicative manner, the reformed liturgy we have.

We can do more with the liturgy. In an article entitled, "Liturgy Hot and Cool," Thomas O'Meara notes that the liturgy in its present form is a "hot" medium.* By this O'Meara means that the liturgy typically is extremely high in content and information. A celebrant can "cool" the liturgy for a "cool" generation by preparing a commentary and perhaps some auxiliary activities for the congregation (for example, a particular kind of offering, or some kind of "kiss of peace") which will focus attention on and develop one simple theme which is particularly significant for the group.

The present liturgy is "hot" also because it is low in personal involvement; it is all laid out beforehand in the rubrics and prayers. A presiding liturgist can "cool" the liturgy by letting the congregation plan the Mass in the sense of cooperatively deciding beforehand the hymns they will sing or will not sing, whether they will have an offertory procession or not, whether they will have a sermon preached or a dialogue homily, what the prayer of the faithful will be, whether they will gather around the altar for the eucharistic liturgy or not, and so on.

The homilist can "cool" the liturgy by making his own words an application of God's word to some experience of the congregation from a very personal perspective (in the style of witness or testimony), rather than leave the liturgy as a proclamation of a message from which he seems detached.

Such imaginative implementation of present rubrical laws is not experimentation. It simply is providing good liturgy, using well what we have, doing something *with* the liturgy. It is, of course, work, and it requires forethought. Obviously, if we embark on a liturgical celebration without forethought, we will revert to old ways or fall into trivial innovations which

---

*Thomas O'Meara, "Liturgy Hot and Cool," in *Worship* 42 (April, 1968):215-222.

will be more distracting than helpful.

Even when the liturgy is reformed, we will still need imaginative implementation. The statement on the place of music in eucharistic celebrations set forth by the previously mentioned Bishops' Committee on the Liturgy notes that with regard to music in the liturgy, three judgments must be made: (1) a musical judgment about quality; (2) a liturgical judgment about which parts are to be sung and by whom; and (3) a pastoral judgment. About this pastoral judgment, the statement says:

> The pastoral judgment must always be present. It is the judgment that must be made in this particular situation, in these concrete circumstances. . . . The signs of the celebration must be accepted and received as meaningful. They must, by reason of the materials used, open up to a genuinely human faith-experience. This pastoral judgment can be aided by sociological studies of the people who make up the congregation, studies which determine differences in age, culture, and education as they influence the way in which faith is meaningfully expressed. *No set of rubrics or regulations of itself will ever achieve a truly pastoral celebration of the sacramental rites. Such regulations must always be applied with pastoral concern for the given worshiping community* [emphasis added].

The problem with liturgical worship today lies as much with people as with the liturgical rites. The legalist mentality, untempered by healthy equity and pastoral concern, still persists In such a mentality, the liturgy is not understood as human communication in which worship rises to God and God speaks to men and inspires them. People and priests still think of themselves as ritualists carrying out prescribed rites, rather than as human beings communicating with one another according to a general procedure. We can do much to further liturgical renewal by implementing the liturgy imaginatively according to the dictates of pastoral concern. Again, this is not experimenting with the liturgy; it is simply doing something pastorally with the liturgy.

Another thing we can do with the liturgy is bring it to bear on life's problems. Psychologists of religion tell us that the function of religion is to integrate the experiences of life and provide meaning and direction for them.[9] Integration, meaning, and direction are important for mental health, which everyone consciously desires and toward which the psyche subconsciously drives. There is a need for religion or some equivalent in people's lives, a need which catechists can exploit to make liturgy relevant and instructive. The liturgy, that concrete vehicle of the Christian religion, must be applied if it is to be worthy of the name "liturgy." In this application, surely, integration, meaning, and direction are urgently needed. After all, in their experiences of self, of society, and of the world, people are thrown into many emotional conflicts; their minds are perplexed by many questions. They are confronted by problems of emotion versus reason, of sexuality and sex, of interpersonal relationships, of freedom and authority, of racial antagonism, of violence in urban, national, and international life. People today are unquestionably looking for meaning, direction, and wholeness in these areas, even though they may not be very conscious of the fact. The liturgy can be used, not to give any final answers, orientations, and balance, but rather to contribute to the resolutions of these problems.

Catechists can help young people, for example, to evaluate the music they enjoy and the feelings and emotions which this music awakens in them by using this music in liturgical worship—or not using it, for our acceptance or rejection of music implies a value judgment. A mass focused on developing positively a theme of sexuality and sex by means of appropriate commentary and a dialogue homily would certainly attract attention; at the same time it would be truly relevant and pedagogical, since it would help people overcome false and

---

[9]Gordon W. Allport, *The Individual and His Religion* (New York: Macmillan, 1950) pp. 6-26; Walter Houston Clark, *The Psychology of Religion* (New York: Macmillan, 1958), pp. 22, 55-82.

dangerous fears and inhibitions and would yield more whole
some, Christian attitudes toward these realities of life. The
shock some catechists might feel at hearing the suggestion o
a mass focusing on a theme of sexuality and on sex is itsel
indicative of a questionable evaluation to which we have
been partially led by never having experienced in the contex
of formal worship a positive consideration of sexuality and sex

The liturgy originally concerned life's problematic experi
ences. A glance at the liturgical books demonstrates this. There
are rites for sickness, which could not be cured by hundred
of drugs available from the pharmacist; rites for childbearing
which was more dangerous to life before the advent of mod
ern obstetrics; rites for planting and harvesting, which coule
not be virtually assured by modern agricultural technology. T
be sure, modern man does not experience the same problems a
those provided for in the liturgical books; yet, it is absurd to
say that modern man has no problems of any kind which re
ligion and its concrete vehicle, liturgy, could help him to cop
with. Such an assertion would be virtually a denial of th
saving power of the word of God.

As important as reforming the liturgy is the serious effort to
discover what problems of contemporary human experienc
need religion and liturgy. Catechists should be alert to discove
these areas of need in the personal lives of people. Then
imaginatively implementing the rubrics of the liturgy, the
should bring the word of God and the sacraments of Chris
to bear on these problematic experiences. In this way liturg
will be relevant and instructive.

Sociologists see a place for religion in social life.[10] They view
religion as helping men to cope with "limit situations" in so
ciety's life. When society encounters problems which canno
be resolved by the resources at hand—foodstuffs, manpower

---

[10]Thomas O'Dea, *The Sociology of Religion* (Englewood Cliffs, Ne
Jersey: Prentice-Hall, 1966), pp. 1-18; J. Milton Yinger, *Religion, So
ciety, and the Individual* (New York: Macmillan, 1957), pp. 49-76.

machines, science, medical skill, technology, and so forth—religion enables men to make some sense out of the situation, to bear the trials which the crisis entails, and to have the hope and courage necessary to carry on with life in spite of obstacles. Religion also provides stability for the institutions of society. It also can act as a catalyst for social change. Religion has no monopoly on these functions; indeed, institutionalized religion sometimes fails to carry out these functions well. A society without religion, however, must find some substitute to perform these essential supporting, stabilizing, and catalyzing functions: it must find some political ideology, national mystique, or popular philosophy of life to hold everything together and keep it moving, so to speak. The main point is, of course, that sociologists recognize that there is a place for religion or its surrogate in social life.

Our task, then, is to discern the "limit situations" in the social life of our people and to insert the liturgy at these points. This will mean taking the liturgy out of the sanctuary into the world where the life of society is carried on and its problems arise. Already, we do this on a limited scale: we expect the mass to be celebrated on the hood of a jeep in a battle area in Vietnam or anywhere else. It may not be an esthetically beautiful liturgy, but it is relevant. Recently more and more bishops have been granting permission to have the eucharist celebrated in neighborhoods in some family's home, or in classrooms, or in other places outside formal churches and chapels. Catechists ought to take advantage of this permission when it is given—and indeed to seek it when permission is not given—in order to bring the liturgy into the places where life is lived and its problems are encountered. Catechists need to release the word of God and the sacraments of Christ from the prison of the sanctuary where they are walled off from the stream of life. How can we expect to have a Christian secularity rather than an atheistic secularism if we isolate the liturgy from the secular realm by tying it down to very special places and times?

There is, then, much that catechists can do *with* the liturgy and will always have to do with it, even after it is reformed. We can follow the reformed rubrics; we can carry out these rubrics in a way that is truly human communication. We can "cool" the liturgy by focusing on themes by commentaries, by dialogue homilies, by involving the people in planning the manner of celebration. We can implement imaginatively the rubrics with pastoral sensitivity for the congregation and the situation. We can bring the liturgy to bear on the real problems of life experienced by individuals and society; we can bring the liturgy into the secular sphere where life's problems arise.

All these possibilities suggest that one of the things catechists ought to do with the liturgy is choose liturgical celebrations more deliberately. We are accustomed to urge people to participate in the liturgy for all kinds of reasons, and then hand them a list of scheduled liturgical services. Instead, we ought to suggest to the people that this or that represents a critical problematic area of personal and social experience, that it might be helpful to see what our Christian religion—or, concretely, the word of God and the sacraments of Christ—say about this area. Then we could invite them or encourage them to celebrate the liturgy in connection with this problematic experience. We then could ask them how they think the liturgy should be celebrated, where and when, in order to be most helpful to them in casting the light of revelation on this face of life. In this way people would build relevance and instructiveness into their liturgical celebrations. Scheduled liturgical worship is no doubt necessary for a number of reasons, but there should be much, much more deliberate choosing and planning of liturgical celebrations. Such a method would help people overcome the feeling that religion is an intrusion into the affairs of life that really concern them and would teach them practically that liturgy is relevant. Surely, all this lies at the very heart of fruitful liturgical pedagogics.

In doing something with the liturgy, we must beware of rationalizing and verbalizing it. The desire to make the liturgy human communication, to "cool" it, to bring it into contact with the problems of everyday life easily leads to a literal liturgy where all is reading, reasoning, and talking. But human communication occurs through the emotions as well as through words and ideas; it takes place nonverbally—through gestures and looks—as well as verbally. Liturgy, whether "hot" or "cool," must awaken intuitive awareness of the mystery of being, existence, life, and human destiny. Liturgy helps us deal with emotions by bringing them into orderly play. Liturgy contributes to resolving life's problems precisely by setting them in the context of reality in all its richness, depth, and transcendence. For liturgy to communicate in this way and to achieve these effects requires time, willingness to wait for insight, patience with what at first sight or sound seems obscure or meaningless, and the courage to expose one's self to the new and unfamiliar. Liturgy is supposed to be a much more profound experience than hearing the crisp, direct words of Malcolm Boyd or exchanging opinions about what the gospel for the day means, valuable though these may be.

Biblical imagery and Christian symbols have roots in man's subconscious, as the researches of depth psychology and the history of religions have revealed.[11] This imagery and symbolism speak to us, evoke responses from us, and orient us in reality at a level which lies below or beyond rational, verbal interpretation. If we too readily thrust aside the symbolic ritual and biblical imagery of the liturgy, in order to come to a liturgy which is relevant and instructive because it deals with life's problems in the familiar words of reason and common sense, we expose ourselves to the danger of an extremely superficial liturgy. The Protestant experience warns us that an exaggerated emphasis on the word can lead down the path to sterile wor-

---

[11]See, for example, Mircea Eliade, *Images and Symbols: Studies in Religious Symbolism* (New York: Sheed & Ward, 1961).

ship, moralism, and a rationalism inadequate to the mystery of life and inappropriate to its Christian interpretation.[12]

In doing something with the liturgy, therefore, we must employ the arts. Music and speech, of course, constitute key arts in this regard. However, the other arts should be utilized as well: architecture and craftsmanship for the place of worship and the things used in worship; sculpture, painting, banner-making, dancing, and so forth. Artistic expression speaks beyond the rational, verbal level, enables us to articulate experiences which words cannot represent, and orients us in the totality of experience about which man is ultimately speechless. If, as Susanne Langer has argued persuasively,[13] the arts are necessary for full appreciation of the totality of human experience, they are necessary for our religious experience, which rises out of the question which the totality of human experience puts to us about its ultimate origin and purpose.

The arts employed with the liturgy must correspond, of course, to the people of our times. Motion pictures or filmstrips can evoke the sense of life's mystery and the place of Christian religion in it for a contemporary congregation as Gregorian chant or a medieval sequence cannot. Care must be taken not to make the liturgy a spectacle; but on the other hand, catechists must help to make it truly gripping and moving. We often feel ill at ease when contemporary arts—movies, slides, dances—are used in liturgical celebrations. Is this because they are not true means of worship, or is it because they confront us so directly with the mystery of life, with the question of God, and with the meaning of Jesus Christ that we feel exposed to them as we are not in ordinary living, yet as we will be on the day of judgment? Are we uneasy because we feel

---

[12]Kenneth G. Phifer, *A Protestant Case for Liturgical Renewal* (Philadelphia: Westminster Press, 1965), pp. 13-20, 137-147; James F. White, *The Worldliness of Worship* (New York: Oxford University Press, 1967) pp. 32-47, 166-168, 178-179.

[13]Susanne Langer, *Philosophy in a New Key*, 2d edition (Cambridge Mass.: Harvard University Press, 1951).

God is embarrassed by us, or because we feel naked before him?

To do the sort of things with the liturgy which we have mentioned, it is necessary that both we ourselves as well as others change our conceptions and attitudes, and also overcome inhibitions which we have about the liturgy. This brings us to our final point: to provide meaningful and instructive liturgy, we must do something *about* the liturgy.

Catechetical Renewal about *the Liturgy*

Catechists must acquire for themselves and pass on to others a sound view of the relationship between liturgy and life, and between the sacred and the secular. Liturgy and life must be kept in continuity with each other, as must the sacred and the secular. Without this comprehensive view which sees the liturgy as integrated with the totality of Christian life, and which sees the secular as radically sacred insofar as it is God's creation and is redeemed in Christ, we are bound to find liturgical celebration irrelevant and uninstructive, and, even if we do something to and with the liturgy, we will be only "playing house."

As the summit of the church's activity, as the aim and object of apostolic works,[14] liturgy intrinsically bespeaks a relationship to that activity and those works. Liturgy which is not the culmination of ecclesial mission and apostolic activity is simply not Christian liturgy.

As the outstanding means of expressing and manifesting the mystery of Christ and the real nature of the church,[15] the liturgy presupposes both that the mystery of Christ is being worked out in the lives of the faithful and that the real nature of the church is to some degree an actuality. Expression and manifestation presuppose that which they express and manifest.

---

[14]Second Vatican Council, *Constitution on the Sacred Liturgy*, article 10.
[15]*Ibid.*, article 2.

If the mystery of Christ and the real nature of the church as expressed and manifested in the liturgy are only abstractions, or ideas, or ideals, or past events, then the liturgy is very much like a stage play about Caesar or Napoleon. The liturgy is meant to be a celebration of the mystery of Christ as it is unfolding now in the members of Christ's Body, the church; it is meant to be a celebration of the love now inspired by the spirit of Christ and binding men to one another in him. The liturgy is meant to be an expression of a concrete, existential reality, of an ideal being realized, an event of the present moment initiated in the past. Liturgy is an unsatisfying, empty gesture unless there simultaneously underlies it, extends before it and after it, the substance of Christian life and community.

Where ecclesial mission and apostolic activity are, where Christian life and community are, there the urge for liturgical expression is also present. That urge can be strong enough to tolerate many inadequacies of ritual and to find deep satisfaction despite these inadequacies.

We can conclude from this line of thought that the approach of liturgical pedagogics to the liturgy can be indirect, that is, can provide meaningful and educative liturgical celebrations by concentrating attention on Christian life and community, on ecclesial mission and apostolic works, all of which come to conscious, explicit, reflective expression in the liturgy. This indirect approach may be called for exclusively in some cases, but it must always be present, for without it the liturgy is bound to be a formality or a theatrical performance. Equally important to catechetical lessons and ritually ideal celebrations of the liturgy is stimulation of dynamic Christian living, of community, of ecclesial mission, and of apostolic works. Apostolic projects by teams whose members, after a time of working together, are gathered together for liturgical celebration can do more to provide relevant and instructive liturgy than hours of lessons and beautiful liturgical celebrations which have no connection with ongoing Christian life because it is lacking.

Pius XII in *Mediator Dei* reminds us of the proper relationship between life and liturgy, specifically the eucharist. He makes the point that the people must add the offering of themselves to their offering of Christ in the mass, if their participation in the mass is to have its full effect. He then goes on:

> This offering in fact is not confined merely to the liturgical sacrifice. For the Prince of the Apostles wishes us, as living stones built upon Christ the cornerstone, to be able as "a holy priesthood, to offer up spiritual sacrifice, acceptable to God by Jesus Christ" (I Pet. 2:5). St. Paul the Apostle addresses the following words of exhortation to Christians, without distinction of time: "I beseech you therefore . . . that you present your bodies, a living sacrifice, holy, pleasing unto God, your reasonable service" (Rom. 12:1). But at that time especially when the faithful take part in the liturgical service with such piety and recollection that it can truly be said of them: "whose faith and devotion are known to you" (Canon of the Mass), it is then, with the High Priest and through him they offer themselves as a spiritual sacrifice, that each one's faith ought to become more ready to work through charity, his piety more real and fervent, and each should consecrate himself to the furthering of the divine glory, desiring to become as like as possible to Christ in his most grievous sufferings.[16]

The liturgy is seen in the above excerpt as an intensification, an explicitation in consciousness, of that faith and of that devotion which inspire all the service involved in Christian life and community, ecclesial mission and apostolic activity. Obviously, if Christian life, community, ecclesial mission, and apostolic endeavor are at a low level, if there is no inspiring faith and devotion leading to service in these areas, then liturgy is not going to be meaningful and instructive no matter what we do *to* it or *with* it, for it will be without substance. It is important in liturgical pedagogics to pay as much attention to

---

[16]Pius XII, *Mediator Dei,* translated by National Catholic Welfare Conference (Washington, D.C.: National Catholic Welfare Conference, 1947), paragraph 99.

the context of life in which the liturgy is celebrated as to the liturgy itself.

The sacred and the secular also must be kept together. We must understand that God's grace comes to us in words, in gestures, in looks, in touches. It came to us that way in Jesus Christ; it comes to us that way now. This is the principle implied in the mystery of the Incarnation. If we can become convinced and appreciative of this incarnational principle and of this understanding of God's grace, then we will be able with more personal ease to incorporate into liturgical celebrations many of those things that I mentioned could be done with the liturgy. We will not feel so uneasy about a dialogue homily if we recognize that God's grace came to the apostles in their discussions with Jesus. We will not feel so uneasy about hearing the words of contemporary songs in the liturgy if we recognize that God's grace came to the poor of Israel in Jesus' parables couched in everyday language.

The Incarnation reaffirms the radical sacredness of human nature and all of creation along with it. Our mission as members of Christ is to continue to reaffirm that radical sacredness of the secular, to bring it out of the darkness into the light. How? Precisely by using creation as the Creator intended it to be used. None of God's creatures is to be rejected as evil, but is to be accepted and used as he intended, thus fulfilling its destiny and realizing God's kingdom and glory.

If we think in these terms, we will not hesitate to assimilate into the liturgy elements of our culture: its music, its signs of fellowship, its arts. Nor will we hesitate to bring the liturgy out of the sanctuary into the home, into the classroom, into the picnic grounds. Only in this way can we do what we are called to do by means of the liturgy: bring into the light again the radical sacredness of all creation by using it for God's praise as it was originally meant to be used. "The whole creation is eagerly waiting for God to reveal his sons . . . creation still retains the hope of being freed, like us, from its slavery to decadence . . ." (Rm. 8:19-21). By incorporating the secular into the liturgy, its eager waiting is answered partially and its hope of being freed is fulfilled partially, even as God's revelation of his sons is accomplished partially in those who confess Jesus as the Christ, are baptized in his name, and give thanks in memory of him.

Conclusion

The crucial problem of liturgical pedagogics, therefore, is practical catechetical preparation for liturgy by providing meaningful and instructive liturgical worship. This we can provide if we begin to think *about* the liturgy in the light of recent understanding of the Incarnation and God's grace, and if we insure the existence of that which liturgy is meant to express, namely, Christian life and community, ecclesial mission, and apostolic activity. We must also do something *with* the liturgy, namely to imaginatively and humanly implement with pastoral concern the liturgical rites. We must also do something *to* the liturgy, namely, take advantage of the reformed liturgy and act politically to bring about further reform. If catechists do not provide relevant and formative liturgy, theoretical catechetical preparation will be in vain, and liturgical worship will not be able to play the role it should in achieving the aim of catechetics: mature Christian response to the gospel of Jesus Christ.

6

Theology of the Word: Implications for Religious Instruction

Bernard Cooke

The Task of Religious Instruction

In any area of human learning or education, the nature and content of a field of knowledge dictate to quite an extent the appropriate manner of teaching. This general principle finds a very special application in the area of religious education: the project of educating faith is unique in the instructional world.

When one realizes that what one is attempting to do in religious education is to give an educated understanding of the process of God's revealing himself to men, one sees that one is attempting to communicate an understanding of a living process of communication: revelation is God's communication of understanding about himself.[1] But more than this, the task of religious education, undertaken by a believer in the context of a community of faith, is itself an integral part of the very process that one is hoping to clarify: the religious educator is himself an element in the mystery whose intelligibility he is hoping to bring to the intelligence of the student, and the student who is receiving this instruction in the context of faith is also a living part of this same mystery.[2] Thus the task of communicating an understanding of faith must fit faithfully into the manner of

---

[1] For a recent study of revelation, see Edward Schillebeeckx, *Revelation and Theology*, 2 vols. (New York: Sheed & Ward, 1967).

[2] For a further treatment, cf. my article "Faith and Christian Personality," in *Catholic Mind*, 57 (October, 1959):450-455.

God's revealing himself to us now in the church, or it will fail utterly in its professed purpose.

Theological Clarification

The topic of this chapter is, then, one that is not at all peripheral to the study of religious instruction. At the risk of otherwise being a fruitless game, religious education must take serious account of the actual operation of the process of divine revelation to man. Any reasonably sufficient theory of religious education must proceed from an accurate theological understanding of the word of God.

Fortunately, we are in quite a good position to approach our present analysis, for there has been a rather active discussion in the past few years of the theology of the word of God. Not that we have a totally adequate synthetic theology of divine revelation, but we are far enough along the road to this goal to make beneficial discussion of the topic possible. Various scripture scholars have clarified for us elements in the biblical mentality about God's word of revelation, and excellent essays have brought together into unity some of this more detailed analytic study. In this regard I just might refer briefly to Father John McKenzie's article in *Theological Studies*,[3] Gerhard von Rad's *Theology of the Old Testament*,[4] or the fascinating book of Alexander Jones, *God's Living Word*.[5] At the same time, eminent theologians—and one can mention Karl Rahner[6] and Hans Urs von Balthasar[7] as two examples—have made important additions to our systematic understanding of the nature

---

[3] John McKenzie, "The Word of God in the Old Testament," in *Theological Studies* 21 (June, 1960):183-206.

[4] Gerhard von Rad, *Theology of the Old Testament,* 2 vols. (New York: Harper & Row, 1963—1965).

[5] Alexander Jones, *God's Living Word* (New York: Sheed & Ward, 1961).

[6] For example, Karl Rahner, "The Word and the Eucharist," in his *Theological Investigations,* 5 vols. (Baltimore, Maryland: Helicon, 1961 —1967), 4:253-286.

[7] Hans Urs von Balthasar, *Word and Revelation* (New York: Herder and Herder, 1964).

and role of God's word in our faith life. So deep is the impact of such biblical and theological studies that it has forced a reassessment of the nature of evangelism and of the role of the strongly evangelical traditions in our current ecumenical developments. Obviously, a theological development so patently related to religious education has influenced considerably the thinking of contemporary catechists—and again, I might just instance the writings of Gabriel Moran as a reflection of this influence.[8]

Sacred Scripture: Old Testament

Any serious investigation of a theology of the word of God must begin, of course, with sacred scripture. This, not just because the bible can lay special claim to being the word of God, but because it is in the historical process of faith reflected in the bible that one can trace the beginnings of such a theology of the divine word. Already in the Old Testament there is a sophisticated understanding of God's word. Linked with prophetic thought, generally—and for the most part accurately—the theological development of understanding about the word of God is not limited to the prophetic traditions. Without going into a technical discussion (for that would take us too far afield from our precise topic), one can see that any current of theology that passes into the Old Testament—and there are a number of such currents—must include a theology of the word. Any reflection, professional or otherwise, upon the traditions of God revealing himself to his people is automatically the attempt to give some further intelligibility to the process of the people's reception and preservation of revelation—therefore necessarily a "theology of the word."

Yet, granted this basic fact, one can speak in more limited fashion of a "theology of the word" in old testament thought. And one can observe a certain progression of such a theology in

---

[8]Gabriel Moran, *Theology of Revelation* (New York: Herder and Herder, 1966); and also his *Catechesis of Revelation* (New York: Herder and Herder, 1966).

the history of Israel's faith life, as this is reflected for us in the pages of the old testament. At the risk of simplification being distortion, we might point to the following steps. In the very early stages of Israel's existence as a people, the word of God, coming to them in circumstances that are not historically ascertainable, provided a guidance that helped bring Israel into being as a people. Much of this early "word" was in one form or another practical prescription. Accompanying this was their faith, due somehow to revelation, that this same law-giving divinity helped protect them from their enemies and provided for their life, even when it required special means—as it did in the giving of the manna.

Apparently, as some of the early prophetic traditions preserved in the book of Kings indicate, a certain confusion entered Israelitic thinking in the more or less settled situation of residence in the promised land. Yahweh Sabaoth remained for them the warrior divinity, whose aid in times of special stress they still sought, but for the ordinary daily sustenance of life they turned increasingly to the vegetation deities of their Canaanite neighbors. It was from this error—or perhaps it was more conscious apostasy—that Elijah called the people; and we are all familiar with the dramatic accounts of how he challenged the power of the Baal, the Canaanite rain divinity, and proved that it was Yahweh alone who controlled not only the rain but all the forces of life.[9]

At this stage we still have not arrived at any noticeable insight into the intrinsic power of the word itself to provide life. This insight comes into being, however, not too long after. The word of God is itself a bearer of life; it not only announces the intent of Yahweh to enliven his chosen people, it actually effects that intent. The well-known passage of the prophetic vocation of Jeremiah is not the first clear indication of such a "theology of the word," but it is one of the most unmistakable: "I have put my words in your mouth . . . to pluck up and to break down . . . to build and to plant."[10] And, of course, the classic

---

[9] 1 Kings 18:20-46.
[10] Jer 1:9-10.

passage which summarizes so much of the prophetic view is found in Isaiah 55:10-11:

> For as the rain and the snow
> come down from heaven,
> and return not thither but water
> the earth,
> making it bring forth and sprout,
> giving seed to the sower and bread
> to the eater,
> so shall my word be that goes forth
> from my mouth;
> it shall not return to me empty,
> but it shall accomplish that which
> I purpose,
> and prosper in the thing for which
> I sent it.

This powerful and life-giving word of Yahweh comes in the challenging oracle of prophetic utterance. It also comes, in a somewhat less striking but also perhaps less important fashion, in the word of the Law and in the celebration of the cult. In many ways it is somewhat artificial to distinguish the manifestation of God's words in these three instances as sharply as we tend to do. Historical studies indicate increasingly the mutual influence of these three. To be sure it was largely in the cultic situations that the laws developed and were promulgated. Much of the growth of prophetism also was connected clearly with shrine situations, and prophetic patterns of thought find important expressions in both law and ritual. For this reason it is inaccurate to find the old testament "theology of the word" only in prophetic books; it is also to be found in important measure in the Deuteronomic and sacerdotal traditions.[11]

---

[11]von Rad, *Theology of the Old Testament*, 1:342-347.

Even when one comes to what is probably among the latest elements in Old Testament thought, the Wisdom movement's reflection on the nature and availability of true wisdom, the "solution" found in Sirach or the Book of Wisdom is a variant of the older traditions about Yahweh's word. True wisdom, which cannot be found among men and which abides only in God, has been partially enshrined by God in the gift of the Law. If a man, or the people as a whole, will only observe with fidelity the word of the Law, this will prove to be a life-giving word.[12]

Sacred Scripture: New Testament

Christian faith sees a qualitatively new phase in the mystery of God's word as having occurred with the historical appearance of Jesus of Nazareth. As Hebrews tells us: "God, who of old spoke to us through the prophets, has in these latter days spoken to us in his own Son." And one needs only to read through the prologue or the sixth chapter of John's gospel to realize how profound and extensive was the early Christian reflection on Jesus as the incarnated word.

In the gospel description of the public ministry of Jesus it is his prophetic character and activity that is stressed. Most of his time and effort is spent in teaching, not as the scribes and Pharisees taught, but with the authority that came from his unique consciousness of the identity and reality of his Father. As no other prophet before him possibly could, he "spoke for God"; for he who is the Son can alone speak properly about the Father, he alone is the Father's own word of self-revelation. His words, then, bear a message of salvation and divine communication that transcends the traditions coming from Moses or Solomon or the prophets. This is the judgment of the new testament literature.

But the gospel narratives are not just collections of the wise sayings of Jesus of Nazareth. The fundamental reason why they

---

[12]Sirach 44-50.

could not be is that the entire human activity and human existing of Jesus is "Word." All of it expresses in human form the
divine identity of the Son who alone can speak with immediacy
about the Father: "No one knows the Father except the Son
and any one to whom the Son chooses to reveal him."[13] Consequently, Jesus fulfills the old testament function of witness
to the covenant God of Israel; he is the supreme witness to the
Father, to the Father's love of men, and to the effective presence within human history of that love. In Jesus, for the first
time, the full dimension of sacrament is realized: he is *the*
sacrament of the Father—"He who has seen me, has seen the
Father."[14]

Precious and inexhaustively instructive as is his public life, it
is only in death and resurrection that Jesus reaches the complete stage of his prophetic witness. Only in his trusting aban-
donment of the known context of this worldly existence and his
pioneering advance into a new life as yet unexperienced by
man did Jesus give the climactic testimony to his Father. Only
in the fullness of risen life is he enabled to send forth his own
Spirit of sonship, so that men can witness to his Father by
themselves becoming sons. Moreover, Jesus' human self-giving
to those who are his brothers and sisters is the sacrament of
the divine self-giving.

The action of the Last Supper, which gives us the key to
understanding Christ's death and resurrection, makes it clear
that death and resurrection are essentially an act of profound
self-giving.

The Church

Having given himself unreservedly to us humans in his Passover
action, Christ does not then cease to be active in our midst.
He abides with his church, and through it with all men. He still
speaks in and through this community of believers, for the

---

[13]Mt 11:27.
[14]Jn 14:9.

church functions as his sacrament, much as he functioned as the sacrament of the Father. Since he continues in the church his own prophetic mission, this Christian community is a prophetic community. The church is meant to speak for Christ, not by way of historical replacement for him who once was in our midst and now is gone to some distant land called "heaven," but rather as his body to which he is constantly and immediately present. This body, the church, Christ animates with his own Spirit, the Spirit of sonship and prophecy.[15]

All Christians, then, by virtue of their entry into union with the risen Jesus through the sacrament of baptism, are responsible for a ministry of the word of God. The basic Christian task of bearing witness to the Gospel—by his words and deeds, ultimately by his own death and entry into new life—is committed to each Christian in his baptism. Providentially our own day marks the end of that narrow vision that limited such prophetic activity to those specially charged with ministry by virtue of the sacrament of orders. We have recovered the realization that, while a special function does attach to those who share in orders, the entire community, the entire people, is a priestly and prophetic people. The mystery of the church being "word of God" embraces the entire life of the Christian, even while it finds more formal expression in the cultic acts of Christian sacrament, particularly in the eucharist.

While it is distressing to have explained the "theology of the word of God" as superficially as we have just done, this may serve at least to review those ideas that contribute to understanding the Christian task of catechesis. Besides, the availability of fuller theological studies—such as those to which we referred earlier in the chapter—can act as a corrective to the insufficiency of our preceding remarks. What I would like to do is to spend the remainder of this chapter in a treatment of some practical implications.

---

[15]On the Christian people's prophetic ministry of the word, see the Second Vatican Council's *Dogmatic Constitution on the Church*, paragraph 12.

IMPLICATIONS FOR RELIGIOUS INSTRUCTION

The practical implications of our theological understanding of the mystery of God's word are limitless, especially as they touch the teaching activity of one who finds himself specially involved in religious education. Among those manifold topics of possible discussion I will choose seven practical conclusions and comment briefly on them—hoping thereby to stimulate further thought and conversation.

Religious Instruction as Word-of-God Experience

The full "word of God," the gospel of Jesus Christ, is a word in itself effective of salvation. Ministry of this word is a ministry of bringing salvation to men. But this salvation comes to men only through God's word. Human words must intervene to give clarification, explanation, and contemporary application; but these human words are not of themselves saving words. They share in saving power only insofar as they bring their hearer into contact with Christ himself.

Christian catechesis must become a situation in which the learning Christian hears Christ himself speaking the mystery of the Father's love. This may sound religiously romantic, or it may sound like plain nonsense, for how actually can we hear Christ, who no longer speaks to us in audible form? Yet there is a reality of Christian religious experience that we must respect if we are not to destroy the most important level of Christian catechesis. Though it be in faith—and faith is meant to be a real way of knowing—the Christian can and is meant to experience Christ as personal. This is not a historical understanding about the early career of Jesus and about its existential implications for us today. It is an acquaintance, a personal friendship, with a man who still is, and who is for me. If Christ is experienced this way, this experience speaks to one about the realities of faith as no verbal presentation of the gospel possibly could.

Yet the process of verbalization, which in large part constitutes religious education, is required to help bring into being the experience about which we have just been speaking. St. Paul himself tells us that such faith comes by hearing—and how shall they hear unless they have the gospel preached to them?[16] What I think needs stressing—for it is so easy to lose sight of—is the fact that our words of catechetical formation are vain if they do not lead the hearer into the deeper level of experiencing Christ himself. We as catechists cannot give them that experience; such is the province of Christ's own Spirit. But we can condition them for it by providing them with the elements of proper understanding that must form part of that experience. And we can refrain at the very least from giving faulty instruction that could block the student's ability to interpret accurately the experience of Christian faith.

Still under this first area of practical application, I would like to advert to the need of prayer as an indispensable element of adequate religious instruction.[17] Unless one has the consciousness of relating in personal interchange with Christ or his Father—and this is what prayer is all about—it is hard to see how one can be experiencing the personal presence of Christ. This prayer need not be formalized, but it must be real. And obviously it cannot be a matter of reciting some "prayers" in conjunction with a session of religious instruction in order "to create an atmosphere of prayer." Generally an atmosphere of prayer should pervade all religious education. Certainly there is nothing reprehensible in reciting formulated prayers. But this type of prayer must be executed with simple and straightforward authenticity, or it will create a sense of artificiality and block real faith-consciousness.

Religious Instruction As Prophetic Witness

If Christ's role in communicating God's word was one of prophetic witness and if the religious educator shares in the con-

---

[16] Rom 10:17.

[17] For an excellent contemporary study of Christian prayer, see Hans Urs von Balthasar, *Prayer* (New York: Sheed & Ward, 1961).

tinuation of this role in the church, it is clear that the function of the religious educator must extend beyond that of mere teacher and be one of witness. This means that the process of religious instruction must be one of "pointing to another." The religious educator must always direct the attention and consciousness of his students to the reality of the living Christ. But here we encounter one of the most demanding requirements of true Christian catechesis, namely that the catechist's own manifest faith must be for his students a living witness to the reality of Christ. The catechist must serve as a criterion for the student in making the personal judgment that Christ is now for him. While much of the religious educator's function is one of conveying an accurate understanding of *what* Christ and Christianity are all about, he cannot escape the need of testifying personally to the fact *that* the risen Christ is.

Even in the area of clarifying the content of Christian revelation, the religious educator must be careful that he speaks for God. His own personal insights about life may be of considerable value to his students, and certainly these will often reflect quite faithfully the basic orientations of the gospel. Yet, he must be careful that he constantly reassesses his own understandings of Christianity, so that these increasingly correspond to the message of the gospel. Only then can he hope to achieve notable fidelity to God's own word as he forms the faith of his students.

Religious Instruction as Real Life

As one looks at the process of revelation during the years of old testament and primitive Christian history, one notices that the word of God that comes to men through Law or prophet or cult or finally in Christ is always a word that deals with the business of living human life. The word of God is always a practical word, challenging human behavior, demanding a response not just to the reality of the divine but to the exigencies of human history and above all to the needs of men. "If anyone says, 'I love God,' and hates his brother, he is a liar.'"[18]

In his task of religious formation, the catechist must take serious account of this aspect of God's word. The word of God to which he ministers is never a static word, never limited to the textual or even ritual formulation in which it is enshrined for us in the church. It always speaks to life as it now is. So the religious educator must go to pains to relate the gospel message to the concrete situations of present-day existence. Again, this never may be a superficial undertaking in which one asks questions such as: What would Jesus do if he were living in our midst today? The fact of the matter is that he does indeed live on in our midst, and does so in order to transform the structures and experiences of our daily existence. Any competent religious educator must have, therefore, an understanding of the purpose and activity of the risen Christ in his present activity in the church and an understanding of the movement of Christ's Spirit in our midst as that Spirit directs us towards the fulfillment of the kingdom of God in our own day.

It follows that all genuine religious education involves a challenge to the students concerned. Perhaps not all of them will welcome this challenge, certainly not all of them will respond generously to it in faith. But if the procedures of religious education do not even raise the challenge, the students do not have the occasion of response, of faith. To speak this way sometimes raises eyebrows among those who insist that good religious pedagogy is an academic undertaking, an undertaking in which—particularly on the higher levels of education—fidelity to "scientific objectivity" is of the essence. But this fear or objection is really a spurious one. By "scientific objectivity" one should mean a scrupulous observance of the methodology intrinsic to any area of human knowing—and one cannot correspond faithfully with the way of human knowing which is Christian faith unless he conveys the challenge of God's word. Religious instruction that is mere information

---

[18] 1 Jn 4:20.

without impact does not deserve to be characterized as "objective"; "eviscerated" would be a much more appropriate adjective.

Religious Instruction as Embracing a Whole Person

Orientated as it is to challenge the believer to response in faith and charity, the word of God demands much more than academic interest on the part of the one who hears this word. There must be on the part of the student who receives religious instruction a personal openness to receiving the word of revelation, no matter what its practical implications. The gospel parable of the seed that fell on stony ground or among thorns or on good ground is related explicitly in the gospel itself to reception of the word of God.[19] Unless the ground, that is, the personal disposition of a person, is prepared to receive the word, even the word of God cannot come to fruition.

What this says to the religious educator is that he must take full account of the background, previous experience and knowledge, prejudices, questions, and so forth of his students. The already present attitudes of these students may condition them very favorably towards accepting God's word, or just the opposite may be true. In either case the alert catechist will fit his religious instruction to the situation, aware of the immense importance of personal attitudes in the process of religious instruction.

Religious Instruction and Scripture and Sacrament

Since God himself is continuously involved in the privileged media of revelation—scripture and sacrament—religious education necessarily must employ those two agencies as part of its own method. In the past it generally consisted in the practice (and we have seen it exemplified in some religion textbooks) of "drawing from" the bible or the liturgy. Clearly, all our religious understandings as Christians should draw from

---

[19]Mt 13.

scripture and sacrament. But what is absolutely essential to the
process of educating faith is that scripture itself be allowed to
form faith, and that sacrament itself be allowed to form faith,
and this as an integral part of the process of religious pedagogy. As a matter of fact, these should be the culminating
aspects of religious education; everything else should prepare
for the immediate and formal exposure to God's word in bible
and liturgy. To arrange a process of religious education without this educated introduction to these primary media of God's
word is as unrealistic as an attempt to teach people how to
swim without ever bringing them to water.

In this regard, of course, many religious educators are at a
distinct disadvantage because they cannot control either the
proclamation of scripture or the celebration of sacrament to
which their students are exposed. Instead they must hope—and
often in vain—that their students will be among the relatively
few who are fortunate to experience adequate liturgy in their
parish church. Granted this problem, the religious educator
must be careful that he does not contribute to this very situation and excuse himself because the parish eucharist is not
in its externals all he would wish it to be. No matter how
externally appropriate a celebration of sacrament would be,
it could not be the kind of authentic liturgical action that
deeply forms faith unless those participating in it knew clearly
what they were doing. This role of forming Christians for a
thoroughly human share in real liturgy by educating them as
to its true nature and purpose is the role proper to the
catechist.

Religious Instruction and Providence

Earlier I mentioned that the word of God always speaks to
the concrete circumstances and demands of life. But life itself,
in the totality of its elements, is also a "word of God."
Obviously life is not "word of God" in the same manner as
scripture or even sacrament. Yet, the happenings of our daily

existence, the elements in our experiences, particularly the fellow beings whose relationships with us so deeply affect our own selfhood, all form part of a providential pattern which can speak to us about ourselves and about God. We must avoid, naturally, the excessive and erroneous view that regards God working specially, almost miraculously, in the ordinary happenings of life. Yet, there is a genuine sacramentalism about human life, based on the fact that there is some degree of personal presence of Christ in the life of every human being.

I am not suggesting that religious educators must possess a sophisticated theology of providence. What I am suggesting is that in religious instruction the insights of faith be brought to bear as far as possible on the life experience of the students. In this way the formal word of Christian revelation can help the student give some Christian form and intelligibility to his own life. Such an approach to religious education presupposes that the catechist knows his students personally. This in turn suggests a relationship between religious educator and student that is one of deep Christian identity and concern. Personal rapport is important in all effective teaching; in religious education it is indispensable.

Religious Instruction as Interiorization

Finally, if religious education is genuinely effective, the understanding it imparts will be one that is interiorized by the learner. That is to say, the student will truly make an act of Christian faith. He will, freely and gratefully, appropriate the meaning of God's word as that word speaks to him in the specific circumstances of his present existence. Joyfully and fearlessly he will let God's word speak whatever it will.

Essentially such an open receptivity to God's word is the result of divine grace. However, the religious educator can do much to create such a disposition. Perhaps the most basic thing that must be done is to respect deeply and obviously the personal freedom and integrity of the student. Genuine faith can not be forced on a person. To attempt to pressure a person towards faith is often to erect a barrier of opposition that makes all further religious instruction fruitless. There is no need to stress the difficulty of forming Christians in true freedom; it is perhaps the most formidable task left to us by the Second Vatican Council. Yet, it is an unavoidable and therefore—if one accepts in faith the power of the Holy Spirit—achievable goal.

Conclusion

These, then, are seven elements of practical procedure that flow from a theology of the word of God. Unquestionably there are many others that might have been mentioned. But these few may illustrate the basic principle that careful and accurate theology should act as a guide to the religious educator, both as to the content he communicates and the method he follows. More specifically, we need to probe yet deeper into the mystery of God's saving word, so that we may with greater fidelity bring this word and its saving power into the lives of men.

Religious Instruction in the Protestant Churches

7

C. Ellis Nelson

Sidney Hook, in an article in the *Harvard Education Review* in 1956, said that one could not work out logically from a metaphysical position a system of education and teaching unique to that philosophical belief. Hook went on to show how educators who disagree on their worldview could agree on certain practices, while others who disagree on practices could agree on their philosophy.[1] Although Hook was not the first to suggest that there was no close, logical connection between belief and educational practices, his article challenged philosophers of education to identify more clearly why their work was important to teachers. That question was answered in part during the annual meeting of the Eastern Division of the American Philosophical Association in 1962 when B. Othanel Smith took the position that the work of the philosopher of education was necessary in order to help teachers think critically about teaching procedures; to give direction to the educational enterprise; to relate properly curriculum, methods, and evaluation of an educational system; and to clarify educational concepts, especially those used in empirical investigations.[2]

We face the same problem in religious education. Both Trinitarians and Unitarians utilize audiovisual materials for in-

---

[1] Sidney Hook, "The Scope of Philosophy of Education," in *Harvard Educational Review* 26 (Spring, 1956):145-148.

[2] B. Othanel Smith, "Views on the Role of Philosophy in Teacher Education," in *The Journal of Philosophy* 59 (October, 1962):638-647.

struction. And it is silly to suggest that theology will give clear solutions to all of the practical problems of religious education. Rather, our theology must be used to help us set goals and critically appraise our teaching and our methods. I wanted to get this basic problem out in the open in the very beginning of this chapter because this essay is intended to deal primarily with the teaching process rather than with the content of Protestant religious education. I agree that these things can be separated for analysis, but from time to time my own theological beliefs will rise to the surface to make judgments about the matters under review. So I invite you to review with me how notions of teaching religion have developed in American Protestantism and how major Protestant denominations conceive of the religious educational process today. Then I would like to share with you some speculations about the future.

THE SETTING

To establish our base line, let us go back to those momentous days of the 1830's when Horace Mann and others established the policy of excluding sectarian religious instruction from the developing public school system. The ethos of the country was Protestant, and the moral instruction that remained in the public schools at that time was Protestant in outlook.[3]

The Protestant strategy in education was formulated between 1830 and the Civil War and it has remained essentially the same until this day.[4] This strategy is based on the assumption of a Protestant ethos and a public school that supports, enhances, or is actually engaged in teaching Protestantism. In this atmosphere the church will teach (through its congre-

---

[3]The public schools in the mid-1900's, even after the elimination of formal church connection, were Protestant in nature. For example, see the "Petition of the Catholics of New York" to the Board of Aldermen of the City of New York, September 21, 1840, in Neil G. McCluskey, editor, *Catholic Education in America* (New York: Bureau of Publications, Teachers College, Columbia University, 1964), pp. 65-77.

[4]William Bean Kennedy, *The Shaping of Protestant Education* (New York: Association, 1966).

gational-sponsored school, communicant classes, and adult groups) the particular theology and sectarian beliefs of the denomination. From the formulation of this strategy until now, the church school, meeting one hour a week, has been the chief agency of Protestant religious education.[5]

For the first three-fourths of the nineteenth century, the Sunday School grew at a fabulous rate, not only because it was the spearhead of the Protestant strategy in education, but also because it was fueled by a strong evangelistic passion to win the new nation to Christ. The Sunday School movement was so powerful that at one time it provided all of the schooling some persons in pioneer settlements underwent. Naturally, in such a situation, nobody was going to pay much attention to instructional methodology, and Protestant historians have labelled this the "Babel" in curriculum. Each group, sect, or denomination taught its own doctrines, usually by means of a catechism, or by just telling bible stories. The instructional methodology was didactic: there was practically no concession adjusting biblical material to the age level of the child. The National Sunday School Convention, meeting in Indianapolis in 1872, brought order out of the wide variety of curricula by adopting a Uniform Lesson Plan. The bible, according to this plan, was assumed to be the textbook for religious education, and most of the content was to be covered in seven years, alternating between old and new testaments. All age levels in Sunday School studied the same bible passage on a given Sunday. Thus, the first instructional principle of American Protestantism was formed: *the bible, as a textbook should be studied systematically*. The formation of the Uniform Lessons quickly stabilized Protestant religious instruction. These lessons have continued to the present day and are still widely used throughout America.

At the turn of the century, two new developments had a

---

[5]Robert W. Lynn, *Protestant Strategies in Education* (New York: Association, 1964).

profound and lasting effect on Protestant religious instruction. The first was the psychological interpretation of religion associated with the names of Edwin D. Starbuck, George A. Coe, and William James. These men analyzed religion in terms of psychological origins, and accounted for religious phenomena (such as conversion) in terms of the individual's psychological needs. They also catalogued and explained varieties of religious experience. Their attention to the adolescent age level and the crisis of belief that Protestants expected at that age level called into question a "conversion experience" as the proper goal of religious instruction. The other development was the child study movement associated with G. Stanley Hall. Although his recapitulation theory did not endure very long, the phenomena he was trying to explain—that children go through rather clearly discernible stages in the process of maturation—was a new factor that had to be considered in any educational process.

Religious educators, following the leadership of those who had developed a psychology of religion and a theory of developmental stages in childhood, began to describe the religious capacities and characteristics of children at different age levels. When the Twelfth National Sunday School Convention met in Louisville, Kentucky in 1908, this study had advanced far enough for them to authorize a graded Sunday School system. Thus there was created the second instructional principle: *the child at his stage of development—his needs, interests, and capacities—should be the criteria by which the materials for religious instruction are selected.*

Viewing the child as a person with varying needs at different ages, rather than as a little adult, recast the whole religious education process. Luther A. Weigle, in his book *The Pupil and the Teacher*, published in 1911, devoted the first half to a description of the pupil at different age levels before discussing the teacher and what is to be taught.[6] George Herbert Betts, in

---

[6] Luther A. Weigle, *The Pupil and the Teacher* (New York: Hodder and Stoughton, 1911).

his book *How to Teach Religion*, originally published in 1910, put it this way:

> Anyone of fair intelligence can master a given amount of subject matter and present it to a class; but it is a far more difficult thing to understand the child—to master the inner secrets of the mind, the heart, and the springs of action of the learner.[7]

To be sure, it was difficult to master the inner secrets of the child's mind; but a brilliant array of scholars such as George Mead and John Dewey had been devoting themselves to the task with the assumption that the self is formed out of social interaction. This meant that there was no natural unfolding of an innate personality that should be enriched and guided by education. Rather, the self was seen as created by society; and education, to be effective, had to be a guided interaction in groups. George Albert Coe, William Clayton Bower, and others applied this social theory to religious education, and in 1922 Bower was appointed chairman of a committee of the International Council of Religious Education to formulate an approach to curriculum along these lines. His description of religious instruction must be quoted in full.

> Christian education is a guided experience in Christian living in which the growing person is assisted in interpreting, judging, and bringing through to Christian outcomes the actual life-situations which he faces in every area of his experience, with the aid of the resources of the past religious experience of the race. The subject-matter of learning from this point of view consists of three elements: the experience of the learner as the starting point, the learner's own past experience, and the accumulated past religious experience of the race, particularly that recorded in the bible. The method of learning, on the other hand, consists of the steps by which persons respond to problematic life-situations in Christian ways: by becoming aware of the problem involved, by analyzing the situation for its factors and possible

---

[7]George Herbert Betts, *How to Teach Religion, Principles and Methods* (New York: Abingdon, 1910).

outcomes, by searching the resources of past religious experience for solutions, by weighing possible outcomes in the light
of Christian convictions and values, by making a choice and
commitment, and by carrying through the decision to action in
changed personal and social living. Thus learning has its beginning and end in experience. The school should be set up as a
laboratory in the midst of life into which all the crucial experiences encountered in living are brought for analysis, interpretation, and resolution at the various levels of growth—a
miniature Christian community in which the growing person
increasingly and effectively participates.[8]

This committee report gives us a third principle of instruction: *the actual life situation a person faces is the place where
religious education takes place; and these situations should be
analyzed in such a way that the person is able to evaluate them
in the light of Christian values and thus improve personal and
social living.*
We can now start our survey of contemporary Protestant instruction with three broad general principles: the bible is the
textbook, the pupil's stage of development controls content and
method, and life situations are the arena in which we work
out Christian meanings with the pupils. I do not mean that
any particular curriculum or any particular denomination has
an instructional methodology that blends all of these together
in a perfect way, even on paper. I mean only that the American
Protestant tradition contains these three broad principles and
that each denomination's formal educational effort is a particular way of putting these three together in an instructional program. But there is one more word of a general nature before
I start an analysis of present programs. Since Protestants often
do not know the scope of their own church education system,
I must assume that Roman Catholics may not know it either.
In 1969 Protestant denominations reported 139,662 Sunday

---

[8]William Clayton Bower and Percy Roy Hayward, *Protestantism Faces
its Educational Task Together* (Appleton, Wisconsin: Nelson, 1949), pp.
61-62.

Schools with a pupil enrollment of 32,014,095.[9] Even after making allowances for the inaccuracy of these data, this is a sizeable group of people assembled week by week for instructional purposes. Now let us go to certain denominational programs to examine their instructional material and see how they deal with the three major curriculum principles we have outlined.

First we will examine the Cooperative Curriculum Project because it is the major cooperative effort in religious instruction fostered through the Division of Christian Education of the National Council of Churches. Educational leaders of sixteen denominations with a total communicant membership of almost twenty-five million, after four years of work, completed in 1964 the outline of a total educational plan. The published volume describing this plan is 813 pages, so it will not be easy to describe it briefly!

The goal of church instruction in the Cooperative Curriculum Project (C.C.P.) is stated as follows:

> The objective for Christian education is that all persons be aware of God through his self-disclosure, especially his redeeming love as revealed in Jesus Christ, and that they respond in faith and love—to the end that they may know who they are and what their human situation means, grow as sons of God rooted in the Christian community, live in the Spirit of God in every relationship, fulfill their common discipleship in the world, and abide in the Christian hope.[10]

The C.C.P. then goes on to identify the scope of the curriculum as man's relationship to God, to his fellowman, and to the world. When the objective is analyzed with relation to this

---

[9]Lauris B. Whitman, editor, *Yearbook of American Churches* (New York: Council, 1969), p. 175.

[10]*The Church's Educational Ministry: A Curriculum Plan* (St. Louis: Bethany, 1965), p. 8.

broad scope, five fairly specific areas of religious instruction emerge. These five areas of instruction are not to be considered separately, but rather, should be regarded as five places from which the church works toward the overall goal. Each of the five areas is broken up into fairly specific concerns or themes. These themes become the place where the pupil, the bible, and the general life situation are all blended into one unit of work about which specific lessons are prepared. The five curriculum areas are: (1) Life in its setting: the meaning and experience of existence; (2) Revelation: the meaning and experience of God's self-disclosure; (3) Sonship: the meaning and experience of redemption; (4) Vocation: the meaning and experience of discipleship; (5) The church: the meaning and experience of Christian community."

METHODIST RELIGIOUS INSTRUCTION

This Cooperative Curriculum Project is typical of Protestant cooperative work in that it is a set of blueprints for the foundation and the steelwork of a building. Each denomination takes the blueprints and erects its own structure: that is, it publishes its own instructional materials based on this design. This means the sixteen denominations will all be working with the same blueprints; but they will make alterations as they go along, and they will give the materials their own slant as it is edited. Materials written on the C.C.P. model are just now emerging from these denominations. In order to get a taste of how this model of religious instruction works, let us examine the Methodist Church's material because this is one of the largest denominations using the material and because they have already completed these materials throughout their children's age levels.

Let us initially sample the material at the first and second-grade level. The spring quarter, 1968, was in area five, "The Church: the meaning and experience of Christian community."

"*Ibid.*, pp. 43, 93, 129, 162, 205.

The lessons are built around the theme expressed in the question "Why do we have churches?" The instructional methodology in this material can be described as having five characteristics.[12]

First, the instructional method starts with the motivation of the teacher, on the assumption that the teacher must see the importance of what he is doing from an adult's point of view. This is done in this particular unit by showing that this unit of work is within the border area represented by questions such as "Is there a difference between the church as an institution and the church as the people of God?" "Is the church out of date?" "How can the church speak to people in today's world?" The teacher is warned that the lesson is not an answer to these questions, but rather is designed so that a first grader can begin to understand that membership in the church has a special meaning. The teacher is told directly that if he can help the children get an accurate understanding of the church, they will not be confused or bewildered about it when they grow up. The teacher is motivated to help the children have a good peer-group experience because it is something they need and because their experience in the church school will become associated in their minds with the word "church." This first step, motivating the teachers, is far more than subject-matter orientation. Underlying this approach is an experiential understanding of religious instruction.

Second, the experiential method is further emphasized by what we call "concomitant" education. The assumption of concomitant education is that religion is related to all of life. Concomitant education is explained to the Methodist teachers of first and second grades by these words: "whatever is happening to your boys and girls in their relationship with the church is likely to make a more lasting impression on them than what you tell them is so—regardless of how right you

[12]Henry M. Bullock, editor, *The Methodist Teacher I-II* (Nashville, Tennessee: Board of Education, The Methodist Church, 1968), pp. 13-27.

are—particularly if what you tell the children is contradicted by their own experiences."

The practical outworking of this educational position is to say that the teacher must be sensitive to what is happening to the children in the whole range of their life. Before the teacher even starts to prepare a specific lesson, he is told to think through the specific attitudes the children would encounter in the congregation from the minister and the adults. The physical environment also teaches; so this idea is reviewed. Practical, inexpensive suggestions are given for making the classroom active, interesting, and informal. Although trying to bring the community into an instructional program for first graders seems formidable, the Methodists do so. They suggest visits to other churches, thus making the ecumenical movement real to children. They counsel the teacher to watch the local newspaper for items that relate to the lesson and to monitor TV programs that may apply.

Third, this instructional model calls for a person-centered instructional method. This is emphasized by telling the teachers they must know the home situation from which the child comes. They insist that the teacher have certain home information about each child by telephoning the parents, visiting in the home, or having the parents help with certain classroom duties on a rotation basis. The teacher is then told that the main source of reliable information is from the children themselves, and so the teacher must observe the ones who can read, those who have special interests, and so on. The teacher is encouraged to have the children ask questions and respond to suggestions in order to get a feel for their particular interests and needs.

Fourth, the classroom is planned around group activities, rather than around a specific amount of information to be learned. Methodists say "children learn through participating in activities that encourage them to think and remember, to grow in their understanding of themselves and show them how to live and work with others, to become more aware of God and his self-revelation in Jesus Christ, and to trust God and His loving care for them." This means that most classroom time is spent doing things such as drawing, acting out ideas, having discussions, or preparing worship materials.

The fifth and final descriptive statement in the educational method is evaluation. The importance of this step can be described as follows: "Experience in teaching is valuable, but experience without a thoughtful analysis of what is done and why it is done can deprive the teacher of satisfaction and growth." Thus the teacher is expected to maintain a record of what he has planned to do, what happened in the class, what was judged to be educationally useful, and what failed and why. This running comment on the classroom session helps the teacher become more objective about his work and more open to suggestion for educational innovation. Education also includes the teacher's relation to the children as individuals. The teacher is urged to observe the children who like to draw, to note the ones who are irritable or quiet, and then to investigate why these children are as they are and what the church could do to help the child change his conduct.

A TYPICAL LESSON

How do these five generalizations about the instructional methodology work out in a particular lesson? As an illustration let us examine the first lesson in this unit entitled "What is the Church?" The teacher is told at the outset that the lesson plan contains more suggestions than he can use, and that he must choose from these suggestions on the twin bases of the life situation of the pupils and of his own skill and interest.

When the children arrive, they are given name tags and put to work at once helping to arrange the worship table or preparing the story paper that will be distributed later. The children are asked to draw a picture of something that makes them think of the church, but the teachers are not to suggest subjects.

The whole classroom is divided into small groups of six or eight and each child explains to the group what he has drawn and why it is connected with the church. The teacher notes the children's ideas but neither corrects them nor expands on their suggestions. The teacher then introduces the theme of the lesson by asking the pupils to think about why we have churches. He initiates their thought patterns by saying that before we can answer the question "why do we have churches," we first need to know what a church is. This will be done through a game. The children are divided into groups, each group composed of two to four students. The groups are asked to think of one thing church people do and then act it out for the other groups to guess. The teacher observes carefully the content of the children's ideas, and then suggests they talk it over with their parents and come back next week with more ideas about what church people do.

The teacher then passes out the pupils' textbooks, has each child turn to the first page where he fills in his name, and tells them to have their parents read the story to them during the week. To provide motivation for the pupils, the storybook contains a puzzle. The teacher suggests first they may solve this puzzle before the characters in this story solve the puzzle, and second that the puzzle will be one of the main things they will talk about when they return next week. Thus, homework has both an intrinsic appeal to the child's natural curiosity, draws the parent into the teaching during the week, and provides continuity with the next week's lesson. The children then learn a song, "We Love Our Church," and sing it through several times. The teacher tells a story, "First Called Christian," which is a bit of imagined dialogue in the home of a Christian in Antioch about the suitability of the name Christian for the new religion. Discussion follows as the teacher makes a clear identification with the bible as the source of truth about Christianity.

The class is concluded with a brief, informal worship, using Psalm 100, read by a child who has been coached to do so in advance. The lesson is reviewed and concluded with prayer and the offering.

At this juncture it might be helpful to look at the child's homework book. The story is about Soko and Dirk, and the illustration shows a white and a dark-skinned boy throwing snowballs. This visual brotherhood is not mentioned in the story. The story concerns the various groups the children in the picture belong to; the puzzle is to determine what is the oldest institution they belong to or attend. The answer is given in the next story if they do not discover that the answer is: "the church."

Now let us sample the instructional methodology for children, ages eleven to twelve in the curriculum of Spring, 1968, to see what is done with this age level when logical reasoning is well established, a sense of history in terms of chronology and meaning is possible, and the pupil has developed a degree of sophistication about life.[13]

The lesson is Unit 2: "The Reality of God: The Meaning and Experience of God's Continuing Revelation." The theme is "How God Reveals Himself in Jesus."

The same five basic characteristics of educational methodology continue in use. First, the teacher's motivation is secured by pointing out that the child of this age is aware of other religions, and the claim of Jesus' uniqueness is something that must be handled in order both to help the child understand his religion and show him that Jesus represents a relationship with God that he (the pupil) should practice. Second, concomitant education is stressed in an introductory article ("A good bargain is the half of it.") in which many environmental factors are reviewed to encourage the teacher to pay attention to the way the environment teaches. Third, the person-centered

---

[13]Henry M. Bullock, editor, *The Methodist Teacher V-VI* (Nashville, Tennessee: Board of Education, The Methodist Church, 1968), pp. 2-22.

instruction has undergone a shift: in the first and second-grade material, emphasis was placed on a child-family milieu, while now, at this higher age level the child is seen as an individual in his own right. The lessons are now full of projects an individual can do in relation to the lesson. This is particularly true in the pupil's book where bible readings, bible crossword puzzles, and tests and other self-instruction devices are used. Fourth, the group activity method of classroom work continues, but there has been a shift from project-type activities such as drama and play to more intellectual activities such as discussions, making a newspaper, developing a TV program or puppet show. Fifth, evaluation continues to be urged as a part of each class session in terms of the development of the pupils as individuals, the adequacy of the instructional method, and the teachers' performance.

Rather than take one lesson from the eleven to twelve material for review, let me say a few things about the lessons in general for this age level. The class material usually starts with some group activity. For example, the first lesson of this unit is on Jesus as a person. Pictures are hung about the room and each student walks around making notes on what Jesus is doing in the picture and what the picture means. Another (lesson 6) starts with a general discussion of Grüenwald's "The Small Crucifixion." The major time is given to a discussion of bible passages, short written assignments, reports from the homework section of the student's textbook, reports from groups of three and four which have worked together for ten minutes on some specific problem or question, listening to a tape-recording or viewing a filmstrip, role-playing of situations, or working on projects such as a map or a time line. The typical session is then concluded with a brief worship, consisting of a hymn, scripture passage, prayers. I found no lesson devoted to lecturing or to any other kind of didactic instruction. In short, instructional methodology is built entirely on student participation. The content of the bible and theology is brought into the process around these individual and group activities.

Hermeneutics is close to methods, so let me say one word about that. Inherent within the Cooperative Curriculum Project, and seen rather clearly in the methods of that instructional pattern, is a hermeneutic that in theological circles was described by Paul Tillich as the method of correlation.[14] By this Tillich meant that philosophy and theology formulated a problem out of life, and the Christian faith, from its sources including the bible, gave its affirmation or belief. This method was picked up by Lewis Sherrill and applied to religious education in his book *The Gift of Power*. Sherrill describes human predicaments and then supplies biblical themes that relate to these predicaments.[15]

This curriculum used that general hermeneutical method. Neither bible nor theology is taught in a systematic way. Rather, the bible and theology are factored into the educational process in relation to a question or life-situation that the learner recognizes as being close to his interest. For example, the purpose of Lesson I is to show the significance of Jesus Christ, and biblical material is suggested to show what Jesus Christ meant to the apostle Paul. The lesson on the baptism of Jesus starts out with a discussion of baptism, the students' own or baptismal ceremonies they have witnessed. Then the discussion focuses on Jesus and what baptism meant to him. The lesson on discipleship starts with a discussion of work camps or other activities of this kind, then goes on to discuss what Jesus said about the kind of service he expects of his followers and concludes with what his followers should do today.

THE LUTHERAN CHURCH IN AMERICA

As I indicated earlier, all Protestant denominations, including

---

[14]Paul Tillich, *Systematic Theology,* 3 vols. (Chicago: University of Chicago Press, 1951—1963), 1:59.
[15]Lewis Joseph Sherrill, *The Gift of Power* (New York: Macmillan, 1955), pp. 92-119.

the few which sponsor parochial schools, depend on church-sponsored schools, usually meeting on Sunday, to teach the Christian faith. There is no real difference between denominations as far as the major means of religious instruction is concerned. However, denominations differ among themselves as to the way they interpret the Christian faith, particularly the bible, and this is quite naturally reflected in their instructional materials and to some extent in their methodology. Let us now look at another denomination which has worked out a different instructional design, even though they use the same basic instructional methods as the Methodists.

The Lutheran Church in America was formed in the late 1950's by a merger of several Lutheran Churches. The instructional design developed by this new denomination is church-centered, and its stated purpose is "to assist the individual in his response and witness to the eternal and incarnate Word of God as he grows within this community of the church toward greater maturity in his Christian life, through ever deepening understandings, more wholesome attitudes and more responsible patterns of action."[16] More specifically, the subject matter of this curriculum is God, Church, Bible, Ethics, Physical World, and Self.

The uniqueness of this instructional design lies not in the subject matter nor in the way the age groups are graded according to ability; rather, the uniqueness lies in the way the planners hope to accomplish this general goal within each age group. The Lutherans have taken the position that the "learning" part of the "teaching-learning process" is the key to instructional methodology. The learner learns when he has to act to satisfy some of his desires, but he acts as a whole person in a total environment. Thus, learning in this model is intensely personal, and the teacher is considered as one who guides the pupil's learning. Problem-solving and instructional methods are

---

[16]W. Kent Gilbert and Wilson C. Egbert, *The Objectives of Christian Education* (Philadelphia: The Board of Parish Education, Lutheran Church of America, 1959).

preferred—or other methods which grow out of the experiences pupils are having in their daily lives.

Given these assumptions, how do the Lutherans design an instructional program? Having identified the world as the place where God is known and the pupil's condition as the key to learning, they have developed a design based on "continual life involvements." This is an adaptation of Florence Stratemeyer's conception of secular education based on "persistent life situations."[17] Continual life involvement as used by the Lutherans means there are general areas of living in which every person is involved; these areas are characteristic of all age levels, although the form of the involvement changes as the life cycle changes.

For example, one's personal identity is a continual life involvement. Although the problems are different in each stage of one's maturation and development, a person has to deal with himself, his conscience, his sex role, and so forth, throughout his life. There are Christian teachings that apply to each of these continual life involvements. Other life involvements are relating one's self to others, to the world, to the social and political order, and to other religions. Life involvement, then, becomes a way of ordering the materials and methods of instruction and providing a rationale by which teaching can be planned.

GENERAL CHARACTERISTICS OF INSTRUCTIONAL PROGRAMS

I could go on to describe briefly the instructional programs of the United Church of Christ, or the Covenant Life Curriculum (which is sponsored by several denominations in the Reformed tradition) or others, but I shall not do so because there is no significant difference in instructional methodology among Protestant denominations. Rather, let me conclude this section

---

[17]Florence B. Stratemeyer, *Guides to a Curriculum for Modern Living* (New York: Bureau of Publications, Teachers College, Columbia University, 1952).

of my chapter with a few generalizations about Protestant instructional programs.

First, almost all major Protestant religious instruction from kindergarten through twelve years of age is "life-situational" in some form. The lessons are conducted with current problems or personal interests in the foreground, and with bible and theology in the background. The educational theory that informs the educational process is that the pupils learn by participation; hence, student activities of all kinds are written into the lessons.

Second, almost without exception the lessons are person-centered. In the kindergarten and first few grades, the material is written to show the importance of the group; pupil activities accentuate group participation. Even so, if one reads through the instructional materials, one finds that the individual has been elevated to an exalted height. From an educational point of view, this is not objectionable, but the question can be raised as to whether it should be that way from a theological point of view. The bible is a history of God's covenant with Israel in the old testament and with the church in the new testament. A Christian is the result of a "cloud of witnesses" from the past and a society of believers in the present; these corporate realities are prior in time and experience to that of the individual. I think we are so "person-centered" because this is one of the latent historical images of American Protestants which has been strongly reinforced by the rugged frontier individualism, because the educational psychology which informs our materials comes from the secular realm where the individual is the unit of education, and because the average classroom teacher can see the rather obvious need of an individual and can work with him to increase his knowledge or develop his devotion. However the religion teacher, who is usually untrained, is not able to cope with educational methods that have as their purpose instilling a sense of reverence and gratitude for the church as a corporate body. Although many group activities are included and games and plays are often suggested, the justification is often to improve the individual's skill or knowledge. In other words, we Protestants often use the group to socialize the individual rather than to help the individual understand and appreciate his connection with the body of Christ—the church.

Third, all instructional materials assume the bible to be the basic textbook. However, there is a wide range in the amount of bible material used and the hermeneutical principles employed. Up to age twelve the bible is not often used as the primary source material for the pupil's textbook. Rather, the stories for younger children are about events that are common to their life, using biblical ideas about love, forgiveness, the nature of God. Sometimes bible verses are appended to the end of the lesson. Material for older children is often more historical and literary; portions of the bible are inserted for comparison and contrast. Very little instructional material for children published today by mainline Protestant denominations uses the bible for the bulk of the lesson. This feature of contemporary instructional material has caused a serious problem. Many adults feel that the bible itself should be the textbook with the teacher's role limited to selecting the material and deciding on methods that will convey the biblical meaning. As a result, there is considerable grumbling among teachers about the "lack of bible" in the new materials. Many churches have abandoned their denominationally prepared materials for materials edited by independent publishers who offer bible materials and simple, easy-to-follow lesson plans.

Fourth, all instructional materials are carefully worked out. It takes a denomination about five to eight years to plan and execute a new curriculum. Special attention is given to a distinctive style or design because the curriculum has to be promoted through the denomination's apparatus and because an army of lay people has to be trained to use it effectively. One might say that most Protestant instructional materials are planned too carefully with the result that the classroom teacher feels guilty if he does not follow the teacher's guide prepared by the experts. It is also characteristic of Protestant instructional materials to contain all kinds of teaching aids. Maps, filmstrips, records, tapes, flat pictures of biblical and contemporary topics, prints of art masterpieces, workbooks, and almost anything else that could be used to aid instruction is available.

Finally, all major Protestant denominations use what we might call a "nurturing" model of religious instruction. The reader has probably noticed, and perhaps was even surprised at, the broad general goals of the Cooperative Curriculum Project and of the Lutheran Church of America. These goals are typical of Protestant instructional programs. They take account of all the factors that go into a person's religious life, including commitment, motivation, and mental understanding. This "nurturing" model was formulated by Horace Bushnell in 1861, and his book *Christian Nurture* continues to have a strong influence on Protestant religious instruction.[18]

In the mid-1960's, this nurturing model came under attack from two sources. The first is from theologians such as Edward Farley, who in 1965 wrote two articles in *Religious Education* in which he attacked the nurture model on theological grounds.[19] Farley is not against Christian paideia. On the contrary, he views the family and the fellowship of the church as indispensable means of nurture. His point is that the classroom activities should not have a nurturing goal but an instructional goal. Farley's basic point is correct. We cannot—in the classroom—do all of the things necessary to nurture children in the faith. And we Protestants are in for a radical reorientation of our educational work when we see what Farley's point means. For example, we justify inexperienced and untrained

---

[18]Horace Bushnell, *Christian Nurture* (New York: Scribner, 1861).
[19]Edward Farley, "Does Christian Education Need the Holy Spirit?" in *Religious Education* 60 (September, 1965):339-347; and 60 (November, 1965):427-437.

teachers in our church school with the notion that their religious life is so fine that the children will "catch" the more important aspects of religion, such as devotion and faith, even if the intellectual work is substandard or the classroom is poorly managed.

The second source of attack on the nurturing model came indirectly. Ronald Goldman, an English professor of education, in 1964 published the result of his research on the cognitive development of children in relation to the kind of religious material that was being taught in the English schools. For over twenty-five years, all English schools have been required to teach a course in religion as an elective course, from a syllabus agreed on by the district school authority and religious leaders. Goldman tested children to see how much of the material they understood, and discovered that a lot of the material was misunderstood or was the source of confusion.[20] Goldman, following the work of Jean Piaget, has asserted that there are three stages of religious development: prereligious from about ages four to seven; subreligious from about ages eight to ten; and religious from about ages eleven to thirteen. Materials must be selected with the child's mental capacity in mind and this will rule out most biblical material until about the age of twelve. Goldman's proposition that we must grade material to fit the child has been widely accepted in America since about 1908, but it is the restricting of materials to those which the child's mind can handle rationally that presents the challenge to Protestant education today. Goldman, like Farley, does not deny the importance of parents or the congregational worship in nurturing the Christian life. He is simply affirming that the classroom should be devoted only to that type of material the child can understand.

A group of religious educators, under Goldman's supervision,

---

[20]Ronald J. Goldman, *Religious Thinking from Childhood to Adolescence* (New York: Humanities Press, 1964). See also *Readiness for Religion: A Basis for Developmental Religious Education* (London: Routledge and Kegan Paul, 1965).

have produced a curriculum based on his assumptions. Entitled "Readiness for Religion," their approach to the teaching task is like the American in that it starts with life. But there the similarity stops. American material is life-situational in that it deals with human relations, human problems, ethical decisions, and moral struggles within the self. Goldman's material starts with ideas, facts, information on contemporary events and then relates these to biblical ideas. For example, one unit of "Readiness for Religion" for junior schools is on "Light." It starts with the source of light, the sun, and then points out the effect of sunlight on the earth and how ancient man used sundials, and then moves the dicussion over to Greek mythology about the sun, and finally begins a discussion of the cosmology of Israel. Within this general setting a connection is made with candles used in worship and then a statement about Jesus being the light of the world.[21]

What effect the Farley and Goldman ideas will have, we cannot say. There is a good possibility that the new instructional materials of the United Presbyterian Church, scheduled to be ready for the Children's Division in 1970, will follow a more instructional than nurture model. This will be done by assuming that the congregation as the sponsor of a school is a dynamic, interacting group of people, building their life together around worship, recreation, and service activities. As such, the adults who shape and administer the church's total program establish and maintain a certain life-style that is communicated to the children in hundreds of informal ways. Moreover, these adults as parents are agents of a life-style in the home, the most powerful social organization we have for shaping attitudes and habits of conduct. For this reason the United Presbyterian Church is publishing its new material for adults first, along with a renewed effort to get the church to see that adult education is the key to the renewal of the

---

[21]William and Inga Bulman, *Light I: The Source of Light* (London: Rupert Hart-Davis, 1966).

church.

However, in the precommunicant ages, the United Presbyterian Church breaks with the standard Protestant instructional design at two points. First, they propose an instructional goal for the church school. This means a serious effort to use church school time for teaching. Their report to the General Assembly last year defined education "as a process in which teachers use various methods of instruction and a selection of relevant resource materials in order to assist students in learning and applying what they have learned."[22] Throughout their design they have emphasized teaching.

Second, they have broken with the almost universally accepted dictum that the lessons should have an objective that is related to the life situation of the child. Rather, they have said that the general goal of religious instruction is to produce adults who are "to participate meaningfully in worship and engage effectively in witness and service" in the world. The goal is not an immediate life situation to which a biblical allusion can be made. The goal is an adult who, after going through the educational program, has developed the following abilities: (1) the ability intelligently to interpret the bible as the unique medium through which God chooses to speak to men, thereby calling his people to active response in the worship and mission of the church in the present world; (2) the ability to understand the beliefs of the church in order to participate constructively in the community of faith through worship, service, and witness; (3) the ability to work for the unity and mission of the Christian Church; (4) the ability to understand the implications and risks of committing one's personal life—in occupation, home, and all other situations and pursuits—as an offering to God in response to his call to faithful service in Christ; (5) the ability to deal with ethical issues and to work toward the solution of contemporary per-

---

[22]*Christian Faith and Action: Designs for an Educational System* (Philadelphia: Board of Christian Education, The United Presbyterian Church, 1967), p. 9.

sonal and social problems.[23]

The characteristics of each age level are taken seriously, but they do not determine the educational enterprise; they only determine the specific outcomes a child is to learn in that stage of his development, outcomes on which can be built other learnings at a later stage of development which in turn lead adolescents to their fully developed abilities. For Protestants this approach represents a new way to set goals and a new way to honor the child's capacity to learn at different stages in the life cycle.

FUTURE TRENDS

This brief look at the new Presbyterian curriculum design, which will not be available for a few years, turns our attention to the future. What are some of the most significant trends in Protestant education that will characterize the 1970's?

First, the role of research in planning curricula is going to be greater. Back in 1959 I helped manage a meeting on research in religious education for the Division of Christian Education of the National Council of Churches. We could find only a few denominations that had anyone on their staff in research.[24] Today, almost every denomination has a department of research, sometimes with three or four highly trained leaders. Although research is carried on for many different problems within a Board of Christian Education, researchers give most of their time to problems related to the instructional program. The new Methodist material for example, carries inside the front cover this statement:

> This unit of study was first developed following extensive experimentation by 1,022 teachers in 255 different Methodist classrooms in 25 states. Further refinement was provided by "Project Feedback" with evaluative reports from 402 representative

---

[23]*Ibid.*, pp. 10-13.
[24]*Evaluation and Christian Education* (New York: Bureau of Research and Survey, National Council of the Churches of Christ, 1960).

churches and 8,032 teachers. Continuing research in evaluation is being carried on through the "National Sample" program of reports and several hundred computer-selected Methodist Churches.[25]

What the Methodists have stated so clearly is now an accepted fact of curriculum building. No major Protestant denomination will ever again formulate an instructional program costing three to four million dollars to design without a thorough testing of the materials. Moreover, this testing and evaluation will continue as the materials are used, in order both to eliminate the units that are not effective and to discover why good units of instruction are useful. But research is not restricted to simply testing and modifying the instructional program. Research is also being used more widely to discover what the child's religious concepts are, what religious problems he has at different age levels, and what effect different methods of instruction have in the educational process.

Second, the problems of education in the churches in the inner city will produce a new style of church education. Thus far in this chapter, I have been dealing with typical white, middle-class Protestant churches, but that image of instruction will not do for the black person living in the inner city.

There is no need to offer details about a situation that is well known to all of us. America is already an urban society. The issue that we face is the condition of the urban poor, usually gathered in residential pockets, often of a common racial or ethnic background. Inner city residents exist in crowded quarters, denied the most elementary public services of sanitation and police protection. Their hope of participating in the bounty of American economic prosperity or cultural life has either failed or disappeared. The American dream of rising to higher social status through self-help is almost unknown. Public education as the standard way to economic self-sufficiency and self-esteem is ineffective. Studies in New York City have shown that the longer a student stays in the public schools

---

[25]Bullock, *The Methodist Teacher.*

in ghetto areas, the further behind he becomes in reading and other basic intellectual skills. Such conditions are the breeding place of crime. *The New York Times* of January 29, 1968, revealed that one-third of all murder, rape, felonious assault, and robbery in New York City is committed in the three major ghetto areas. Crime is related to the use of drugs and alcohol, which are used to escape the frustrations of living in the ghetto. The social situation, compounded by a racial caste system, makes the educational ministry of the church in the ghetto seem weak and timid. Indeed, the church itself seems almost an anachronism in the modern inner city situation.

The Board of Education of the United Presbyterian Church commissioned Edward A. White, Charles Yerkes, and Gerald Klever to study for a three-year period the nature of the church's educational ministry in an urban setting. Their report, entitled *Education in the City Church,* is a brilliant analysis of the total social and religious situation.[26] The recommendation of this report about education would drastically affect our interpretation of religious education and our methods of training leaders for inner city situations. In brief, the main part of this report is as follows.

The inner city problem is primarily one of powerlessness, which breeds despair, emotional impotence, and helplessness. Lying, cheating, and stealing are normal ways of carrying on the battle for the elementary needs of food, shelter, and a little bit of spending money. The only way the church can get at this situation is to help "empower" the people of the slums.

A goal of "empowering" people is complicated and has many psychological and social dimensions. But at this point let us restrict ourselves to the way this goal required a different view of church education. The question becomes: "What can the church do to help these people achieve self-respect and under-

---

[26]Edward A. White, Charles Yerkes, and Gerald L. Klever, *Education in the City Church* (Philadelphia: Board of Christian Education, United Presbyterian Church, U.S.A., 1967).

standing of their world?" rather than, the restricted question of: "How can the church teach its beliefs?" These questions are not mutually exclusive, but the traditional answer to the latter question often rules out the former question.

The writers of this study see three major changes in church education that will be necessary to empower the poor. The first is a change in administrative structure. No congregation in an inner city situation has the resources for good education even if it tries to do no more than carry on a traditional program. Therefore, clusters of churches of various denominations or an area wide judicatory, such as the presbytery, will have to be the agency to formulate and administer the educational program. Second, teachers will have to be trained to make learning interesting and exciting, and it is proposed to supplement voluntary teachers with public school teachers who may want to have a "moonlight" job on Saturdays in the church school. But these teachers ought not to be trained in the usual way—they are to first become a community of teachers capable of starting their educational work without any preconceived formal curriculum. Third, the report deals with the intent and content of church education. The church must use all of its facilities and leadership to enrich the lives of inner city people, and particularly to offer children tutorial and counseling services. The content of education must connect with life as the boys and girls have experienced it. This means church education must contain a study of the history of the poor, how to make changes in living conditions and in Negro areas a study of the Negro heritage. Church education must bring to the surface and help people overcome the ideological structure that has been used to keep them powerless, such as the notion of racial superiority, equal opportunity, and the fiction that any individual can succeed if he tries hard enough. Moreover, the theory of objective tests, particularly IQ tests based on the verbal behavior of middle-class children, has to be explained and discussed. Few of these topics are now treated in a systematic fashion in our church school curriculum. Christian education, according to this approach "is a reeducation in power."

The 1970's will probably be the time when Protestants break up their long-established tradition of having one major pattern of religious instruction. There will be an increased recognition of the tragic life situation of the urban poor. Rather than trying to transplant the middle-class lessons into terms the poor can understand, the church will attempt to develop an instructional program that will take their plight seriously.

Third, the 1970's hold out the promise of genuine cooperation among Protestants and Roman Catholics in religious instruction. The split of 450 years ago seemed, up to the Second Vatican Council, to be a permanent division in Christendom, but the changes that have occurred in and between our churches in the last few years are nothing short of miraculous. And the end is not yet. The coordination of seminary training of Roman Catholics and Protestants is moving at a rapid rate. We may see the development in the 1970's of coordination of religious instruction in some of our communities. It is too early to predict, but it is not too early to note that when it comes down to classroom instruction Protestants have the same problems which Catholics have. Although much has been done to understand the teaching of religion to children at different age levels, a great deal is still unknown. Perhaps now is the time for Protestants and Catholics to pool our resources to do basic research in religious instruction so that each faith may develop a more effective program, pending that day when our differences will be less formidable and we are able to teach our common faith together as today we serve the same Lord.

8 Religious Instructional Materials

William B. Friend

Introduction

Teaching someone to learn of God, rather than simply *about* God recognizably involves more than mere memorization of doctrinal capsules or of nicely wrought polemical rationalizations. As Pierre Babin observed, the teaching of religion must help the student to experience Christ and his kingdom in such a way that an integrated understanding and appreciation of a relationship with God progressively takes form.[1] A student who is sensitive to the mystery connected with an active response to God opens himself to a process of discovery wherein he not only unfolds self, but also cultivates opportunities for interacting and interrelating with others. He follows the urge to grow and develop, and to become.

Gabriel Moran[2] and others have pointed out that earlier developments in the teaching of religion in this century have stressed either the product content matter of what is to be taught—thereby dissociating doctrine and life to a great extent —or have oversimplified the situation by attempting to reduce the directions for Christian formation to a methodological approach that worked to the frequent exclusion of the truths and the factual realities belonging to the object of faith. Today, it appears that there is need for researching and developing a new

---

[1] Pierre Babin, *Options* (New York: Herder and Herder, 1967), p. 173.
[2] Gabriel Moran, *Vision and Tactics* (New York: Herder and Herder, 1968), p. 158.

style of thinking as well as a way of communicating that will utilize the inner relationship of message and method. Moran calls this needed development a concern for "sophisticated methodological questions."[3] Put another way, what is needed is a process-oriented and a student-centered approach to the teaching of religion which will reflect the best in modern theological understanding of revelation. Emphasis is placed on process simply because therein is found the cluster of diverse procedures which surround the acquisition and utilization of knowledge. The highest form of content is that which is acquired and effectively translated into shaping behavior so that one can ultimately attain personal sanctification. From the works of educationists, such as Skinner, Bruner, Getzels, Suchman, Miller, Gagné, and Ausubel, stem proposals for self-directed learning, for the discovery method, for inquiry learning, for the reconstruction of concepts on one's own terms, for motivation, for distinctive conditions and cumulative learning, and for subsumption. Carl Rogers once observed that "the only kind of learning which significantly influences behavior is self-discovery or self-appropriated learning-truth that has been personally appropriated and assimilated in experience."[4] An individual learns at his own rate of speed according to his own particular style, and indeed may learn many things simultaneously.

The religion teacher who recognizes that learning is an active process more readily assumes the role of diagnostician, organizer, or manager of functionally varied learning experiences. No single process, experience, or medium appears to him as being sufficient for generating all the specific learning objectives, or for developing all desirable attitudes or appreciations. On the contrary, no single teacher can or should attempt to employ every instructional mode or medium; he advisedly

---

[3]*Ibid.*

[4]Carl Rogers, "Personal Thoughts on Teaching and Learning," *Improving College and University Teaching* 6, no. 1, Corvallis: Graduate School of Oregon State College (Winter, 1958):45.

selects the most appropriate available resource, plans for its effective utilization, and evaluates its efficiency and acceptance in terms of the kind, quality, and extent of learning desired.

FUNCTIONS OF INSTRUCTIONAL MATERIALS—MEDIA

From the beginning of the 1960's, instructional materials have come to be viewed in a different way. A change in research and reporting emphasis is evident, for example, from a comparison between the April, 1968, edition of the cyclical issue devoted to instructional materials of the *Review of Educational Research*[5] and its counterpart published in 1962. In the earlier edition, with James D. Finn and William H. Allen acting as cochairmen of the issue, principal consideration was given to theoretical formulations in audiovisual communications, textbooks, instructional television, language laboratories, self-teaching devices and program materials, and the administration of instructional materials. The 1968 publication evidenced a transfer to the problems-approach or the systems-approach to instruction. Chaired by Gerald Torkelson, this edition explored design and selection factors, utilization and management of learning resources, learner variables and educational media, and educational media as they relate to educational objectives. The central theme of the 1962 work was primarily concerned with the programming or comparative aspects of research, while in 1968 the *Review* considered different types of problems connected with integrating modern technology and the total learning environment. Today, one can often hear a warning to the effect that unless there is a wiser utilization of technology in education, each will go separate ways, and technology will advance far beyond present expectations to the detriment of education.

In the first section of his excellent book on the history of

---

[5]*Review of Educational Research* 38, no. 2, Special Issue, "Instructional Materials: Educational Media and Technology," Washington, D.C.: American Educational Research Association (April, 1968):186.

instructional technology, Paul Saettler identified two basic approaches or concepts associated with the materials for learning experiences. One he called the media concept or the physical science concept, and the other the behavioral science concept. The media concept, he said, "views the various media as aids to instruction and tends to be preoccupied with the effects of devices and procedures, rather than the differences of individual learners or with the selection of instructional content."[6] Indeed, this concept has generally been promoted by practitioners in the audiovisual movement and by the electronic media industry. The behavioral-science concept of instructional technology, on the other hand, states that educational practice should be more dependent on the methods developed by behavioral scientists in the broad areas of psychology, anthropology, sociology, and in the more specialized areas of learning, group dynamics, semantics, communication, administration, systems, perceptions, and psychometrics. This second approach is much more demanding and requires thoughtful consideration of educational goals and planning designs. The direct target for the behavioral scientist-educator is the learner, how to effectively reach him and bring him to experience the need for self-initiated change or advancement.

Educators advocating the systems approach consider instructional materials as an integral part of the teaching-learning experience, rather than as simply an adjunct to it. No longer called "aids," the materials for learning experiences are basic essentials for effective dynamic instruction—they become rightly viewed as means to an end and not an end in themselves. The systems approach to instruction includes the planned, validated selection of media, methods, equipment, facilities, and people used in performing activities to achieve the objectives of instruction. Such an approach also incorporates within itself the capability of providing continuous self-cor-

---

[6]Paul L. Saettler, *A History of Instructional Technology* (New York: McGraw-Hill, 1967), p. 399.

rection and improvement. Admittedly, this approach to instruction is broadly concerned with all elements of instruction, of which media are but one part. It is in this approach, however, that media are given due consideration and incorporated as a necessary part of instructional planning. The extreme opposite viewpoint suggests teachers just let matters existentially evolve and have unplanned, unstructured learning experiences occur through a chance happening.

Most of the current uses of the systems approach to instruction cluster around two different kinds of educational problems. John Pfeiffer observed that the first employs simulation and model building of the system in order to identify effects of alternate courses of action and facilitate decision-making.[7] The second type of systems approach strives to identify modes and media capable of satisfactorily instructing each student, and endeavors to generate a synergy of technology and teaching strategies in order to facilitate learning. It is the last type of systems approach that more directly relates to modern catechesis.

Curriculum designers and catechetical specialists who are confronted with the task of carefully reviewing educational modes and trends also have the sometimes overpowering charge of appraising a vast quantity of varied and often complicated media available in today's technological market. Moreover, religious educational processes are much more complicated than some of the other instructional areas; in religious education there is much less understanding of the component parts and variety of interactions between the divine and the human.

Presently in religious education circles there often abounds considerable emotion about media. Some who are devoted to the spread of new media claim learning outcomes far beyond the data reported by careful research. Defense of the traditional

---

[7]John Pfeiffer, *New Look at Education: Systems Analysis in Our Schools and Colleges* (New York: The Odyssey, 1968), p. 162.

media incorporating lecture, laboratory, and text also is voiced. Donald Tosti and John Ball observed that when the extant literature was examined from the standpoint of what is known about the learning process, "ineligible data, faulty generalizations from learning theory, and appeals to the emotions or artistic inclinations are apparent."[8] They see as the major fault in instructional design today the frequent failure to recognize the distinction between three separate design elements: the medium, the presentation form, and the content. The media in instructional systems, according to their observations, carry not only the data of the instructional message but also data on students' responses and various bits of information necessary to maintain the operation of the systems. It is the structure by which the information is carried that is called the presentation form. In their eyes a student does not learn from the media, he learns from the presentation form. Media do little more than deliver the information to be learned in whatever presentational form was previously decided upon. This point, while it may appear insignificant to some, especially to those who completely discount the behavioral view, is considered crucial because in current research there is often a failure to treat presentation variables. Sometimes such variables are confused with product content or they are categorized incorrectly. If the form of the presentation, for example, involves a lecture by a competent, personable, and dynamic teacher, the overall learning outcome may differ than if just the medium and product content were to be studied.

The observations presented by Tosti and Ball are in need of careful consideration by both the religion curriculum designer and by the teacher. For if it is true, as behavioral engineers claim, that by utilizing effective presentational design theory and known techniques for modifying behavior a technology can be developed to overcome most limitations of media, then

---

[8]Donald T. Tosti and John R. Ball, "A Behavioral Approach to Instructional Design and Media Selection," *AV Communication Review* 17, (Spring, 1969):6.

it is not so much the constant introduction of new media alone that will benefit education, but rather a sounder evaluation and utilization of the media currently available. To the typical religion teacher, this means that we should not wait for the magic medium that will supposedly solve all instructional problems, but rather, we should study intensively ways of effectively employing what is now available. Curriculum designers, for their part, ought not to be misled by the intrinsic advantages of the medium which can be often quite superficial to a learning task, but rather should look even more to the presentation in light of the specific goals of the instruction. Basically one must recognize that media have limitations; some occasions demand substitutes for the customarily expected media or require the introduction of additional media. Media have to be evaluated not in respect to their own functions alone, but more importantly in light of their capability and success in producing the desired learning outcomes. However, the selection of media and the definition of media limitation are not the only factors to be carefully investigated, for it is the effective presentation form that must also be ascertained. Likewise, it is equally important that the very concept of evaluation itself be more readily associated with the use of media and presentation.

SELECTED TRENDS AND NEEDS
ASSOCIATED WITH MEDIA

The current generation in America is the first in history to be reared on television. The frequently cited studies at Fordham University's department of communications indicate that the average young person today from birth to high school graduation experiences about 15,000 hours of television and views between 400 and 500 motion pictures—as compared to 12,000 hours of classroom work. While this observation is occasionally challenged, it is safe to say that children have considerable exposure to these media. As Paul Schreivogel commented, "we have to abstain from further alienating youth with outdated teaching methods. School learning ought to consist of analyzing and synthesizing things learned outside the classroom to enable the young to see themselves in the role of humanity."[9]

Perhaps our preoccupation with product content forced upon us by a linear, logical, visual, print technology, alienates many of us completely from the instant-message of the electronic environment. However, we may well discover that the straight-line theory of development, together with the logical and chronological uniformity it dictates, is out of touch with the needs of many young learners.

The Textbook

Henry Ruark contends that teachers often find themselves using media of all types in various combinations, seeking motivation and stimulation from one medium, special presentation of important data from another, and complementary content open to individual inquiry and development from still another. This is the practical beginning of the so-called "multi-media method," which can be defined as the functional utilization of more than one form of medium to accomplish a teaching-learning result.[10] The impact on teaching is thought by many media specialists to be especially strong today because some of the new media are identified as causing catalytic and synergistic effects when combined with good teaching strategies. In many learning situations involving the teaching of religion, the practical problems connected with time, finances, and adequate planning diminish the overall effect which could otherwise be realized from a well designed and executed utilization of creative combinations of media. The level of preparation and professionalization of the average catechist and religion teacher must also be regarded. Because of such limitations, most often the basic

[9]Paul A. Schreivogel, speech delivered at the meeting of the Division of Christian Education, National Council of Churches, Dallas, Texas, February, 1968.

[10]Henry C. Ruark, "Editorial," *Educational Screen and Audio-Visual Guide* 46 (October, 1967):21.

textbook and its supplementary materials will continue to have an important role to play in religious programs throughout the nation. Textbooks provide continuity and organization as well as an outlined and detailed sequence and developmental pattern around which other media can be woven to take their own significant role. The textbook can and often should remain as the basic tool for the student, unless well organized and designed handout material can be produced to replace it.

Presently religion textbooks are published by some fourteen firms in the United States. A review of all available textbooks reveals a wide variety in content, approaches, composition, strong points, and weak points. Textbooks are available for children from preschool age through the senior year in college. There are likewise textbooks for boys and girls enrolled in classes of the Confraternity of Christian Doctrine programs and special religious education programs. Supplementary printed materials are available in the form of homework books, weekly periodicals, paperback books, guides for parents of children in the lower elementary grades, and illustrated materials.

Besides the recent doctrinal developments and the psychological orientation woven into most of the new texts, an outstanding new characteristic of some series is their excellent art and composition, together with the emphasis placed on the utilization of the art medium as a tool for learning. In some textbook series, the art for children in the lower elementary grades is impressionistic rather than realistic, and is of the kind with which small children can easily identify. A gradual progression through types of art usually leads to the wide usage of photographs and symbols in the upper-level grades. In experiencing the lesson through pictures, a child is helped in learning to be aware and to observe, to categorize and to establish sets of priorities, to creatively execute and relate the world around him as he perceives it. Children in the upper-level elementary grades can develop a lesson which includes not only these functions, but also includes verbal and written explanations and reflections. Thus, a complete learning experience can be realized through the use of the medium of graphic art.

The Learning Activity Package

Another significant characteristic of some new textbook series is the inclusion of response sequences in the children's edition of the text series. Some of the response sequences are comparable to the "experience kits" referred to in professional literature; some strive to approximate the composition of the "learning activity package." While some of the so-called kits in religion are still in the primitive stages psychologically, they do inaugurate a trend which should prove to be significant in the future. It would appear that religion programs will continue to be influenced by developments in programmed and computer-assisted instruction.

Strictly defined, a learning activity package consists of learning materials which provide each student with a plan that includes a careful programming of a series of learning activities leading the student through different types of educational experiences most relevant to his interests and goals at any given time. In addition to a range of learning activities, the package includes a clearly defined rationale for the selection of the particular concept or major theme, a carefully selected range of behavioral goals, opportunities for student self-assessment, and teacher inventories.

Jan McNeil and James Smith, in describing the "multi's" at Florida's innovational Nova School, speak of the learning activity package as a broadly programmed set of materials that provide each student with alternatives of how, what, when, and where to learn while utilizing efficiently a whole range of learning measures.[11]

A typical learning activity package viewed in an ongoing

[11]Jan McNeil and James E. Smith, "The Multi's at Nova," *Educational Screen and Audio-Visual Guide* 47 (January, 1968):16-17.

process commonly would include a procedure wherein students work through a similar set of learning activities at the same pace and level, directed at all times by a teacher. Students would then be divided into groups for reading assignments, for viewing a film, for viewing filmstrips and slides, for listening to a recorded program, or for working directly with the teacher, either in small groups or individually. Such students would be required to produce a written assignment, a creative presentation, or a similar outcome before returning to the total group and meeting with the teacher.

McNeil and Smith reported that at Nova School students customarily meet with the teacher, have a discussion, proceed to visually oriented media, and continue to either listen to sound recordings, read, or conduct an experiment. Following these activities students summarize and creatively give their responses, and then meet with the teacher.[12]

At the present time, designers of programs for religious education are only beginning in terms of multi-sensory or multi-media programs to be used in conjunction with or without text-books or weekly periodicals. As religion textbooks begin to reflect more and more a trend toward making adaptations from programmed instruction textbooks with their methods of composition and programming, religious educators will be faced with the challenge of defining more specific instructional goals. In this connection catechetical specialists will begin to have a more serious concern for selectivity, for specificity, and for sequencing of learning materials and subject-matter content.

Catechists also will have to continue exercising the teaching function of harmonizing the goals of a prepackaged system and those of the particular group of students with whom they meet. As the level of sophistication in software design develops for each of the various available media, the catechist will face an ever increasing need to advance professionally in the study of identifying pupil strengths or deficiencies. An ever increasing

---

[12]*Ibid.*

concern, it seems, will be given to engineering the environmental factors involved in the teaching process. Utilization of various group patterns, settings, and activities will come to be recognized as not simply a device for occasionally upsetting the monotonous routine of a class, but will be recognized for its true pedagogical value.

As the trend toward miniaturization and simplicity in media hardware design continues, teacher attention will hopefully shift from an overconcern about the way audiovisual devices are operated toward the basic teaching-learning possibilities inherent with the equipment. As certain types of equipment and services become increasingly available, such as access information systems, teachers will merely afford students the opportunity to help initiate use of the system and concentrate on conditioning and working with them on other learning goals. Use of such traditional media as textbooks, therefore, will not be limited necessarily to the practice of utilizing them as readers, as in the past, but rather textbooks can become the resource manual, the program outline, designed for aiding the learner to know how to utilize other media and experiences more efficiently.

Some media available for use in the learning situation of formal classroom teaching are designed to present materials of a kind that would not otherwise be available to the student in the ordinary school experience. Educational films, television, various projection materials, sound recordings, and the like are the pedagogical tools by which the student is given a vicarious though direct experience of events or reality. Jerome Bruner points out it does not serve much to dismiss such materials as "merely for enrichment," since it is obvious such enrichment is one of the principal objectives of education.[13] Marshall McLuhan would emphasize such material is not necessarily an adjunct to the learning situation, but is actually that

---

[13]Jerome S. Bruner, *The Process of Education* (New York: Vintage, 1960), pp. xvi and 97.

which principally produces the vehicle for learning.

Connected with the use of such a method, there is a certain inherent flexibility which simultaneously can be controlled effectively by the teacher in the classroom. There can also be artful and effective combinations and designs for learning experiences which typically are based on available materials and local creativity.

The key to the selection of the appropriate instructional media to use in any particular teaching-learning situation lies in the relative effectiveness of that medium to accomplish the desired educational objective. William Allen found that little experimental evidence points the way for the making of such instructional decisions.[14] The task awaiting religious educators is that of orientation to the advantages and disadvantages in using each distinct type of medium, designed materials, and programs which will produce the desired learning outcomes, and developing an understanding about the interrelationship of content, medium, and presentation form.

The popularity and utilization of audiovisual apparatus will continue to increase as more understanding about their effectiveness for learning becomes known. Since all learning is rooted in sensation, there is obviously great pedagogical advantage to utilizing sensory experience materials. Researchers such as Henry Ruark have found audiovisuals provide concretized sense experiences that command attention and underline all true learning.[15] When functionally combined in a carefully planned and programmed presentation, such materials can and do stimulate motivation of the learner to the point that often a whole chain of learning activities is triggered into action.

The Motion Picture

Of all the advantages for using educational films as listed by

[14]William H. Allen, "Media Stimulus and Types of Learning," *Audiovisual Instruction* 12 (January, 1967):27-31.
[15]Ruark, "Editorial."

Edgar Dale in his classical work on audiovisual methods, perhaps the most important for the religious educator is that the use of motion pictures heightens reality for the viewers and creates the spatiotemporal experiences so frequently needed in religious educational programs, experiences which could not otherwise be produced in the ordinary learning center.[16] Until quite recently most educational films were considered for enrichment only; consequently, they were produced for that purpose. Such motion pictures were necessarily self-contained. Since the producer was uninformed of what his potential viewers had previously learned or what they would learn, he could neither build upon the learners' immediate past nor lay the groundwork for their immediate future. In recent years another kind of educational film has made an appearance in educational circles. Influenced a great deal by television programming, producers of educational films now tend to produce a film series embodying an entire course of study. Stephen White, for example, has produced a film for high school physics based on data furnished from those programs developed by the personnel of the Physical Science Study Committee (PSSC).[17] His film series were so designed as to further the presentation of the PSSC course as a whole. White observed that motion pictures fit into the complex of interacting agents, namely, the student and teacher, the textbook, laboratory experimentation, and classroom atmosphere. Further, he noted that the film series enhanced rather than disrupted the teaching-learning process.

It has been discovered that in evaluating programs such as the one mentioned above, motion pictures need to follow the textbook's developmental sequences, spirit, and vocabulary. More pedagogically effective films direct attention to those aspects of the subject matter that best stimulate classroom dis-

---

[16]Edgar Dale, *Audio-Visual Methods in Teaching* (New York: Holt, Rinehart & Winston, 1959), pp. 218-219.
[17]Stephen White, as cited in Bruner, *The Process of Education*, pp. 85-87.

cussion and fruitful responses from the learners. The more recently produced films sometimes contain response frames which call for students to employ a previously prepared cue sheet to indicate their immediate response to an experience or to an item of information which previously has been programmed in such a way as to require a student reaction.

Perhaps the most important contribution which films can make is the setting of level and tone to a learning situation. Motion pictures can direct attention to an important question or problem. They can help assure in some measure that all the great mass of factual information, concepts, theories, and applications that constitute any field of knowledge will fall into a coherent pattern in which the more important aspects will be clearly delineated from the less important. This, as Jerome Bruner has observed, "is most difficult to achieve with the printed word, yet on film it can be accomplished with a mere gesture."[18] A film's capacity to communicate feeling certainly places it rather importantly on the scale of affective learning experience.

Religion teachers now have a variety of films available for use in the religion class. While a number of the motion pictures are still representative of the traditional type of film-making and sometimes lacking in quality of production or content, there now exists a few films which have the "new look" and are of high quality. Since there is some research which indicates the advantages of films of brief length and in color, educational film-makers are tending toward eight millimeter films. New projection equipment facilitates the use of such a medium.

Some religious educators are presently experimenting with the showing of films which are not primarily intended for use in a religion class, but which communicate an example or model for students of religion to study. If such use of motion pictures is made in connection with carefully planned preparation and follow-up after the viewing of the film, effective

---

[18]Bruner, *The Process of Education.*

results undoubtedly can be realized. Extensive use of motion pictures of this type involves high rental costs to obtain the film and can fail miserably as a learning experience unless it is planned in accordance with clearly defined pedagogical objectives and related to other teaching techniques. Researchers point out that a protracted use of even the best teaching films, unrelated to other methods, can produce a great degree of passivity among learners.

When using an educational film, William Hockman advises that the teacher always keep specific educational objectives in mind in preparing readiness remarks for students viewing the film. Likewise, he advises teachers to carefully keep in mind what they will do immediately after the film is viewed so that learners will meaningfully transfer from one experience to the next. The actual readiness remarks should take cognizance of the characteristics and needs of the viewers. In addition, such teacher remarks should mention the reason for the film, include a few significant insights, comment on any difficulties or unusual circumstances, suggest responses, and call for applications.[19]

In commenting on the Yale Motion Picture Research Project, Mark May and his associates concluded that previous instruction on the content of the motion picture greatly increased pupil learning from the film.[20] This observation would seem to be in disagreement with comments made in the late 1960's by certain religious educators who dismiss entirely the need for preparing students who are to view a film as part of a learning experience.

While some religious educators today are employing films to a larger extent than ever before, it would appear efficient pedagogical use of such films has yet to be fully realized. Often there appears inadequate planning for the use of films and how

---

[19]William S. Hockman, "How to Introduce a Film," *Educational Screen and Audio-Visual Guide* 47 (June, 1968):20.

[20]Mark A. May, et al., *Learning From Films* (New Haven, Conn.: Yale University Press, 1958), pp. 115-122.

they relate to definite learning objectives. Moreover, some teachers fail to inform students what definite behavioral outcomes are expected from the lesson which utilizes the film medium. As a result, students are left to guess what they should attempt to learn from a particular presentation, and often have to wait until the viewing of the film has been completed before giving any response that can be adequately evaluated. Such unstructured learning experiences can bring confusion, passivity, and bewilderment to the learners.

The Filmstrip

Excellent filmstrips for the religion class are now readily available from a number of commercial producers. Any number of such filmstrips are accompanied by sound recordings and teacher's guides. Probably one of the most useful resources available to catechists at the present time is the excellent work edited by William Dalglish.[21] This work gives succinct yet excellent reviews of various types of media, provides an excellent subject index of evaluated materials and provides information as to media libraries and resource centers. Ratings are given from the Audio-Visual Resource Guide of the National Council of the Churches of Christ and the Media for Christian Formation, Glenmary Home Missioners. Film guides were provided through the cooperation of the National Center for Film Study and by William Kuhns. In this work over four hundred concepts or subjects are indexed and hundreds of filmstrip programs are to be found distributed under the various subject topics. Mary L. Allison has also published a work reviewing and evaluating educational materials for use with prekindergarten through grade twelve.[22] The two source books just mentioned provide catechists with excellent information concerning visual programs that might well be used in teaching

---

[21]William A. Dalglish, editor, *Media for Christian Formation* (Dayton, Ohio: Pflaum, 1969).

[22]Mary L. Allison, *New Educational Materials, Pre-Kindergarten Through Grade Twelve* (New York: Citation, 1967).

religion. Catalogues and reviews are obviously available from distributors. Professional journals in religious education and in general education provide a regular flow of information concerning newly published materials.

Some of the more recently developed filmstrip programs include built-in response frames which allow time for students to react to what has been presented, which call for him to write a response to that frame before the next one is presented, and finally, which continue through a self-correcting process to the next frame that gives the correct answer. The sequence continues on to present the next step or item of information. As can be noted, this type of filmstrip owes much to the automated tutor or teaching machine for its procedures.

Many visual presentations offer a great deal of factual data often enriched with feelings, which, if they are to be learned, must be responded to by students. Filmstrips readily allow for such responses since the teacher controls the rate of advancing the learning sequence, and can at the appropriate time introduce discussion, research activities, or other activities designed to build the proper responses in the learners.

Robert Bisson reports that there is a definite need for teacher procedures to control pupil responses in the learning setting. Often only the more articulate students respond; others remain silent. He maintains that pedagogical procedures for eliciting responses from each viewer should be developed in such a way that every viewer responds to every important item considered in the learning program. Bisson further maintains that the ordinary procedure should follow the pattern of stimulus, cue to the expected response, the response itself, and the correction of the response.[23] Teachers might find it helpful to write the response cue either on a chalkboard, on an overhead transparency, or use a cue sheet prepared prior to the time of class and upon which the students can write their responses. Like

[23]Robert Bisson, "Filmstrips and Active Responding," *Educational Technology* 8 (April, 1968):16-17.

other visual aids, the filmstrip provides experiences that learners could not otherwise have in a classroom. William Grindeland suggests that the use of filmstrips depicting scenes from the local community or some other highly localized milieu has a distinct advantage over commercially prepared programs.[24] Obviously the nature of the lesson would determine to a great deal the practicality of such a suggestion. Most professional visual media specialists hesitate to recommend such a procedure unless the filmstrips used are of exceptionally high production quality and are really relevant to the lesson.

The Overhead Projector

J. Lloyd Trump and Delmas Miller, among others, report that the overhead projector is probably the most widely used of the newer technical aids to teaching.[25] One fault common to religious educators employing this new medium is the hesitancy to utilize it in a way other than like a chalkboard. This is hardly an exciting addition to the teaching process. Rather than simply using the overhead for outlines, Trump and Miller recommend utilizing more symbolic materials to stimulate creativity, introducing different colors to emphasize ideas, and developing other imaginative approaches to augment pupil interest and make better learning opportunities available. Some commercially prepared transparencies for religion classes are already available from such sources as the 3M Company. More such programs will be developed as the consumer demand continues.

Television

Another medium reflecting new trends for program designers and teachers of religious education is television. Today, there are a number of television programs produced by various

[24]William I. Grindeland, "The Community Can Be Your Classroom," *Educational Screen and Audio-Visual Guide* 47 (March, 1968):26-27.
[25]J. Lloyd Trump and Delmas F. Miller, *Secondary School Curriculum Improvement: Proposals and Procedures* (Boston: Allyn & Bacon, 1968), pp. viii and 408.

agencies and organizations of the church. These are viewed by many persons in various cities. What appears needed in this programming is the coordination with other educational activities conducted by the church. For example, it seems that a series of instructional television programs on the sacramental life in the church would be much more profitable for everyone if it were to complement basic outline structures and product content contained in textbooks used in elementary and secondary school programs. Such a practice would reinforce learning which is already experienced or which is in the process of being experienced. While not necessarily presenting the same product content in a similar way, such programs would assist what is being done in schools and in C.C.D. Special programs in this medium seem very much needed for children. Preschool children, especially, could benefit from programs designed for them, since little is being done for them other than what parents are presently able to do. Parents and children could become involved in a learning experience at home. Undoubtedly the greatest advantage is the capability television has of getting into such a large number of homes and being warmly received. Only a few dioceses have found the resources of personnel and finances to develop their own closed-circuit educational television systems.

Basically there are two different forms of educational television. "Televised instruction" denotes a formal classroom lecture approach, while "instructional television" is a term used to describe a viewing of some scene, drama, event, or the like. Closed-circuit programming usually employs both methods or approaches.

Since most educational agencies interested in religion have limited budgets, the open-circuit and closed-circuit television production procedures always will present problems. However, there is an excellent opportunity for using videotape or kinescope as a medium for at least introducing teachers to self-development programs. This would appear to be more effective than the present practice of requiring noted theologians and educators to lecture in various places around the country. In such a practice, as is currently in vogue, not only is the energy of the specialist dissipated but only the few who enjoy ample resources (such as financial) are able to benefit. A series of videotapes, on the other hand, might serve somewhat the same purpose if not in quality of experience, at least in a more equitably distributed benefit to more learners. Console players for the videotape are becoming more reasonably priced and are easily operated.

It is not my purpose here to discuss all the advantages and disadvantages of employing television as a pedagogical tool. The vast majority of research investigations comparing educational television with conventional teaching reveal no statistically significant gains or losses in pupil learning as measured by standardized or typical teacher-made tests.[26] And for practical purposes, one has only to observe a small child who typically has viewed 4,000 hours of television prior to entering the first grade in school to note that he has very well received the messages of many of the commercials broadcast daily on television. Should not such a child also be able to learn something of Jesus from the same medium?

The Radio

Although radio has been in existence for many decades, there is known to be little work done with this medium for the religious education of children. To be sure, radio enjoys great popularity among children and youth, who can often be seen listening to a radio that is playing a decibel or so too high. Programs for adults and so-called general audiences are utilized by some religious denominations, but there appears little done specifically for the young Christian. Perhaps it has been supposed that programs for general radio audiences will of themselves attract young people as well. If this be the hypothesis, perhaps now is the time for reevaluation. Certainly there is

---

[26]See, for example, *Ibid*.

need for some type of general planning and coordination of efforts in using such a powerful medium as radio.

The Tape Recording

As magnetic tape recordings continue to be developed for programs in religion, definite guidelines will have to be developed for teachers. More than likely, a programmed learning approach will be utilized in such a teaching-learning strategy. Something more than simply listening to a lecture on tape will have to be developed if this medium is to reach its potential. The Argus Communications Corporation is doing excellent work in this area of media. Disc sound recordings, already widely used in conjunction with filmstrip programs and for the purpose of teaching liturgical music, will understandably broaden in usage as catechists learn to effectively use recordings from drama, English, or social studies to enrich a religion class and provide an example or model.

PRACTICAL PROBLEMS IN EMPLOYING VARIOUS INSTRUCTIONAL MEDIA

In his study on the use of media, Charles Streeter found that a teacher's competence in media and the subject he teaches are important variables affecting the frequency of using media.[27] Other studies substantially support this finding.

The utilization of various media in instruction requires a level of competencies described by John DiSanto as beyond those normally practical in the conventional classroom.[28] Involved in the process is the selection of appropriate media and methods, the preparation and construction of instructional materials, the operation of electronic equipment, the integration of materials and media for effective presentation, and the evaluation of

---

[27]Charles Edward Streeter, "A Study of Relationships Among Selected Factors Affecting Media Use by Classroom Teachers Within Selected School Systems," unpublished doctoral dissertation, Michigan State University, 1967.
[28]John D. DiSanto, "A Unique Coadunation," *Educational Screen and Audio-Visual Guide* 46 (October, 1967):22, 46.

multi-media presentations. The building of such competencies seems to be a top priority to be considered by contemporary religious educators. Administrators of religious instruction programs will have to seriously plan for such needs in the very near future.

In order to develop quality instructional materials for religious instruction, the recommendations of Louis Bright might well be considered here. He recommends that an inter-disciplinary team should consist of a subject matter expert, a media specialist, a programmed-instruction designer, and an experienced religion teacher. Such a team would undoubtedly not all be found in the ordinary school, but it might be made available on a consultative basis or as a service from the office of the chief school administrator.[29]

A few school systems have solved a great many of their problems with instructional materials by establishing instructional materials centers. While this may not be new to many areas of education, it is still absent from programs for religious education. The addition of a specialist in illustration and graphic material is often a welcome asset to such a center. Often religion teachers have need of visuals that fit the lesson plans or the local scene, and they would find the services of a specialist of immense assistance.

Catechists using various modes and media in instruction will still have the very important job of carrying on the diagnostic work customary to their routine task performance. While some of the work involved in this process might be handled through automated methods and with consultation of instructional team members, the final task of making judgments and recommendations concerning appropriate learning experiences for his students will be left to the individual religion teacher.

In the work religion teachers will do with individuals and groups, there will be a need of employing only the best in

[29]R. Louis Bright, "The Place of Technology in Educational Change," *Audiovisual Instruction* 12 (April, 1967):340-343.

educational psychology. Called upon as they will be to engage in group work, they will have to be both prepared and experienced in effective group dynamics. Cooperation too with professionals of both the educational team and those teams supporting educators will be a great demand on the teachers of the near future, even more so than at the present time.

Catechists will no longer be asked to spend their time distributing preinterpreted information or supervising lockstep drills; rather, they will be asked to help students learn how to learn so that once their students complete formal schooling they can go on learning more than they might have been taught.

In making assignments that will involve student reporting, religion teachers might well suggest to their students that they utilize various media in both researching and presenting the discoveries they will make.

Catholic school and C.C.D. libraries will have to expand their roles, however, if what is suggested in this chapter is to take place. Rather than simply emphasizing books and periodicals, these libraries will have to become expanded reservoirs of accessible photographic prints, projection and recorded materials, microfilm and microfiche, and eventually adequate information retrieval systems. Incorporated into all of this necessarily will have to be instructional and learning materials for religion, and these to a more realistic extent than is ordinarily found in most learning centers today.

All of this cannot be accomplished without adequate research and development. It is in this area that some of the major Catholic universities can be of immense service to the people of God. The challenge involved in designing and producing adequate educational programs for the new media will be one that will take a great amount of cooperation and coordination on the part of many professional teams. Those centers that have developed great advancements in studying mass communications media need to relate to those specializing in the area of directly connected instructional materials. And both of these areas will have to relate in more meaningful ways to theologians, to religion teachers, to psychologists, and to all other specialists for the common interest of effectively teaching children Christ and his kingdom. One of the major research areas still in need of further attention is that of value education. If there comes a wider usage of mass media for religious education, as is expected, then intensive study will have to be given to the analysis of values, the effective ways to teach values in light of various and diverse cultures and religions, the integration of values with various life styles and numerous other areas of vital interest.

Concern will continue over the needed production of media and modes of instruction for youth and adults of disadvantaged educational backgrounds. Special efforts will be particularly needed in this area for the next few years.

As serious objections continue to be advanced by the more conservative and extreme tradition-minded Catholics to the newer textbooks and materials, there will be more obviously evidenced the need for the proper interpretation of teaching emphases to parents and to members of the community at large.

While religious educators view the ever increasing complexity of their work they are to be reassured by the fact there are many more resources being assembled to assist them.

Hopefully, within a few years teachers will have a national resource center for securing information, media, and services designed to assist them to facilitate learning. A major accomplishment for religious education in the United States came when portions of the Vatican Library Collection and the Ambrosian Collection were microfilmed and placed in depositories at St. Louis University and the University of Notre Dame respectively. This has been only a beginning, however, and there remains a great deal yet to be accomplished along these lines. Not only is there needed a widespread dissemination of information concerning the availability and indexing of material available at such depositories, but there is needed additional services in religious education that will complement what has been undertaken at the Educational Research Information Center (ERIC). Indices of all materials should be made available and where practical, microfiche or microfilm service provided. This is quite a large order, to say the least. But if religious educators are to maintain their own professional growth, and encourage authenticity in research material, it appears that definite measures will have to be taken for providing more data at reasonable costs than is now available. Since the average religious education program cannot afford extensive investments in local resource centers, wide use of resources such as those just mentioned will serve as a solution. The Cunningham collection, possibly the largest single repository of research data on Catholic education and religious instruction in America, might serve as a useful model in this connection. This collection is sponsored by and housed at the Department of Graduate Studies in Education at the University of Notre Dame.

Once the church in the United States reawakens to her prophetic mission in the world and willingly employs adequate means to secure desired outcomes, then resources of personnel and technology will be employed in the work of religious education as has never before been witnessed in the history of man. The reservoir of technology and the sciences allied to the educational process await the invitation.

9 Research and Evaluation in Teaching Religion

David Elkind

Introduction

Research and evaluation in religious instruction is an enormous topic and one which can be approached from a number of different directions. Not all of the paths to the problem, however, have received equal commerce. While there is a long history of studies, which date back to Hall,[1] Preyer,[2] and Sully,[3] that deal with the content and product dimensions of religious growth and instruction there are, with but one or two exceptions, no studies that deal with the process of religious instruction.[4] We are thus in the peculiar position of having a variety of methods and instruments for assessing religious educational outcomes but almost no data on the process of religious instruction itself.

In view of this situation, I will not attempt in this chapter to review and evaluate the most recent and most sophisticated studies of the outcomes of religious instruction such as the

---

[1]G. Stanley Hall, *Adolescence II* (New York: Appleton, 1908).

[2]W. Preyer, *L'ame de l'enfant* (Paris: Ancienne Libraire Germer Baillere, 1887).

[3]James Sully, *Studies of Childhood* (New York: Appleton, 1903).

[4]André Godin, "Importance and Difficulty of Scientific Research in Religious Education: The Problem of the Criterion," in S. W. Cook, editor, *Review of Recent Research Bearing on Religious and Character Formation* (New York: Religious Education Association, 1962), pp. 166-174.

Notre Dame study[5] or the work of Erickson,[6] Goldman,[7] Johnstone,[8] and Greeley and Rossi.[9] While these studies have implications for religious instruction, they do not deal with the "how" of the educational process. Instead of covering these studies, what I intend to do is to draw upon and review the mistakes and successes of process research in secular education in order to suggest the most fruitful directions that might be taken by future research and evaluation in religious instruction.

In brief, the plan of this chapter is as follows: In the first section the process of instruction will be analyzed into its four major components, each of which will be described in somewhat general terms. Then, in the next section, the most recent research trends relative to each component will be reviewed with an eye towards the implications of this work for research and evaluation in religious instruction. A final concluding section will review and summarize the major points of the presentation.

THE COMPONENTS OF INSTRUCTION

When one looks at the history of research in education and psychology, the error which stands out most boldly is the tendency to approach the problems on much too broad and global a level and without sufficient analysis of the variables and factors involved in phenomena of investigation. The studies of the effects of nursery school instruction upon the child's IQ is a case in point. Literally hundreds of studies were done on this question but the results were so varied and contradictory that

---

[5]Reginald A. Neuwien, editor, *Catholic Schools in Action* (Notre Dame, Indiana: University of Notre Dame Press, 1966).

[6]Donald Erickson, "Religious Consequences of Public and Sectarian Schooling," *School Review* 72 (Spring, 1964):22-23.

[7]Ronald Goldman, *Religious Thinking from Childhood to Adolescence* (New York: Seabury Press, 1964).

[8]R. Johnstone, *The Effectiveness of Lutheran Elementary and Secondary Schools as Agencies of Christian Education* (St. Louis: Concordia Seminary, 1966).

[9]Andrew M. Greeley and Peter H. Rossi, *The Education of Catholic Americans* (Chicago: Aldine, 1966).

the only valid conclusion one could reach was that the effect of nursery school education depends upon a great many other factors including the nature of the school, the background of the children and so on. As a consequence of such fruitless endeavors, the course of research has been toward progressively more circumscribed and more answerable questions. Current research on nursery school education is concerned with the effects of specific types of instruction upon specific types of academic skills.

Although it is impossible to avoid the problem of globality in research in a new area, we can profit nevertheless from the history of educational and psychological research by attempting to analyze in as great a detail as we can the phenomena that we want to investigate. Such an analysis must of necessity be preliminary and subject to continual revision and refinement. With this reservation in mind, I want to suggest that within any instructional enterprise one can distinguish at least four major components: the agency, the agent, the media, and the object of instruction. Let us consider each of these components in a little more detail.

The Agency of Instruction

By an agency of instruction, I mean any social institution or organization which has as one of its major functions the dissemination of information. According to this definition, the school, the family, the church, and the mass media of television, radio, and cinema are all agencies of instruction. There are, in addition, less formal agencies of instruction such as the peer group, boy scouts, church groups, and so on. Obviously, these agencies differ in their orientation towards, and commitment to, instruction as well as in the types of instruction and kind of information they are concerned with disseminating.

There is, moreover, considerable overlapping in the instructional activities engaged in by these agencies. The family supplements the instructional activities of the school and church, while the peer group often supplements the instruction provided in the family. The mass media in turn reinforce the instructional activities of family, school, church, and peer group. While such complementarity of functioning may be beneficial from an instructional point of view, it poses serious problems for the research investigator. In such a situation, the instructional effects of any agency are inevitably confounded in inextricable ways with the effects of every other agency so that it becomes next to impossible to trace the effects of any agency in particular.

It is this confounding which makes the results of survey research on the effects of parochial school attendance upon religious practices and belief so ambiguous. Is it the instructional practices of the school which accounts for the increased religiosity of such children, or is it the fact that they come from religious homes, or that they have peers more interested in religion, or that they are more attuned to mass media communications dealing with religion? As empirical research in this area stands now, there is little possibility of disentangling the threads of causation and correlation in these investigations.

The Agent of Instruction

In speaking of the agent of instruction, I have in mind the particular individuals who staff the agencies. An agent can be a teacher, a parent, a TV broadcaster, the author of a book, or a member of the peer group. It must be emphasized that the term "agent" refers to a role which an individual may play under certain circumstances and that it is not a fixed attribute of the individual. The teacher is an agent in the classroom but not necessarily at her bridge club or while attending a concert. In short, a person is an agent of instruction only at those times when he or she takes on the mantle of a teacher or purveyor of information.

Just as there is overlapping of functions among the various agencies of instruction, so is there a similar overlapping among the agents of instruction. There is, in addition, the consideration that a particular individual may be an agent of instruction under some circumstances and an object of instruction under other circumstances. The teacher who attends graduate courses at night to attain additional academic credit is a case in point, as is the child who instructs his peers in the rules of the game which he in turn has learned from his parents.

The efficacy of any particular agent as a purveyor of information will depend upon a host of different factors. It will depend upon the authority of the agency for which the agent works or which she represents; upon the agent's personality, intelligence, and style; and upon the particular materials and conditions under which she must work. Even the most skilled teacher working in a dark and colorless room with few instructional aids will have a harder time of it than a teacher operating in more favorable circumstances. The teacher's effectiveness will also depend upon the congruence between her own personality and the personalities of the subject she is to teach, as well as her understanding of her students' strengths and weaknesses as learners. The assessment of the efficacy of a particular teacher is thus an extremely complex but not an insurmountable task.

The Media of Instruction

In speaking of the media of instruction, I have in mind all of the paraphernalia utilized by agents in their efforts at instruction. Media include such things as verbal instructions and illustrations, pictures, books, excursions and sight-seeing trips, as well as the technical aids of television, rearview projectors, tape recorders, and similar apparatus. The designation of particular materials as instructional media does not mean that they need be entirely instructional. Indeed, the most effective media are often just those which are entertaining as well as instructional. Furthermore, instructional media may be formal as in the case of the curriculum materials prepared especially for training in particular subject matter or informal as in the case of the fish tank or "ant city" brought into the classroom by an enterprising teacher.

As in the case of instructional agents, the efficacy of particular instructional media will depend upon a variety of different factors. It will vary with the intrinsic interest value of the materials and with their appropriateness for the subjects toward whom they are directed. Likewise, the efficacy of the materials will vary with the skill and expertness of the agent who employs them. Even the most elaborate and interesting media may lose their effectiveness if employed clumsily or inappropriately by the instructional agent. Accordingly, while the nature of instructional media is important, its effectiveness can be ascertained only within the total context of the instructional enterprise.

The Subject of Instruction

Within the purview of the present discussion, the object of instruction is the individual toward whom the activities of the instructional agency and agent are directed and for whom the instructional media have been created. Children are the predominant objects of instruction, but it must be remembered that, as in the case of the agent of instruction, the term object of instruction refers to a role which an individual plays at certain times. Just as the agent of instruction can become an object of instruction, so can the reverse hold true. The child who, on returning from school, commences to teach his younger brother the alphabet has in those moments taken over the role of the agent of instruction. In such circumstances, in fact, the child is both agent and object since he often learns a good deal through his attempts at teaching. Likewise, the child can become an agent of his own instruction when, for example, he goes to the dictionary to look up words and thus to acquire information on his own.

The extent to which the object of instruction will acquire

what he is taught will depend not only upon the agencies, agents, and media to which he is exposed but also upon his own level of intellectual development, his motivation for learning, and his personality. What the object of instruction will learn will depend also upon his individual style of learning and upon the previous experiences he has had with instruction of various kinds. In short, the end product of the instructional enterprise, what the object of instruction actually acquires, must of necessity have been filtered through the sieves of instructional agencies, agents, media, and the subject himself, each of which progressively modifies the content of instruction and adds its unique coloration to the instructional product.

I hope I will be excused for this somewhat tedious recitation of the components of instruction, but I do believe it is important and necessary not only to distinguish among these components but also to underline their complexity. While this analysis of the instructional enterprise has been less than fine-grained, it nonetheless reveals the difficulties of attributing the products of education to any particular component. There can be no sidestepping or blinking at these components and their complexity if we wish not only to assess the effects of religious instruction but also to improve the process of instruction. In science the most difficult problem is always that of finding and asking the right questions and in such a manner that they can be put to test. It is in this spirit, the spirit of providing a context for finding meaningful questions, that the foregoing analysis was presented.

In the next section each of these components will be discussed with respect to some of the current psychological and educational research regarding their role in the process of instruction. Wherever possible I will try to draw the implications for religious instruction.

NEW LIGHT ON THE COMPONENTS OF INSTRUCTION

The Agency

Many of the recent innovations in instruction in general education have been made at the level of the agency of instruction. Reducing the size of the classroom, the utilization of team teaching, and the formation of ungraded classrooms are all attempts to affect instruction through the organization of the instructional agency. While the effects of these manipulations have still to be evaluated thoroughly, they are procedures which could be adapted to religious instruction and their efficacy assessed in this domain.

There are, of course, very practical problems in adapting such procedures to religious instruction. Within Catholic parochial schools, which are hard-pressed for classroom space and qualified teachers, reduction in the size of the classroom may be a practical impossibility, particularly if one adheres to the principle of "Every child in a Catholic School." In a like manner, the Protestant Sunday school may not have the child for a long enough period of time to make team teaching or ungraded classrooms a worthwhile procedure. In principle, however, even in the Sunday school it might be possible to group children according to their level of proficiency in bible studies rather than with respect to age. Hopefully, the effects of such a procedure would be compared with those obtained from children receiving instruction in graded classrooms.

Another recent innovation in classroom organization has to do with the establishment of "interest areas." In the "World of Inquiry School" in Rochester, New York, for example, each classroom has a science area, an arts area, and a stage for dramatic activities. In addition to the routine group work within the classroom, children can sign up for science, art, and library work during the day and can go on their own to those areas. The value of this arrangement seems to lie in that it permits the child to follow his own spontaneous interests for an uninterrupted period of time.

Allowing the child to engage in activities for as long as he wishes would seem to have significant educational benefits. We have all experienced that exultation which comes from total engrossment in some activity and during which we forget about meals, television programs, and rest. These are often the periods of our most productive and creative endeavors. Too often in the school setting, however, a child is torn away from an activity in which he is totally engaged because it is time to take up another subject. It is not surprising that under such conditions many children soon lose their zest for learning and consider school a bore. They are unwilling to invest in an activity because they do not want to experience the pain of giving it up in the middle. In this regard they are like children who have been shifted from one foster home to another and who will not allow themselves to become attached to foster parents in order not to be hurt when they are again separated. Such children have been called "emotionally burned" in metaphorical comparison to the child who avoids the fire because he has been burned by it. I am afraid that not infrequently we produce "intellectually burned" children who fear becoming totally involved in an intellectual activity.

To be sure, not all children thrive under the relatively free and unstructured atmosphere of the "interest area" arrangement. Some children need a great deal of structure and are lost without it. For these children the traditional classroom arrangement with its regularly scheduled activities, twenty minutes for reading, twenty minutes for spelling, and so on, provides a needed sense of stability in their lives. When introducing innovations in classroom organization, then, it is important not to ignore individual differences and the fact that for some children the innovations in question may pose a very real threat. This is but another way of saying that the efficacy of any innovation in the instructional agency is always relative to the needs and abilities of the particular child.

The Agent of Instruction

The problem of the teacher in religious instruction often has been discussed. Within the Catholic parochial schools, the

presence of both lay teachers and religious makes for a hetero-
geneity of outlook and background that is perhaps far wider
than is true for the faculty of a public school. The effects of
having both types of instructor within the same school has
yet to be evaluated. Within the Protestant Sunday school, the
problem is of a somewhat different order. For the most part,
teachers in the Sunday school are volunteers who may have had
little or no formal or practical training in education. While
persons without formal training are by nature sometimes gifted
teachers, this tends to be the exception rather than the rule, and
it is difficult to control the quality of instruction. Similar problems are faced by the Jewish parochial and weekday afternoon
schools.

Within public education the role of the teacher is coming
under increasing scrutiny not so much from the standpoint of
her teaching skills as from the perspective of her behavior as a
person. In addition, the quality of the teacher-learner interaction as a factor in learning also is being investigated. It may
well turn out, in fact, that person-variables are more important
in determining the teacher's effectiveness than the extent to
which she conforms to some abstract ideal of a skilled instructor. The teaching process, it is now recognized, is never a one-
way street, and the teacher often gets as much as she gives in
the way of warmth and need satisfactions. Let us look at some
of the research in this area which may be relevant to the
teacher in religious education.

To illustrate the intricacies of the teacher-as-person variables
in interaction with her pupils a study by Heil, Powell, and
Feifer is instructive.[10] The study was done with elementary
school children and teachers. The teachers were categorized as
either *turbulent* (outspoken and objective in evaluation, and
status-striving) or *self-controlling* (practical, dominant, orderly,

---

[10]L. M. Heil, M. Powell, and I. Feifer, *Characteristics of Teacher Be-
havior and Competency Related to the Achievement of Different Kinds of
Children in Several Elementary Grades* (New York: Office of Testing and
Research, Brooklyn College, 1960), mimeographed.

and dependent upon authorities) or *fearful* (plagued with anxiety resulting from fear, and who are nurturant). Students, in contrast, were labelled as *conformers* (high in social orientation, strict control of impulses, emphasis on mature behavior) or *opposers* (pessimistic, intolerant of ambiguity, disappointed, and frustrated in self, in others, and in objects) or as *waverers* (anxious, ambivalent, fearful, floundering, and indecisive) or as *strivers* (striving for recognition relative to school achievement, and exhibitionistic).

When the achievement test results of the children in these various categories were compared with the teachers under whom they had been instructed, the following results were observed: Self-controlling teachers (those who were practical, orderly, and dominant) produced the greatest amount of achievement in their students regardless of student type. Turbulent teachers had almost as much success as self-controlled teachers with youngsters classed as conformers or strivers but not with children classed as opposers and waverers. Finally, the fearful teacher was as effective with children classed as strivers as the other two teachers but was less successful than the others with children grouped in the other categories. These results are of interest because they suggest that while some children—the strivers—will achieve under a variety of teacher regimes, other types of children will respond differentially to the teacher-as-a-person.

Other studies have shown similar relationships between dimensions of teacher personality and school achievement. Active classroom participation on the part of children, for example, has been shown to be related to the amount of flexibility, originality, and democracy exhibited by the teacher.[11] In a like vein, the authors of a study on the effects of teacher personality upon classroom interaction concluded that: "A teacher must, in short, care; must not have this concern blocked by her in-

---

[11]David G. Ryans, *Characteristics of Teachers* (Washington: American Council on Education, 1960).

terpersonal tensions; and must be relatively free of distorting mechanics and be able to enter honestly into relations with others which facilitate skillful interpersonal relations with students."[12]

Still other studies can be cited. Flanders[13] explored the interaction between teacher and pupil behavior with the aid of Withall's[14] distinction between learner-centered versus teacher-centered behaviors on the part of the instructor. The major findings were as follows: (1) teacher behavior, described as directive, demanding, and deprecating, elicits hostility toward self or toward the teacher and produces withdrawal, apathy, aggressiveness, and even emotional disintegration upon the part of the pupil, and (2) teacher behavior, described as supportive, elicits problem orientation, decreased interpersonal anxiety, integration, and even emotional adjustment on the part of the pupil.

Additional studies could be mentioned, but these should suffice—even acknowledging their methodological limitations—to suggest the importance of the teacher-as-a-person and the quality of teacher-learner interaction upon the student's achievement and upon adjustment within the classroom. Similar relations most surely would be found in parochial and Sunday schools. Such relations are, moreover, particularly important in religious instruction. The child's feelings towards the teacher are necessarily comingled with his feelings towards the subject matter which she teaches. How much of the child's religious feeling is colored by the personality of the agent who instructs him in this domain? We do not know. But it certainly would be of interest and importance to study, within the context of re-

---

[12]Norman D. Bowers and Robert S. Soar, "The Influence of Teacher Personality on Classroom Interaction," in *Journal of Experimental Education* 30 (June, 1962):309-311.

[13]Ned A. Flanders, "Personal Social Anxiety as a Factor in Experimental Learning Situations," in *Journal of Educational Research* 45 (September, 1961):100-110.

[14]John Withall, "An Objective Measurement of Teachers Classroom Interactions," in *Journal of Educational Psychology* 47 (April, 1956): 203-212.

ligious instruction, the effects of the teacher's personality upon the religious knowledge, attitudes, feelings, and behavior of her pupils. The results of such studies would not be simply negative in providing criteria for screening teachers but could also be positive if they were used in training teachers to exhibit the kinds of behavior most likely to induce pupil cooperation and achievement.

Not only the teacher's personality but also her expectations with respect to her pupils will influence children's achievement. In a recent study by Rosenthal and Jacobsen,[15] teachers were told the IQ scores of their pupils. These IQ's, however, were false and did not really represent the true abilities of the children. At the end of the semester, children whom the teacher assumed were better than average in intellectual ability had gained an average of ten IQ points whereas children whom the teacher believed were average or below average in intellectual ability made no such gains. In short, how the child is labelled may determine the teacher's expectations and her behaviors towards the child, which in turn may affect his achievement. What is mystifying about all of this is that the teacher is unaware that she is behaving differently towards some children, and even objective observers are hard put to specify the mechanisms by which the teacher differentially encourages or inhibits her pupils.

I have had a personal experience which adds weight to the evidence which indicates the importance of the teacher's expectancy upon her evaluation of teacher behavior. Several years ago, I spent a week at the Mission School, which is run by Jesuits, on the Sioux reservation at Pine Ridge, South Dakota. One of the teaching priests asked me to attend his class because he knew I was interested in reading problems, and he felt he had a great number of them among his students.

---

[15]Robert Rosenthal and Lenore Jacobsen, "Teachers' Expectancies: Determinants of Pupils' IQ Gains," in *Psychological Reports* 19 (August, 1966):115-118.

When I sat in the class and heard the young people read, I was amazed at how good they were. Compared to the inner city youngsters with whom I had been working, these adolescents read like angels. The priest, however, had just come from teaching at a prep school in the East, and compared to the youngsters he had taught there, the Indian children were doing poorly indeed. The significance of this experience, or so it seems to me, is not so much in the fact that the priest and I had set up different standards on the basis of our previous teaching experience but, rather, that we had set up expectancies as to how all children should behave, based on those standards. How such expectancies color our evaluations and affect our teaching is a very ripe area for investigation in both secular and religious instruction.

In summary, then, the effects of the teacher-as-a-person, her warmth, style, and expectations with regard to her pupils probably play a very important part in determining the extent and quality of educational outcomes. The effect of the teacher-as-a-person variables in religious education must be at least as great as it is in secular education. Certainly one of the most important directions which future research and evaluation in religious instruction must take is towards the study of the effects of the teacher-as-a-person upon the cognitive and affective achievements of her students.

The Medium

Both within the secular and religious spheres, the most active efforts for change in education have come in the domain of instructional media. This is, after all, not surprising. It is the one component in the process of instruction which is easiest to manipulate and control. While it is hard to reorganize classrooms and modify teachers as people, it is relatively easy to revise textbooks and curriculum materials. While curriculum revision and new instructional aids are frequently of value, much of that value is often lost because the other components of the instructional process are ignored or paid slight heed. It often happens, for example, that curricular and technological innovations in education are far in advance of the teacher's readiness or preparation for such innovation. In actual practice new curricula often are bypassed or sabotaged, and new equipment and machines frequently lie quietly gathering dust and rust in supply closets in schools all over the country.

It is not possible and probably unnecessary to review the innovations in hardware that have come upon the educational science over the past few years. Their relevance for religious education will depend in part upon the availability of funds for their purchase and upon the availability of persons who can program religious materials. Furthermore, I am not convinced that programmed instruction is every child's cup of tea nor that it may not have negative consequences. One of the most important characteristics of human thought is that it often arrives at solutions by indirect and novel means. It is at least possible that programmed instruction can overchannel the child's thought and remove that flexibility and spontaneity which differentiates between what the mind can do from what can be accomplished by a computer. Programmed instruction may well be appropriate for some children and for some kinds of material, but it is far from being the panacea for all of our educational ills.

Far more exciting than the new hardware, at least in my opinion, is the work on curriculum revision currently being undertaken in the field of science and social science. What is exciting about these curriculum revisions is that for the first time educators genuinely are trying to gear the materials and the instruction to the thinking of the child. Thanks largely to the work of Piaget and his colleagues, we now have a general picture of intellectual growth which maps out the child's assets and liabilities at different age levels. This information has been invaluable not only in providing a basis for ordering the presentation of the materials at different grade levels but also in alerting us to the kinds of difficulties children may encounter in dealing with them.

Similar curriculum work is now also being undertaken in the religious sphere and often with the same emphasis of fitting the instructional materials to the mind of the child. The work of Goldman[16] and my own investigations[17] have provided evidence that Piaget's stages have relevance for the understanding of religious concepts and materials. There is, then, an empirical basis for assuming that religious materials can be graded meaningfully with respect to the child's level of mental development.

Constructing new curricular materials in conformance with our knowledge of mental growth is not, however, a particularly easy task. For the past couple of years, I have been working with the Presbyterian Church in the writing of new texts for the elementary, intermediate, and high school age groups. We have gone over not only the content of the texts but also the various devices to be used in the process of instruction. In each case we have been guided by the characteristic needs and interests of the particular age period as well as by the modes of thinking and learning which current research suggests holds true for the different age periods.

One of the big problems we encountered was the selection and placement within the curriculum of the various biblical materials: Which bible stories should be taught, and should they be presented in their entirety, or should only those parts be included which the children would be able to understand? We came into conflict here with the theologians who argued that particular stories, such as that of Jonah, had to be presented whole if their religious significance were to be retained. The teachers, on the other hand, were concerned that latter

[16]Goldman, *Religious Thinking from Childhood to Adolescence.*

[17]David Elkind, "The Child's Conception of His Religious Denomination I: The Jewish Child," in *Journal of Genetic Psychology* 99 (December, 1961):209-225; David Elkind, "The Child's Conception of His Religious Denomination II: The Catholic Child," in *Journal of Genetic Psychology* 101 (September, 1962):185-193; David Elkind, "The Child's Conception of His Religious Denomination III: The Protestant Child" in *Journal of Genetic Psychology* 103 (December, 1963):291-304; D. Long, David Elkind, and B. Spilka, "The Child's Conception of Prayer," in *Journal for the Scientific Study of Religion* 6 (1967):101-109.

sections of the Jonah story, which contain the metaphor of the worm and the gourd, would not be understood by the children who could still appreciate the early part of the tale. In truth, of course, there was speculation on both sides because there was no real empirical data for either position. Such questions are of considerable importance in religious instruction and are the sort of queries for which research and evaluation into religious education could provide meaningful answers. If research into such questions seems too circumscribed, perhaps it is well to recall that studies of much broader issues frequently produce highly ambiguous results. And, it should not be forgotten, studies of smaller issues frequently have implications for larger questions.

The preparation of curricular materials was, however, but one part of our task. We also had to prepare teacher manuals which would instruct teachers in the use of the new materials. Instructional materials for teachers are as important and present as many problems as the preparation of materials for children. In some ways the problems were even more complex. It seemed that the writers and theologians involved in constructing the materials were less traditional in their views than many of the congregations and teachers for whom they were writing. It was thus necessary to take the teacher's theological position into account. Since many of the teachers probably will not have had any formal training in education, it was also necessary to go into detail with respect to teaching techniques. My own role was to provide general descriptions of mental development which would provide teachers with a better understanding of the subjects with whom they would be working. Here again, the usefulness of the teacher handbooks is based upon our a priori assumptions about what teachers need and want to know. Research and evaluation in this domain might be very useful, indeed, in improving the teacher's effectiveness with the new curricular materials.

There are, then, a great many problems within religious

curriculum development which could be profitably researched. I am well aware that funds and personnel for such research in religious education are not always available, or available in insufficient quantity to do the job as well as it needs to be done. Nonetheless, considering the amount of money that has been spent upon large-scale survey research, I wonder whether some funds might not be directed toward more specific and practical questions regarding the educational process, such as those raised above. My guess is that the results of such studies would be more useful and less equivocal than the large-scale studies. I do not mean to imply that large-scale survey studies should be discontinued but rather to suggest that there are other directions which research in religious education profitably might take.

The Subject

Some of the most exciting changes in psychology and in education over the past decade have occurred in the conceptions of the learner and of the learning process. Psychologists are at last beginning to break out of the bonds of a rigid behaviorism which for so long tied them to a limited and restricted view of the human learner. In this section I want to describe some of the changes which have taken place and what seem to me to be the implications of these changes for the process of religious instruction and for research and evaluation of this process.

One of the changes that have come about in our conception of the learner derives from the work of Piaget, and from investigations such as White,[18] Berlyne,[19] and Hunt,[20] all of whom have postulated that the child, as well as the adult, has needs and desires to learn, which cannot be reduced to such motives as

---

[18]Robert W. White, "Motivation Reconsidered: The Concept of Competence," in *Psychological Review,* 46 (1959):297-333.

[19]Daniel E. Berlyne, *Structure and Direction in Thinking* (New York: Wiley, 1965).

[20]Joseph McV. Hunt, *Intelligence and Experience* (New York: Ronald, 1961).

hunger, thirst, and sex. It is hard to overemphasize the significance of this point since we, at least in psychology, are so accustomed to thinking of rewards and punishments as the prime movers of learning. What this new conception says is that the child finds learning pleasurable in itself and that if we play our cards right, that is to say, if we select the appropriate materials and modes of instruction, then children will learn without the promise of rewards or the threat of punishment. What we are beginning to understand, if not to apply, is the idea that the progressive disinterest and dislike of schooling so common in children as they move up in the grades is a failure of our teaching and not an inevitable consequence of a built-in resistance to learning.

Another change in our conception of the learner has come about as a result of psychology and education's new involvement with the inner city and with the disadvantaged child. Up until a decade ago, child psychology was really the psychology of the middle-class child. Once we became acquainted with disadvantaged children it was immediately obvious how inadequate and narrow were our traditional ideas about childhood. Experience with inner city children has forced us to revise one of our cherished conceptions, namely, that of *readiness*. In dealing with middle-class children, it seemed clear that these youngsters were developing at a maximum rate and that there was no value in pressuring them to go faster and further than they had gone on their own. Readiness for academic instruction was thought to be a spontaneous unfolding which each child experienced in his own way and at his own pace. What we did not recognize was that this readiness was in fact the product of considerable instruction at home and which Strodtbeck[21] has called the "hidden curriculum" of the middle-class home. The highly verbal, achievement-oriented, considerably socialized youngster, which

---

[21]Fred L. Strodtbeck, "The Hidden Curriculum of the Middle Class Home," in H. Passow, Miriam Goldberg, and E. J. Tannenbaum, editors, *Education of the Disadvantaged* (New York: Holt, Rinehart & Winston, 1967), pp. 244-259.

is the norm for the middle-class five-year old, is not, we now appreciate, the spontaneous outgrowth of "unfolding from within," but rather the product of five years of intensive and extensive instruction and socialization on the part of his parents.

This becomes obvious when we deal with disadvantaged children who frequently come from homes where there is no father, in which the mother works, and in which the oldest children often bear the responsibility for the younger children. Such children are frequently far below middle-class children in language skills, in perceptual ability and in social control, while at the same time far more advanced than middle-class children in the mature understanding of the harsh facts of existence. The most striking thing about disadvantaged children, in my experience, is their tremendous needfulness. It is not because they are unloved at home that they are needful, but rather because even at four and five they sense their second-rate citizenship. They are tremendously needful of acceptance and recognition to bolster the injury to their pride and self-esteem which comes from bearing the stigma of being a Negro. After working with these children we can never again regard readiness as a spontaneous unfolding from within which is uninfluenced by the reality in which the child is reared.

Still another change in our thinking about the child as a learner is due largely to the work of Hunt[22] who has marshalled impressive evidence against the notion of fixed intelligence. Whereas, heretofore, intelligence was regarded as a relatively fixed and unalterable characteristic of the individual, Hunt has shown how often the IQ can be modified to a considerable extent by experience. Here again we have been trapped by our focus upon the middle-class child. Among middle-class children, who have had every opportunity to realize their intellectual potential to the full, the IQ does tend to remain relatively stable. Heredity still sets limits for intellectual growth; that much is undeniable. But for children who have grown up in less than

---

[22]Hunt, *Intelligence and Experience.*

an optimal environment, the limits of this potential are far from having been reached; hence, the possibility of remarkable changes in IQ on the part of disadvantaged children. Therefore, we cannot be certain that the child is operating at the upper limits of his ability until we have provided him with the optimal environment for realizing his talents. And, it must be admitted, we are still a long way from knowing just what that optimal environment is like.

In addition to the changes in our conception of learner have come changes in the learning process itself. Many of these changes have come about as a result of the computer and of the information-processing models which it provides for looking at the learning process. This is not the place to go into detail with respect to such models and I can only note that they give a much more detailed and complex picture of the learning process than is provided by the standard Stimulus-Response learning theories. Information-processing models of learning place heavy emphasis upon the encoding of information and upon its storage and retrieval. The implications of such models for our conception of learning and for instruction are still in their infancy, but they bode well to revolutionize our whole conception of learning in children and in adults.

What do these changes in our conception of the learner, the object of instruction, and of the learning process mean for religious instruction and for research and evaluation in religious education? First of all, with respect to the child as a self-motivated learner, it suggests that children have a spontaneous interest in and curiosity about religious matters. This fact must be taken into account in any attempt to reorganize the classroom and to devise new teaching strategies and fresh curricular materials. The aim should always be toward building upon and further stimulating the child's religious interest and curiosity. I believe that with sufficient care it will be possible to construct materials for each level of development which are both theologically sound and intrinsically interesting.

The implications of our changed conception of readiness for religious instruction are, or so it seems to me, that we need to reexamine our approach to preschool religious instruction.[23] The move towards preschool instruction in public education is gaining increased momentum as states such as California, Massachusetts, and New York begin to make preschool education available for all children. Without entering into the controversy as to whether pushing academic training into the preschool years is bad or good, it behooves us to look at our preschool programs in the light of our new awareness that "readiness" is itself a result of instruction.

Perhaps waiting until the child is "ready" for religious instruction misses an opportunity for more adequate preparation during the preschool period. This is not, after all, a new idea. Both Froebel[24] and Montessori[25] have stressed the importance of religious preparation in the preschool child. The most adequate means for such instruction, its quantity and extent, needs to be studied systematically; but it certainly is possible that beginning religious instruction in early childhood would greatly facilitate the whole later course of religious growth. One reason that religious families routinely produce religious children is probably the fact that the child is exposed to a religious orientation and to religious practices at an early age. Indeed, it could well be that research and evaluation of religious instruction during early childhood is the most imperative need in religious instruction today.

The alterations which have come about in our notion of intelligence are of particular relevance to the religious instruction of the disadvantaged child. The danger with such children is always that of underestimating their intellectual potential be-

---

[23]David Elkind, "Preschool Education: Enrichment or Instruction?" in *Childhood Education* 45 (February, 1969):321-328.

[24]Frederick W. Froebel, *The Education of Man* (New York: Appleton, 1893).

[25]Maria Montessori, "The Child in the Church," in E. M. Standing, editor, *The Child in the Church* (St. Paul, Minnesota: Catechetical Guild, 1965), pp. 1-64.

cause of their language difficulties and disruptive behavior. We need to train teachers to cope with such children and who can understand and respond to their needfulness, who can give them both warmth and direction, and who can stimulate them intellectually and settle them behaviorally. It is a challenge to the church's ministry and a challenge which must be accepted.

SUMMARY AND CONCLUSIONS

In the foregoing pages, I have described the basic components of the educational process: the agency, agent, media, and object of instruction, and some of the new trends of thought and research which pertain to each of these components as well as the implications of these new trends for religious instruction and for research evaluation in religious education. The present section briefly will summarize the discussion and highlight the major conclusion of this chapter.

With respect to the agency of instruction, it was pointed out that major innovations have come in the form of organizational changes within the classroom such as team teaching, reduced class size, ungraded classrooms, and the establishment of interest areas both within and without the classroom. While, for practical reasons it may not be possible to try out some of these innovations in parochial or Sunday schools, some aspects of these programs might be incorporated and evaluated in religious instruction. In particular, the provision for children to follow through for long periods of time on a particular activity would seem to be essential if we wish to keep alive his spontaneous interest in and enjoyment of learning.

Perhaps the most significant trend in evaluation of the agent of instruction, the teacher, has come in the consideration of the importance of the teacher-as-a-person. Such factors as the teacher's warmth and concern for her children, her flexibility and originality, her democratic attitudes, and her familiarity with her subject all play an important part not only in determining what the child learns but also in his attitudes and feelings about the subject matter. Within religious education we need to begin to look at the teacher-as-a-person variables both in terms of screening of candidates and also with respect to training teachers in the most effective classroom attitudes and strategies.

With regard to instructional media, one of the major innovations is the construction of curricular materials in conformance with the child's modes of thinking and with his spontaneous interests and inclinations. A similar approach can be and is being taken in the construction of materials for instruction in religion. One of the real needs in this area is for research on the effectiveness of these materials and also of the effectiveness of materials designed for teachers.

Finally, with respect to the object of religious instruction, the child, innovations have come about because of our altered conceptions of the child as a learner and of the learning process. We now recognize that the child is motivated to learn and does not have to be threatened with punishment or beguiled with rewards. In addition, we now appreciate that readiness is in large measure a product of instruction in the home and that intelligence is much more malleable than was heretofore assumed. As concerns the learning process, computer models have altered and expanded our conception of the learning process in irrevocable ways. All of these changes in our conception of the learner and of the learning process have important implications both for the construction of religious materials and for the age groups towards whom religious instruction and evaluation should be directed.

In concluding this chapter on research and evaluation in religious instruction, I would like to emphasize the need and importance of investigations aimed at particular problems in the domains of the instructional agency, agent, media, and object. If we are to profit from the mistakes made in other disciplines, it will perhaps be necessary to forego the large-scale investigations such as those dealing with parochial school attendance and religiosity. Even if such studies were to demonstrate unequivocally that religious education has no effect upon the religiosity of those who have been exposed to it, religious education would not be disbanded or given up. What would happen would be a tremendous effort in the direction of improving religious instruction. If we accept the fact that religious education and instruction is important and here to stay, let us then direct our efforts towards making it maximally effective and not spend our energies in a practically meaningless discussion of the necessity for religious instruction. In this regard, the most effective approach might well be the initiation of relatively circumscribed investigations of the instructional process, which will give us that foundation of valid knowledge upon which a scientific pedagogy of religious instruction can one day be erected.

Afterword

Patrick C. Rooney

Toward a Future for Religious Education has attempted to present a point of view which can be termed "the social science approach to religious instruction." It would be pretentious, at this time, to suggest that the essays presented here are anything more than a preliminary statement of this viewpoint. The question arising naturally from this book is: Where does the social science approach go from here?

It seems to me that teachers and specialists within the area of religious education can respond to the social science approach in at least two basic manners. They can ignore it, either passively or actively, by making the claim that religious education is so obviously a theological discipline that a radical restructuring of the area along social science lines would be the height of irrelevancy and destructive of the small degree of focus which religious educators have struggled to gain in the recent past. In other words, it could be claimed that the social science approach tends to confuse the issues and presents a strange orientation to a field that simply cannot support any more confusion or different orientations.

To some degree these claims can be justified, and, therefore, I would hope that religious educators will respond to the present work in an entirely different manner. I believe that in particular the essays in this book, and in general the social science approach itself, offer to religious education a tremendous opportunity for growth and advancement. But this opportunity rests upon the assumption that religious educators, be they of a markedly theological orientation or of the social science variety, are capable of a professional discussion, dissent, and dialogue among themselves. It is no secret, at least among Catholic religious educators, that there has been a rather pitiful lack of meaningful discussion concerning the nature, purpose, and thrust of the catechetical enterprise during the past few years. What discussion, and at times dissent, have appeared seem to center around such matters as classrooms methods and curriculum materials. A relatively few catechetical leaders have determined the basic questions to which religious education must address itself, and with almost a frightening ease the mass of Catholic religion teachers in the field has assented to these questions as their own. This phenomenon has occurred undoubtedly because the questions articulated by leaders in the field correspond to the real doubts, problems, and needs felt in the hearts of most Catholic catechists. The point here, and I think, the point of the social science approach, is to re-examine the basic questions posed by theologically oriented catechetical leaders, and to do so from a radically different point of view. The social science approach, therefore, offers the occasion to question the basic questions, and indeed to question the questioners in the modern catechetical movement. The social science approach can effect this result, of course, only if it is carried to the marketplace of the area of religious education where in a spirit of sincere dialogue, authentic dissent can be utilized as a creative catalyst within the area itself.

There are two reasons why this dialogue should occur. First, no one leader or group of leaders in the catechetical movement could, or in fact, do claim that their particular perspective is the *only* valid one. Second, it is an undeniable fact that the social sciences are playing an increasingly important role in the intellectual life of the United States, especially in the educational enterprise. I think this latter phenomenon must now be both examined and ingested in the areas of religious education and of theology. This stance actually has been promoted in the recent past, but unfortunately not very widely. Among Catholic educators in Europe perhaps the leading exponent of the social science orientation has been André Godin of Lumen Vitae.[1] Social scientists like Talcott Parsons are claiming that:

> . . . the social sciences must soon in some sense assume the position, among the secular discipline groups, which has, in relation to theology, been historically occupied by the humanities. For theologians to center their worldly cognitive attention only on the humanities is too easy, since they are basically "religious" anyway. It is in the social sciences that the intellectual battles concerning the meaning of the relation between the ordered "creation" which is independent of man, his interests, and his will and the process of "creative action" in which man is the divinely appointed responsible agent will have to be worked out.[2]

I must add that what these claims amount to must yet be worked out, and perhaps *Toward a Future for Religious Education* constitutes the beginning of this process. Much remains to be said, and a great deal of clarification is called for, but the challenge presented in this book can hardly go unheeded in the field of religious education. Religious educators are now given through this volume the opportunity to question their assumptions and to investigate their starting points. It is the hope of the editors and contributors that the dialogue will begin and grow so that it might become a dialogue of the type characterized by Paul Tillich as "a dialogue done in listening

---

[1] See especially, André Godin, editor, *From Cry to Word* (Brussels: Lumen Vitae Press, 1968), pp. 13-16.

[2] Talcott Parsons, "Social Science and Theology," in William A. Beardslee, editor, *America and the Future of Theology* (Philadelphia: Westminster Press, 1967), p. 155.

love, which can become a tool of providence and a channel of the divine Spirit."[3]

³Paul Tillich, "Appreciation and Reply," in Thomas O'Meara and Donald M. Weisser, editors, *Paul Tillich in Catholic Thought* (Chicago: Priory Press, 1964), p. 311.

Profiles of
Contributors

PATRICK C. ROONEY is Instructor of Education at the University of Notre Dame. A member of the Dominican order, Father Rooney received a bachelor's degree in philosophy from the Pontifical Faculty of Philosophy (River Forest, Illinois), a master's degree from the Aquinas Institute of Theology (Dubuque, Iowa), and a *Diplome de Catéchèse* from the International Centre for Studies in Religious Education (Brussels). He is a specialist in religious education, with a particular interest in the philosophical ecology of catechetics in the United States. Father Rooney has taught religion in Fenwick High School (Chicago), and has been engaged in various diocesan and parish level roles in the Confraternity of Christian Doctrine. He is a member of the Religious Education Association, the Society for the Scientific Study of Religion, the National Catholic Educational Association, and the National Education Association.

JEFFREY KEEFE is Staff Member in the Psychiatric Outpatient Service at St. Vincent Medical Center of Richmond (New York), Professor of Pastoral Psychology at St. Anthony-on-Hudson (Rensselaer, New York), Lecturer in Psychology at Notre Dame College (Staten Island, New York), and Associate Professor of Education in the summer session at the University of Notre Dame. A priest of the Order of Friars Minor Conventual, Doctor Keefe received a bachelor's degree in philosophy from St. Anthony-on-Hudson, a licentiate degree in theology from The Catholic University of America (Washington), a master's degree in education from The Catholic University of America, a master's degree in psychology from Fordham University (New York City), and a doctor's degree in clinical psychology from Fordham University. Serving his clinical psychology internship under David Wechsler at Bellevue Psychiatric Hospital (New York City), Doctor Keefe held a post-doctoral fellowship at the Staten Island Mental Health Society. He has previously taught at Trenton Catholic Boys High School (New Jersey) and at St. Francis Preparatory Seminary (Staten Island, New York). Father Keefe serves as a consultant for psychological screening and assessment for several religious institutes in the United States. In 1969 he acted as *peritus* to the General Chapter of the Order of Friars Minor Conventual in Rome. He is a member of the American Psychological Association and the American Catholic Psychological Association. His articles have appeared in the *Catholic Psychological Record, Homiletic and Pastoral Review, Worship,* and in a book, *Readings in Guidance and Counseling,* edited by James Michael Lee and Nathaniel J. Pallone (New York: Sheed & Ward, 1966, 562 pp.).

JAMES MICHAEL LEE is Professor and Chairman of the Department of Graduate Studies in Education at the University of Notre Dame. He is a specialist in the teaching process dimension of religious education. Professor Lee received a bachelor's degree in philosophy-psychology from St. John's University (New York), a master's degree in history from Columbia University, and a doctor's degree in education from Columbia University. He has taught in the New York City public school system at the secondary school level as well as in the adult education program. Professor Lee has also been Lecturer in Education at Seton Hall University (South Orange, New Jersey), Lecturer in Education in the Graduate School of Hunter College (New York City), and Assistant Professor of Education at St. Joseph College (West Hartford, Connecticut). He has served as an evaluator of a federally funded education program for disadvantaged children and youth, a project consultant for the United States Office of Education, a special consultant for a national research project on Roman Catholic seminaries, and currently is a member of the Board of Lay Consultants, Education Section, of the National Conference of Catholic Men. Professor Lee is a member of the Religious Education Association, the Society for the Scientific Study of Religion, the American Educational Research Association, the National Catholic Educational Association, and the National Education Association. His books include *Principles and Methods of Secondary Education* (New York: McGraw-Hill, 1963, 619 pp.), senior editor of and contributor to *Seminary Education in a Time of*

Change (Notre Dame, Ind.: Fides, 1965, 590 pp.), senior author of *Guidance and Counseling in Schools: Foundations and Processes* (New York: McGraw-Hill, 1966, 612 pp.), senior editor of and contributor to *Readings in Guidance and Counseling* (Sheed & Ward, 1966, 562 pp.), editor of and contributor to *Catholic Education in the Western World* (Notre Dame, Ind.: University of Notre Dame Press, 1967, 324 pp.), and *The Purpose of Catholic Schooling* (Dayton, Ohio: Pflaum, and Washington: The National Catholic Educational Association, 1968, 80 pp.). Professor Lee's articles have appeared in numerous journals including *Catholic Educational Review, National Guidance Conference Journal, Herder Correspondence, Review for Religious, Theological Education, Catholic Counselor, Nation's Schools, Catholic World, Today's Catholic Teacher, Ave Maria, Clearing House*. He also contributed an article to the book, *The Parish in a Time of Change*, edited by Marvin Bordelon (Notre Dame, Ind.: Fides, 1967, 227 pp.). Professor Lee is listed in *Who's Who in America*.

DIDIER J. PIVETEAU is Professor of Catechesis and Education at the Institut Catholique de Paris, and Professor of Education in the summer session at the University of Notre Dame. He is also Editor-in-Chief of *Orientations,* one of France's leading journals on Catholic education. A member of the Brothers of the Christian Schools, he received his doctor's degree from the Institut Catholique de Paris. Professor Piveteau has served as Dean of Studies at St. Gène's High School (France). Currently Lecturer in Education for American Catholic agencies in Europe, Doctor Piveteau has twice been a Fulbright scholar, and three times acted as the official French delegate to the International Conference on American Studies held annually in Salzburg (Austria). He has been a grantee of the British Council and of the Swedish government. Professor Piveteau is also Director of Education of CODIAM, a French government organization for promoting schooling in French-speaking black Africa. As Brother Didier he is a *peritus* to the Brothers of the Christian Schools in Rome. Books by this French educationist include a series of textbooks for Catholic schools (Ligel, 1952-1962), *Actualité des langues vivantes* (Ligel, 1953), *Equilibre affectif et sexuel de l'Ecolier* (Centre Cath. Educ., 1962). He is the coeditor of *Le Pretre educateur* (Mame, 1964). His articles have appeared in many journals, including *Le Maison Dieu, Pédagogie, Catéchèse, Catechistes, Orientations, La Famille Educatrice,* and an article in the book *Catholic Education in the*

Western World, edited by James Michael Lee (Notre Dame, Ind.: University of Notre Dame Press, 1967, 324 pp.).

CHRISTOPHER KIESLING is Professor of Theology at the Aquinas Institute of Theology (Dubuque, Iowa). A priest of the Dominican order, he is a specialist in systematic theology and liturgy. Professor Kiesling received a bachelor's degree from the Pontifical Faculty of Philosophy (River Forest, Illinois), a licentiate degree in theology from the Pontificum Collegium Angelicum (Rome), and a doctor's degree in theology from the Pontifical Faculty of the Immaculate Conception (Washington). Professor Kiesling has taught theology at St. Xavier College (Chicago). He is a member of the International Liturgical Commission of the Order of Preachers, and a member of the special subcommission of the United States Catholic Conference for Educational and Interreligious Affairs specializing in consultations with the Reformed and Presbyterian Churches in the United States. He is a member of the Liturgical Conference, Catholic Theological Society of America, and the Society for the Scientific Study of Religion. Doctor Kiesling's first book was *The Spirit and Practice of the Liturgy* (Chicago: Priory Press, 1965, 143 pp.), and he currently is working on a volume dealing with the future of the Christian Sunday. He has written numerous articles for theological journals including *Theological Studies, Worship, Journal of Ecumenical Studies, Review for Religious, Homiletic and Pastoral Review, Thomist, Chicago Studies, The Living Light,* and *Cross and Crown.*

BERNARD COOKE, now at Yale University, was formerly Professor and Chairman of the Department of Theology at Marquette University. He is a specialist in sacramental theology. Professor Cooke received a bachelor's degree in theology from St. Louis University, a master's degree in theology from St. Louis University, and a doctor's degree in theology from the Institut Catholique de Paris. He also holds an honorary Doctor of Letters from the University of Detroit. Professor Cooke is a member of the national board of directors of the Society of Catholic College Teachers of Sacred Doctrine, a professional association of which he has served as national president. He also holds memberships in the Catholic Theological Society of America, the National Liturgical Conference, and the Catholic Biblical Association. His books include *Formation of Faith* (Chicago: Loyola University Press, 1965, 107 pp.), *Christian Sacraments and Christian Personality* (New York: Holt, Rinehart & Winston, 1965, 278 pp.); *Christian Involvement* (Chicago: Argus, 1966, 72 pp.), *Challenge of Vatican II* (Chicago: Argus, 1966, 72 pp.), *New Dimensions in Catholic Life* (Denville, N. J.: Dimension, 1968, 126 pp.), and *The Eucharist: Mystery of Friendship* (Dayton, Ohio: Pflaum Witness Book, 1969, 128 pp.). Professor Cooke's articles have appeared in a wide variety of journals including *Theological Studies, Religious Education, Journal of Ecumenical Studies, Worship, Christian Century, Theological Education, Commonweal, Diakonia, Lutheran Quarterly, Catholic Mind, Perspectives, Theology Digest, Human Rights, Spiritual Life, Chicago Studies, Focus, The Way,* and the *Bulletin of the National Catholic Educational Association.* Books in which Professor Cooke's articles have appeared include *Modern Catechetics,* edited by Gerard Sloyan (New York: Macmillan, 1960, 381 pp.), *The Church as the Body of Christ,* edited by Robert Pelton (Notre Dame, Ind.: University of Notre Dame Press, 1963, 152 pp.), *Readings in Sacramental Theology,* edited by C. Stephen Sullivan (Englewood Cliffs, N. J.: Prentice-Hall, 1964, 236 pp.), *Pastoral Catechetics,* edited by Johannes Hofinger and Theodore Stone (New York: Herder and Herder, 1964, 287 pp.), *Apostolic Renewal in the Seminary,* edited by James Keller and Richard Armstrong (Christophers, 1964, 305 pp.), *Spirituality in the Secular City,* edited by Christian Duquoc (New York: Paulist Concilium, 1966, 184 pp.), *Wisdom in Depth,* edited by Vincent F. Daues (Milwaukee: Bruce, 1966, 260 pp.), *Revolution in Missionary Thinking,* edited by William Richardson (Maryknoll, 1966, 261 pp.), *Vows But No Walls,* edited by Eugene Grollmes (St. Louis: B. Herder, 1967, 230 pp.), *Ecumenism, the Spirit and Worship,* edited by Leonard J. Swidler (Pittsburgh: Duquesne University Press, 1967, 258 pp.), and *New Themes in Christian Philosophy,* edited by Ralph McInerny (Notre Dame, Ind.: University of Notre Dame Press, 1968, 416 pp.).

C. ELLIS NELSON is Skinner and McAlpin Professor of Practical Theology at Union Theological Seminary. He is a specialist in religious education and in the educational mission of the Church. An ordained minister of the Presbyterian Church (U.S.), Reverend Nelson received a bachelor of arts degree in history and English from Austin College (Texas), a bachelor of divinity degree from Austin Presbyterian Theological Seminary, a master's degree in education from the University of Texas, and a doctor's degree in education from Columbia University. He also holds an honorary doctor of divinity degree from Austin College. Professor Nelson has served as associate minister and director of student work for the University Presbyterian Church (Texas), chaplain of the State School for the Blind (Texas), Director of Youth Work for the Board of Christian Education of the Presbyterian Church (Virginia), and Director of Research for the Texas Legislative Council's Study of Higher Education in the State of Texas. Professor Nelson has taught at the Austin Presbyterian Theological Seminary and at the University of Texas. He is a consultant to the Board of Christian Education for both the Presbyterian Church (U.S.) and the United Presbyterian Church (U.S.A.), chairman of the Commission on Research and Counsel of the American Association of Theological Schools, and Secretary to the Executive Committee of the Religious Education Association. Professor Nelson is a member of the North American Committee of the Word Council of Christian Education, the Association of Professors in the Practical Field, and the International Commission to Study Education. His books include *Love and the Law* (Richmond, Va.: John Knox, 1963, 93 pp.), editor of the four-volume series *Monographs in Christian Education* (New York: Association, 1964-1966), *What's Right?* (Richmond, Va.: John Knox, 1966, 186 pp.), *Where Faith Begins* (Richmond, Va.: John Knox, 1967, 231 pp.), and *Issues Facing Christian Educators* (World Council of Christian Education, 1968, 40 pp.). Professor Nelson's articles have appeared in numerous journals including *The International Journal of Religious Education, Religious Education, Theological Education, The Christian Century, The Christian Century Pulpit, The Presbyterian Review, Princeton Seminary Bulletin, Religion in Life, Union Seminary Quarterly Review, Presbyterian Action,* and *Colloquy.* Books in which Professor Nelson's articles have appeared include *Wider Horizons in Christian Adult Education,* edited by Lawrence C. Little (New York: Association, 1962, 338 pp.), *The Westminster Dictionary of Christian Education,* edited by Kendig Brubaker Cully, (Philadelphia: Westminster, 1963, 812 pp.), *An Introduction to Christian Education,* edited by Marvin Taylor (Nashville, Tenn.: Abington, 1966, 412 pp.), *Grolier's Encyclopedia,* and *The Future Course of Christian Education,* edited by Lawrence C. Little (New York: Association, 1969, 322 pp.).

WILLIAM B. FRIEND is Acting Director of the Office for Educational Research at the University of Notre Dame. A priest of the diocese of Mobile-Birmingham (Alabama), Father Friend received a master's degree in education from The Catholic University of

America. He is a specialist in religious education. Father Friend has taught religion in Catholic high schools in Florida and in Alabama. He has served as a principal in a Catholic high school, as assistant superintendent of schools for the diocese of Mobile-Birmingham, and as chairman of the Mobile-Birmingham Diocesan Religion Committee. Father Friend is a member of the Advisory Board of the Southeastern Regional Educational Laboratory (Auburn Component), and a member of the Advisory Board of the National Catholic Educational Association's Data Bank of Information Concerning Private Education. He also holds membership in the Society for the Scientific Study of Religion, the Religious Education Association, the National Catholic Educational Association, the American Educational Research Association, and the National Catholic Guidance Conference. Father Friend has authored *A Report of Studies and Surveys of Religious Education in the Diocese of Mobile-Birmingham, 1963-1966* (Artcraft, 1967, 221 pp.).

DAVID ELKIND is Professor of Psychology and Director of Graduate Training in Developmental Psychology at the University of Rochester. He is a specialist in developmental psychology with a particular research and teaching interest in the cognitive processes in children. Professor Elkind received a bachelor's degree in psychology from the University of California at Los Angeles (UCLA), and a doctor's degree in psychology also from UCLA. He did postgraduate work under Jean Piaget in Geneva. Professor Elkind has taught at Wheaton College (Norton, Massachusetts), at the U.C.L.A. Medical School, and at the University of Denver. He is the program chairman for Division 7 of the American Psychological Association, and holds memberships in the Society for Research in Child Development, the American Educational Research Association, the Society for the Scientific Study of Religion, and is Foreign Affiliate of the British Psychological Association. Professor Elkind's books include editor of *Six Psychological Studies* (New York: Random House, 1967, 250 pp.), and senior editor of *Studies in Cognitive Development* (Oxford University Press, 1969, 500 pp.). Articles by Professor Elkind have appeared in many journals including the *Journal for the Scientific Study of Religion, Journal of Religious Research, Lumen Vitae, Journal of Educational Psychology, Journal of Genetic Psychology, Journal of Abnormal and Social Psychology, Child Development, Science, Mental Hygiene, Young Children,* and *Childhood Education.*

Index of Names

Index of Subjects